Fundamentals in computer understanding: speech and vision

Fundamentals in computer understanding: speech and vision

Edited by

J.-P. HATON

Centre de Recherche en Informatique de Nancy

The right of the
University of Cambridge
to print and sell
all manner of books
was granted by
Henry VIII in 1534.
The University has printed
and published continuously
since 1584.

CAMBRIDGE UNIVERSITY PRESS

Cambridge

London   New York   New Rochelle

Melbourne   Sydney

Published by the Press Syndicate of the University of Cambridge
The Pitt Building, Trumpington Street, Cambridge CB2 1RP
32 East 57th Street, New York, NY 10022, USA
10 Stamford Road, Oakleigh, Melbourne 3166, Australia

First published 1987

Printed in Great Britain at the University Press, Cambridge

British Library cataloguing in publication data
Haton, Jean-Paul
Fundamentals in computer understanding:
speech and vision.
1. Computer vision   2. Automatic speech recognition
I. Title
006.3'7   KT7882.S65

Library of Congress cataloguing in publication data available

ISBN 0 521 30983 2

CONTENTS

CONTRIBUTORS

Jean-Paul Haton
CRIN-INRIA, BP 239, F-54506 Vandoeuvre Cedex, France

James P. Delgrande
Department of Computer Science, University of Toronto, Toronto,
Ontario M55 IA4, Canada

John Mylopoulos
Department of Computer Science, University of Toronto, Toronto,
Ontario M55 IA4, Canada

Roberto Bisiani
Computer Science Department, Carnegie-Mellon University, Pittsburgh,
Pennsylvania 15213, USA

J. C. Sperandio
Université Paris V, 28 rue Serpente, 75006 Paris, France

D. L. Scapin
INRIA, BP 105, 78153 Le Chesnay Cedex, France

C. Y. Chrisment
Laboratoire CERFIA-CSI, UA CNRS 824 Toulouse, France

G. Zurfluh
Laboratoire CERFIA-CSI, UA CNRS 824 Toulouse, France

H.-H. Nagel
Fraunhofer-Institut für Informations- und Datenverarbeitung (II TB),
Sebastian-Kneip-Str. 12–14, D-7500 Karlsruhe 1, Bundesrepublik Deutschland.

O. D. Faugeras
INRIA, Domaine de Voluceau, Rocquencourt, BP 105, 78153 Le Chesnay
Cedex, France

Renato De Mori
Department of Computer Science, Concordia University, Montreal,
Quebec H3G IM8, Canada

Lily Lam
Department of Computer Science, Concordia University, Montreal,
Quebec H3G IM8, Canada

David Probst
Department of Computer Science, Concordia University, Montreal,
Quebec H3G IM8, Canada

F. Lonchamp
Institut de Phonétique, Université de Nancy II, BP 33-97, 54015 Nancy Cedex,
France

Stephen E. Levinson
Speech Research Department, AT & T Bell Laboratories, Murray Hill, New
New Jersey 07974, USA

G. Perennou
Laboratoire CERFIA, UA CNRS 824, Université Paul Sabatier, 118 Route de
Narbonne, 31062 Toulouse Cedex, France

J. M. Pierrel
CRIN, University of Nancy, BP 239, F-54506 Vandoeuvre Cedex, France

INTRODUCTION

Jean-Paul Haton

This book is the result of a course sponsored by the European Economic Community (the CREST Committee) and the INRIA, that took place in Versailles, France (from May 28th to June 7th, 1985).

The course and the book originate from a very ambitious and difficult challenge :

bringing together researchers and students concerned with most aspects of man-machine communication, more precisely : the design of computer understanding systems, with an emphasis on speech understanding.

Much may be gained from a close comparison between approaches and methods used in the related fields of speech, vision and natural language. This book, which is a collection of lectures from well known specialists in the various disciplines concerned, may be regarded as a fairly comprehensive introduction to the design and development of man-machine communication systems.

The contents can be divided into three parts.

First, chapters one to five, deal with general problems and analysis methods. At present, the design of understanding systems appears as one of the most difficult tasks in artificial intelligence. On the one hand, the data to be processed are often erroneous or incomplete, especially in the fields of vision and speech ; on the other hand, it is necessary to take into account varied large knowledge sources, in order to accurately account for an utterance, a scene or a written sentence. Knowledge-based techniques provide an efficient framework for the formal description of knowledge and development of systems.

Chapter 1 by Jean-Paul Haton is devoted to an overall survey of the domain : system architecture allowing the cooperation of knowledge bases (e.g. the blackboard model), search strategies, use of expert systems for solving subproblems, etc. are briefly discussed and illustrated with examples from the fields of speech understanding and computer vision. Some of these notions are fully explained in subsequent chapters.

In chapter 2, John Mylopoulos deals with a crucial problem in the design of knowledge-based systems, i.e. the representation of knowledge sources. He reviews most current approaches : logic formalism, production rules, structured descriptions, with particular emphasis on semantic networks.

With respect to implementation, the view commonly held now is that today's Von Neumann architectures are not well suited to symbolic computation nor to artificial intelligence system implementation. The design of custom VLSI chips and specialized or parallel architectures appears as a key issue for the future development of artificial intelligence applications, especially in a real time environment. Roberto Bisiani in chapter 3 describes some promising architectures that may prove efficient solutions to implementation problems, not only for speech processing but also for other artificial intelligence applications ; convincing examples concerning the speech domain are given to support this assumption.

Most computer understanding systems are intended to become vital parts of man-machine communication processors. Human factors involved in such interactions are outlined by Jean-Claude Sperandio in chapter 4. From a practical point of view this aspect cannot be ignored and should be carefully considered by designers, most of whom still underestimate it.

One of the major applications of man-machine communication using speech, image and written natural language is the design and manipulation of new generation multi-media data bases. C. Chrisment (chapter 5) brings out some aspects of the research done in this area : integration of images, spoken documents, texts, etc. within a single model ; definition and implementation of multi-media interfaces and suitable manipulation languages.

Part 2 (chapters 6 and 7) focuses on another aspect of computer understanding : image analysis and vision.

The numerous applications of image recognition and computer vision in robotics, medicine, geology, etc. are well known. In this field we are confronted with problems similar to those encountered in speech understanding (cf. chapter 1 by Jean-Paul Haton), especially since computer vision usually appears as a twofold process including a perceptive or low-vision component interacting strongly with a high-level vision component.

Hans Helmut Nagel in chapter 6 studies the various operations involved in the detection and localization of low-level descriptors on images. He also approaches the problem of relating local features to scene descriptions, thus establishing a link between his contribution and chapter 7. In the latter chapter, Olivier Faugeras describes various approaches for the symbolic interpretation of images and/or scenes. The basic principles of computer vision are clearly stated and illustrated thanks to the analysis of numerous examples of 2D and 3D images ; these examples too point out the usefulness of knowledge-based approaches in this area. Although the complexity and diversity of computer vision would justify a whole volume, chapters 6 and 7 may be considered as a well documented introduction to this pluridisciplinary field of research.

Part 3 (chapters 8 to 12) concerns another pluridisciplinary domain, i.e. speech recognition and understanding.

Low-level speech processing like image analysis cannot be achieved without a close cooperation between sophisticated signal processing techniques -that are not described in this book- and processors using varied knowledge sources. Thus Renato de Mori, in chapter 8, details a knowledge-based approach for the acoustic-phonetic decoding of speech, which constitutes one of the major bottlenecks in continuous speech understanding. This approach based on the notion of plan generation involves an "expert society" as a paradigm.

The main difficulty to overcome when designing an acoustic-phonetic decoding expert system is the elucidation of the expert's knowledge. One interesting way of acquiring such an expertise is to analyze the activity of an experienced spectrogram reader. In chapter 9,

François Lonchamp expounds his point of view as an expert phonetician involved in the design of an acoustic-phonetic decoding system and reviews the different problems he encountered while trying to explain his competence as a spectrogram reader.

Statistic methods provide another way of acquiring the knowledge relevant to phonetic decoding and facilitate its integration into a speech recognition system, especially a speaker independent one. Steve Levinson (chapter 10) discusses two solutions :

- data analysis (clustering) techniques, which allow the processing of very large amounts of data,
- stochastic models such as hidden Markov models.

Lexical processing plays a central part in speech understanding. Chapter 11 by Guy Perennou provides a fairly exhaustive survey of this area, including lexical decomposition and derivation, semantic description of words, morpho-phonological transformations, etc. Numerous examples from the French language are used to illustrate his lecture.

Finally, oral man-machine communication systems should aim at task-oriented dialogue understanding rather than confine their capabilities to mere sentence recognition. Jean-Marie Pierrel, in chapter 12, outlines the different components that should be included in an efficient system. These general views are illustrated by a brief description of the dialogue managing system now under development at the CRIN.

KNOWLEDGE-BASED AND EXPERT SYSTEMS IN UNDERSTANDING PROBLEMS

Jean-Paul Haton
CRIN - INRIA, B.P. 239, F-54506 Vandoeuvre Cedex

1. INTRODUCTION

Knowledge-based systems have led to considerable changes in approaches to a number of problems and are largely responsible for the recent successes of Artificial Intelligence (AI) in a number of domains : expert systems, natural language understanding, speech recognition, computer vision, etc., even though important problems still remain unsolved.

The present success of AI therefore mainly results from the design of new system architectures which are able to use all the knowledge, including human expertise, available in a given domain. That is, these knowledge-based systems thus take human expertise into account in order to improve their own performances. In this chapter we will consider the application of knowledge-based techniques to understanding systems, especially speech understanding and computer vision where the basic problem consists of interpreting input physical data. In these two related fields there exists a close interaction between numerical data-processing (perceptual aspects such as in signal processing and pattern recognition techniques) and symbolic computation (cognitive aspects). Moreover, it is difficult to implement reasoning processes, due to the multiple knowledge sources and to the fact that data are incomplete and/or erroneous. The solutions which are found in these fields are therefore often original and powerful, and they are then used in other domains of AI.

After having presented the fundamentals of expert systems, we will concentrate on two major questions, i.e. the representation and use of knowledge and the structures for controlling efficient search strategies. The principles presented will be illustrated by practical examples from the fields of speech and vision.

2. BASIC PRINCIPLES OF UNDERSTANDING SYSTEMS

The first step in the design of an understanding system consists of collecting the various relevant knowledge sources (KS) and of designing a structure for the efficient cooperation of these KSs. Figure 1 illustrates the situation, with several knowledge sources, KSi, each having its own activation mechanism , Mi.

Figure 1. Overall blockdiagram of an understanding system.

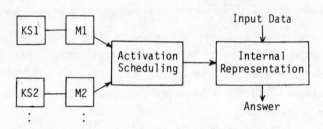

This structure is applicable for several domains of AI where the complexity of the task makes it mandatory to use several types of information, such as speech understanding vision, natural language processing or signal interpretation.

For instance, in vision, the localization and recognition of objects on an image - or a fortiori on a 3D scene - is not only a problem of matching some parts of the scene against stored prototypes, since problems of object-orientation, illumination, etc. can cause important variations in the perception of a given object. A classical solution consists of representing an object or an image as a relational graph. These graphs are then compared during the processing of a scene. Similar methods are used for the representation of words in a lexicon.

A very common strategy used in these fields relies on the so-called hypothesis-and-test or prediction-verification paradigm. In this strategy, hypotheses are emitted at the various processing levels according to both the available knowledge and to various indices. These hypotheses are then verified or cancelled by other knowledge sources. We will often encounter this strategy in this chapter.

A large amount of our knowledge about speech comes from linguistics. The speech signal is encoded at various levels during the speech production process and the automatic decoding will have to take into account the corresponding KS :

- = <u>acoustics</u> : for handling signal preprocessing and feature extraction,
- = <u>phonetics</u>, which is related to the transcription of the speech signal into discrete phonetic units,
- = <u>phonology</u> : together with phonetics, this component deals with alterations of sounds (accent, etc.) and with contextual variations (liaisons, assimilations, co-articulations, etc.),
- = <u>prosody</u> : these features are specific to speech communication and highly important in speech understanding for a human listener,
- = <u>lexicon</u> : the word is an essential element of sentence structure,
- = <u>syntax</u> : related to the structure of a message according to the grammar of the language,
- = <u>semantics</u> : representing the meaning of words and conceptual dependencies,
- = <u>pragmatics</u> : more specific than semantics, this KS is associated with the context of the application.

Most of these KSs also play a role in written language understanding. Results obtained in this domain can therefore be re-used to a certain extent in speech understanding. However the specificity of oral language and the indeterminism which appears during the understanding process makes it necessary to design new models or at least to adapt them.

Indeterminism is inherent to most domains of signal understanding. It basically comes from two sources :

(i) errors in the identification of low-level primitives (phonemes in speech or basic patterns in an image), due to the variability of signals and to noise,

(ii) errors in high level interpretation, due to the continuous character of signals (erroneous spotting of a word in a sentence or of an object in a scene), or to ambiguities and imprecisions in the KSs (for instance prosody obviously plays an important role in speech understanding but no theory has yet been able to formalize this KSs satisfactorily).

These different errors are then propagated throughout the interpretation process and thus make the problem a very difficult one.

As far as speech is concerned it is important to notice the fundamental role played by words and the lexical level. Word hypotheses are emitted in both a bottomup or data-driven mode from the acoustic data and in a top-down or model driven mode from context and high level KSs.

A similar situation exists in computer vision, except that the linguistic models available for speech are more operational than those for vision. A computer vision system can be described (figure 2) as a set of interrelated processes which progressively transform sensory data in accordance with different models (perceptual, fonctional, etc.) that incorporate the knowledge available at the various levels in order to yield a symbolic and finally semantic description of the scene.

Figure 2. Principle of a computer vision system.

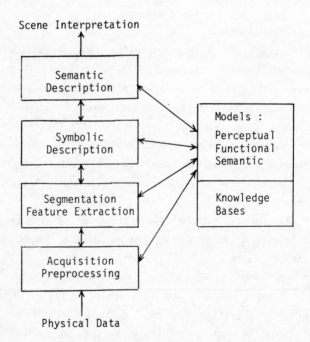

In this case the interaction between low level and high level processing involves objects which play a similar role to that of words in speech. We will see later on that very similar models have been used in speech understanding and in vision.

It is important to note that the distinction between perceptual or low level (i.e. pattern recognition) and cognitive or high level (i.e. artificial intelligence) is only used for the sake of simplicity. In fact, during the human understanding process there is a very high degree of interaction between the sensory organs and the brain. Figure 3 is an attempt to summarize this situation.

Figure 3. Schematic blockdiagram for a human understanding process.

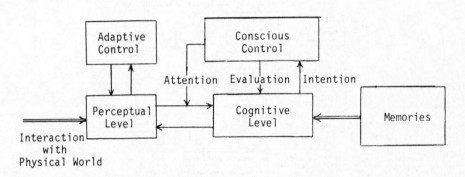

This perceptual, or rather sensori-motor, level is controlled by an adaptive system which mostly works in an unconscious way. It is tightly coupled with the cognitive level and the memories. This latter level is controlled by a conscious system which corresponds to some of the fundamental mechanisms of audition and vision such as evocation, intention or attention. These mechanisms are not yet very well understood, and attempts to implement them in automatic systems have been far from satisfactory.

One way of characterizing low level and high level processing is in terms of knowledge available. High level processing carries out reasoning by taking into account the various domain-specific knowledge sources (syntax, semantics, etc. in case of speech, or symbolic and semantic description of objects in case of vision). Low level processing, on the other hand, works directly on physical data with general models which are usually less dependent on the domain of application (signal processing techniques, segmentation, etc.).

In the case of speech, the central role of the lexical level is clearly illustrated in figure 4. This figure in no sense represents the architecture of a speech understanding system : rather it indicates the various processes involved in the operation of such a system and the roles of the various KSs concerned.

<u>Figure 4</u>. Typical processes in continuous speech recognition.

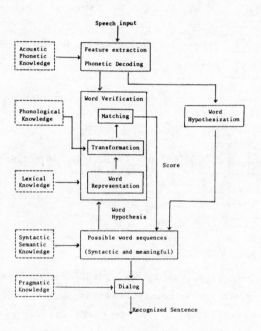

Most complex understanding systems can be similarly organized into successive levels corresponding to a progressively more and more symbolic description of initial data. In order to avoid a combinatorial explosion of possible solutions, several techniques are used at each level for decreasing the ambiguities. Such techniques do not always come from the AI field. For instance, dynamic programming is widely used in speech understanding for spotting speech units precisely (syllables, words) within a sentence. Similarly, relaxation techniques make it possible to improve the results of low-level image processing : contour extraction, etc. (Zucker 1976). These techniques can also be used for solving ambiguities at a higher level of abstraction, e.g. in object labeling (Barrow 1976).

3. KNOWLEDGE REPRESENTATION AND USE

3.1. General Models

The performances of an understanding system are highly dependent on the choice of efficient representation schemes for the various KSs. There exist two extreme solutions :

- the first is to define a unique structure in which all available knowledge will be integrated,

- the second is to keep the various KSs totally independent, and hence increase the modularity of the system.

Representing knowledge in a single structure is the solution that was chosen in the HARPY speech understanding system (Lowerre 1976). In this system, all available KSs - from acoustics to semantics are precompiled into a huge network which contains all the phonological variations of the various sentences allowed by the grammar of the language. The recognition of a sentence consists of finding the optimal path in this network. HARPY uses a heuristic beam search strategy which retains only a small number of the best solutions, at each step thus avoiding a combinatorial explosion. This strategy is a sub-optimal solution of a dynamic programming algorithm initially developed in the DRAGON system. A similar solution has been implemented in the ARGOS system for computer vision (Rubin 1978). HARPY was the system which best matched the initial requirements of the ARPA Project on Speech Understanding (Newell 1973) : precompiling knowledge is definitely a more efficient solution than using it in an interpretive mode. However this solution is very ad hoc and presents important drawbacks. First, every change in the language (or in the user) makes it necessary to recompile the network. That always means a lot of work, even though it can be partly automatized. Secondly, this solution is only tractable for simple situations, e.g. in highly constrained languages or simple and repetitive scenes. For instance it would be impossible to represent in this way all the KSs necessary for understanding pseudo-natural languages.

The second extreme solution consists in defining a system architecture in which each KS behaves completely tely independently of all the others but can communicate with them. However, a completely

¡heterarchical model with connection between all pairs of KSs would be too complex to implement. The blackboard model represents a good compromise. In this model, the different KSs are independent processes which communicate with each other only through a common database called blackboard. The HEARSAY II speech understanding system (Lesser 1975), for instance, has been built on this model.

The role of the blackboard is twofold :

- it ensures the passage of a message (i.e. an hypothesis) from one KS to another : every KS asynchronously emits hypotheses at its own level of expertise (phoneme, syllable, word, phrase, etc. for speech) and posts them on the blackboard. A hypothesis emitted by a particular KS Si may activate another KS Sj. The activation of a KS is thus pattern-directed : certain preconditions have to be fulfilled in the blackboard in order to activate a given KS. This notion has been very fruitful in AI (Waterman 1978). We will come back later on to this "Condition-Action" structure of KSs in HEARSAY II. In such cases, the action of a KS consists of creating, modifying or cancelling one or several hypotheses on the blackboard,

- it contains the partial interpretations of a sentence in terms of sets of hypotheses.

The blackboard model is general, and has been applied to various domains of AI : computer vision (Prager 1977) (Nagao 1979), signal interpretation (Nii 1978), cristallography (Engelmore 1979). This is not surprising if one considers the analogies which can be found between domains like speech or vision which were mentioned above. It is interesting to notice that there exist large similarities in the structure of the blackboard of the HEARSAY II system and of the VISIONS system for image understanding (Hanson 1978). However, there is an important difference in that the blackboard data base in HEARSAY II has a time dimension (speech is a time varying process) whereas VISIONS is only able to process static scenes.

Several intermediate solutions have been used for representing knowledge in understanding systems. The most usual model is a hierarchical one operating under the control of a supervisor, instead of the asynchronous, pattern-directed control of the blackboard model. Systems like HWIM (Woods 1976), ESOPE, KEAL, LITHAN, MYRTILLE I and II in speech understanding are good illustrations of this model. We will see in the next section the control structures which can be associated with this solution. Similar exemples could be given from other fields of understanding.

The idea of integrating a certain amount of knowledge by precompilation is also often used. For instance, phonological knowledge which is responsible for phonetic alterations of words in context can be represented in terms of contextual rewriting rules which apply to word entities in the lexicon (Shoup 1980). This application of phonological rules to basic word-forms in the lexicon can be done either during the understanding process at each access to the lexicon or all at once in a single, preliminary phase. This phase consists of a precompilation of the set of phonological forms of the words. This latter solution is much more efficient as far as the computation time is concerned and is used in several large systems for speech understanding, such as HWIM.

Similarly, the use of some kinds of precompiled knowledge increases the efficiency of vision systems. The MIRABELLE system (Masini 1978) we have developed in our group uses a compiler of descriptions for interpreting handwritten drawings. In a preliminary phase this compiler extracts information from the structural description of the class of drawings to be recognized. This information is then used during the recognition process in order to control the analysis. We have extended this idea to the interpretation of 3D scenes in the TRIDENT vision system (Masini 1984). Precompiling a knowledge base (e.g. a set of production rules) also contributes to efficiency, as for example in the PROSPECTOR system (Konolige 1979).

3.2. Knowledge-Based and Expert Systems

We have already noted the present tendency in AI to design systems which are able to solve problems in very narrow domains by using knowledge specific to these domains. In such knowledge-based systems a very common paradigm for representing knowledge is the production rule paradigm (Davis 1977).

Let us briefly recall the basic principles of production-rule systems. A production rule is of the form :

IF Condition THEN Conclusion

where "Condition " represents a conjunction of predicates which have to be verified to order to enable the rule to be fired. The application

of this rule results in "Conclusion", i.e. emission or modification
of an hypothesis or a fact. This way of using a rule is referred to
as forward- or data-driven chaining. It is also possible to use a rule
in a backward-chaining mode. It consists of taking the "Conclusion"
part of a rule as a goal to be reached and of considering the verification
of the predicates in the left-hand side of this rule as new sub-problems.

A production system can be regarded as a simple example
of a pattern-driven system like HEARSAY II, even though the knowledge
sources in HEARSAY are much more complex. This system has been rewritten
as a pure production-rule system (Mc Craken 1981).

One model proposed for knowledge utilization in human brain
has been based on the idea of very rapid and frequent transfers between
a long-term memory which stores knowledge and a short-term memory which
uses it. Production rules can be considered as implementing these
knowledge transfers (Newell 1976).

An important characteristic of knowledge-based and expert
systems is that they represent a large amount of knowledge by breaking
it down into small chunks, such as production rules, which are easy
to formalize and to manipulate. This interesting property can be taken
into account in understanding systems for solving specific problems,
provided that human experts are able to solve these problems and to
formalize their expertise. This is particularly important for areas
in which the human expertise involves some kind of visual reasoning
about data (vision, signal interpretation, etc.). As an example we will
now present the case of acoustic-phonetic decoding of speech or, more
precisely, of speech-spectrogram reading.

Present automatic phonetic decoders only achieve about 65
to 70% of correct recognition for a single speaker. They are all based
on a more or less sophisticated phonetic model, for instance :

- a set of reference patterns which are tentatively matched
against speech segments (in a pattern-recognition approach to the
problem),

- a set of hierarchical decision rules (in the AI approach),

- a homogeneous stochastic model, e.g. a Markov model (in
the information theory approach) which makes it necessary to process
very large amount of speech data in order to tune the parameters of
the model.

It is worth noticing that these models are in no way incompatible : a satisfactory solution might consist of combining rule-based reasoning with a certain amount of (eventually stochastic) pattern matching.

Rule-based models have proven reasonably efficient, particularly when one can incorporate in the rules the human expertise accumulated through the examination of a large number of cases. One way of capturing such an expert knowledge consists of considering the activity of a phonetician while reading a speech spectrogram (Zue 1979). The acquisition of this expertise, and more generally of different kinds of knowledge about speech, will certainly help significantly in improving the segmentation and phonetic labeling of speech (Memmi 1983) (Caelen 1983) (Gillet 1984) (Meloni 1985) (Mizoguchi 1984).

The problem of spectrogram reading is conceptually difficult, since it combines cognitive reasoning processes with the perceptual aspects of visual inspection. However the expression of this problem in terms of image processing and vision is quite unhelpful. Moreover, recent studies (Bush 1983) have shown that an expert is able to adapt his expertise in order to decode not only "classical" spectrograms but also LPC spectra (Makhoul 1975) or tables of numerical values. The central question is, therefore, to capture the knowledge and metaknowledge that enable the expert to develop sophisticated decoding strategies. In the SYSTEXP project we are developing in Nancy at present (Carbonell 1984), we have put particular emphasis on this transfer of knowledge, which turns out to be more difficult than in more usual expert systems. Expert system technology provides a powerful tool for improving our knowledge of the speech decoding process, even though, for reasons related to the efficiency of the machines available at present, the final implementation of a speech recognition system will probably take the form of a procedural system (Haton 1984).

The expertise of the phonetician can be formalized into classical production rules of various kinds :

- phonetic class identification rules,

- exclusion rules,

- contextual rules (the most common ones), for instance :

IF   Right Context = /i/
AND Formant 2 is increasing
AND Formant 3 is increasing

```
AND First formant visible above 1000 Hz = 2200 Hz
AND No Discontinuity with formant 2 of /i/
THEN /m/ .
```

- meta-rules expressing the choice of various strategies according to the actual situation.

These rules are also useful in speech recognition tasks other than those involving phonetic decoding. We have, for instance, implemented a 2000 isolated word recognizer which uses the same expert knowledge base for the selection of small subsets of phonetically similar words (Mari 1984).

A knowledge-based approach has also been used in the field of pitch detection (Dove 1983). In this case knowledge engineering once again provides an efficient framework for mixing signal processing methods and human expertise.

The segmentation of the speech wave into phonetic units can also largely benefit from a knowledge-based azpproach. This segmentation can be carried out either by merging together small elements of speech (e.g. centiseconds) or by finding boundaries in the speech **continuum**. A **similar** alternative exists in image segmentation, where we can merge pixels or small parts according to their similarity, or progressively split an image into smaller regions. Image segmentation can thus be solved by an expert system approach (Nazif 1984). A common characteristic of the two domains is the non-unicity of the segmentation obtained. That makes further processing more complicated and necessitates the handling of multiple partial solutions throughout the understanding process.

The formalization and exploitation of phonological constraints can also be thought of in terms of knowledge-based systems (Oshika 1984). A fundamental phase consists of collecting an exhaustive base of rules representing the morpho-phonological phenomena of the language (Pérennou 1982).

More generally the problem of understanding complex "objects" as encountered in the domains of speech or vision can be solved by knowledgebased systems. For instance, expert systems have been designed for the image interpretation of aerial photographs (Mc Keown 1983). When the complexity of the tasks increases it becomes necessary to use a number of different knowledge bases and, therefore, a single expert system is no longer sufficient. Several models have been proposed, both for object identification (Kim 1984) (Reynolds 1984) and for the more general problem of scene interpretation (Riseman 1984) (Barrow 1976). We have already seen the interest of the blackboard model at this level. That model represents an efficient framework for an asynchronous, partially data-driven solution to the understanding problem. It has a number of important characteristics, including real cooperation between processes, the possibility of combining partial solutions for incrementally building up the interpretation of complex objects, problem solving at various levels of abstraction, etc. These characteristics are important in all domains of knowledge engineering and therefore a number of tools for building knowledge-based systems have been founded on them, such as HEARSAY III (Balzer 1980) or AGE (Nii 1979).

In fact the blackboard model is not the only one that has been proposed, particularly for KS cooperation. For instance, in the expert society model each expert has its own internal reasoning logic and control structures and communicates directly with the other expert modules (cf., for instance, (De Mori 1983) for an application to speech understanding). The model proposed by Nazif and Levine in their vision system (Nazif 1984) is a slightly different version of the blackboard model. In their system (figure 5) various processes responsible for different understanding tasks such as system initialization, line processing, region processing, general control, etc. communicate through two different blackboards :

- a short term memory (STM) which contains the data and facts about the actual problem (initial data, segmentation results and final interpretation),

- a long term memory (LTM) which contains knowledge and metaknowledge in the form of rules.

Figure 5. A vision system based on a two-blackboard model.

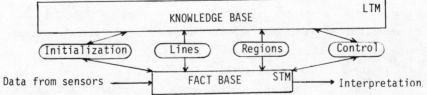

4. SEARCH STRATEGIES AND CONTROL STRUCTURES

In order to use various KSs efficiently, it is necessary to implement sophisticated control structures for controlling the interpretation process. Moreover, the combinatorial explosion of solutions has to be reduced by means of appropriate search strategies. We will now discuss these points and show their influence on the overall architectures of understanding systems.

4.1. Models for Control Structures

As we have seen, indeterminism and uncertainty are inherent to understanding problems. One way for coping with this consists of using hypothesis valuation techniques and of propagating "confidence factors" during the interpretation process. The implementation of sophisticated control structures is also of primary importance. There are two basically different philosophies for control structures :

- bottom-up or data driven control, which emits hypothesis in accordance with the input data and tries progressively to build up the interpretation of the object (sentence, scene, situation, etc.) under consideration,

- a top-down or model driven control, which consists of emitting hypotheses about the input data by taking into account high level knowledge available. This type of control can be associated with the classical AI notion of problem reduction.

When the KSs are coded under a Condition-Action form (like production rules or the blackboard model) these two control structure classes correspond to a forward and a backward chaining respectively.

In fact, the two methods refer to the same KSs and manipulate the same intermediate notions (e.g. phrases, words, syllables, etc. for speech or objects, regions, lines, etc. for images) and they mainly differ in the order in which the different processings are carried out and in the degree of detail into which they enter. The notions of bottom-up and top-down control are an oversimplification of the implementation of processing levels interaction in actual systems. In the human brain the control structures reach still much higher level of sophistication (Geschwind 1980).

In a bottom-up speech recognition system, a word lattice containing all the possible occurrences of words within a sentence is

built up from the acoustic data and the lexical knowledge. Syntactic
and semantic KSs are then used to select the most plausible sequence
of words that will represent the actual interpretation of the sentence.
This method is interesting, since it is not too sensitive to noisy data.
However it becomes untractable when the size of the application (number
of words, complexity of the language) increases, due to the large number
of possible solutions. The same situation exists in vision : a purely
bottom-up approach consisting of starting from pixels in order to build
up to a scene is only valuable in simple industrial applications where
adequate illumination conditions make it possible to only manipulate
binary images.

In top-down approaches, high level knowledge about the
application universe is used for making assumptions about the constituents
of a sentence or of a scene. The predictive aspect of top-down control
makes it possible to cancel a large number of hypotheses. This point
is particularly interesting in large applications where there is a high
number of possible combinatorial solutions. On the other hand, a purely
top-down control is relatively more affected by noise in the incoming
data.

The representation of knowledge in frames provides an
efficient way of implementing top-down control. Frames were initially
proposed for natural language processing (Schank 1975). They represent
for instance models of classes (Brachman 1978) and correspond to a less
fine granularity of knowledge than production rules. This representation
scheme features the important notion of procedural attachment, a notion
that makes it possible to activate procedures when the interpretation
process needs it. We have used this approach for controlling the
acoustic-phonetic decoding of speech in a knowledge-based system (Haton
1985). A somewhat different, but related, solution was proposed by (Green
1984). It consists of defining an intermediate representation structure
("Speech Sketch") in terms of frames and of trying to instantiate a
frame prototype within a sketch. The interpretation of other kinds of
objects, e.g. ECG signals (Lee 1984) can also be approached in this
way as well as the classification of objects in a vision system. The
use of representation structures in vision, as initially suggested
by (Marr 1982), seems as promising in this field as it does for speech.

Frames represent one particular case of object-oriented

representation of knowledge. The use of so-called object-oriented languages is of interest to understanding systems from at least two points of view :

- they provide the software environment for representing in a structured manner and for using the different entities which are manipulated (phonetic and supraphonetic units, objects of a scene, etc.),

- the basic mechanism of message-passing that underlies all these languages is well suited to the cooperation of KSs on a prediction-verification scheme cf., for instance, the cooperation of KSs in the blackboard model by emission of hypotheses, i.e. messages. It is moreover adapted to a parallel hardware implementation.

For simple applications an understanding system may operate in a structly bottom up way. On the other hand, it is very rare to find purely top down systems. An example is one version of the HWIM speech understanding system based on Klatt's analysis-by-synthesis model (Klatt 1975). In this version, the top down assumptions about words are pushed down to the level of acoustic signal by means of a speech synthesis system. A word assumption is then verified by dynamic comparison of its acoustic spectrum with a position of the input sentence. This solution is not computationnally efficient but it is interesting at the level of principle. One version of the ESOPE speech understanding system (Mariani 1982) is also based on a similar idea.

In most cases, systems based on top-down control structures incorporate some bottom-up process. The most commonly encountered arrangement consists of deriving a bottom-up symbolic description of the input data that corresponds at a same time to an important reduction of these data. This description might take the form, for example, of a phoneme lattice in the case of speech or a set of lines, regions or partially identified objects in vision. These preprocessed data are then taken into account by top-down processors.

As far as speech understanding goes, bottom-up or partially top-down systems are almost equally efficient for processing sentences of artificial, highly constrained languages (see, for instance, the MYRTILLE I system (Pierrel 1975) for a typical example). But for pseudo-natural languages it is absolutely necessary to implement much more sophisticated control strategies that combine bottom-up and top-down methods. Such structures can be found in the systems we have already mentioned : HEARSAY II, HWIM, MYRTILLE II, etc.

It is interesting to consider the development of understanding systems during the past fifteen years, both in vision and in speech. The first systems that were built relied heavily on a bottom-up methodology which consisted of extracting the maximum amount of information from the data by the use of powerful but blind techniques of signal processing and pattern recognition.

As we have already seen, except in simple cases (binary images or artificial sentences), such methods cannot handle the combinatorial explosion of possible solutions. They were therefore abandoned and replaced by top-down methods and then by mixed methods for understanding as in the case of the ACRONYM system (Brooks 1981). This system is based on a geometrical description of objects which is independent of the application domain. However, these models are not yet completely satisfactory and there is now a tendency towards basic studies about the physical and physiological phenomena that are involved for instance in the process of image or speech production and perception : properties of objects (luminosity, brightness, textures, geometry of surfaces, etc.), vision process (Brady 1981), etc. on the one hand, phonetic and phonological properties of sounds, phonation and audition processes, etc. on the other. This promising new tendency calls on a number of very different disciplines and necessitates the elucidation of diverse knowledge and expertise domains.

4.2. Search Strategies

At each step during the understanding process a potentially large set of partial solutions has to be examined. In order to restrict this set to a computationnally reasonable size and to avoid any combinatorial explosion, sophisticated search strategies have to be implemented so that an acceptable interpretation of the incoming data -though not always the optimal one- is finally reached. The search problem is well known in AI and it has been addressed a great number of times. Search strategies are crucial in complex problems like speech understanding or vision since the solution space is very large, whereas in more restricted tasks such as diagnostic expert systems (e.g. the MYCIN system (Shortliffe 1976) which was among the first systems developed) an exhaustive search throughout the solution space is practicable.

Dynamic programming yields an optimal solution to the search problem. For instance, it has been implemented by IBM (Jelinek 1982) in association with a Markov model of the language by using the Viterbi algorithm. Relaxation techniques used in image processing are approximately equivalent to this algorithm.

Dynamic programming algorithms have a complexity proportional to n^2 where n represents the number of states to be explored. They are therefore often much too time-consuming, in which case it is necessary to use suboptimal but faster heuristic search strategies.

This means that, instead of a global strategy, we have a sequence of local decisions which will hopefully lead to a global acceptable solution in accordance with the general prediction-verification paradigm. Two widely used strategies are :

- a best-first search strategy with backtracking : it consists of keeping the most promising solution at each step and of developing it as far as possible. If this becomes impossible, a backtracking algorithm is activated for considering another solution. This strategy can be found in numerous systems, since it is easy to implement and efficient for small-and medium-size applications,

- a beam-search strategy : this consists of simultaneously retaining the k best solutions and developing them in parallel, without any backtracking.

This strategy is usually more efficient than the best first strategy, especially in the case of speech understanding (Quinton 1982). It is the strategy used in the HARPY system.

These two strategies are very popular in various domains of AI and have been adapted in a number of different ways. Specific constraints of speech and vision have led to the design of a new class of search strategies, called anchor-point or island-driven strategies. The basic idea consists of starting the interpretation of a sentence or an image from one or several reliable anchor-points. Such strategies are rather complex to implement but prove to be very useful for processing pseudo-natural sentences or images and handwritten sketches (Haton 1976).

5. CONCLUSION

Knowledgebased techniques have led to significant successfull applications of AI in various domains. We have shown in this chapter the importance of such techniques in computer understanding systems, especially in the fields of speech and vision. These fields are characterized by a close interaction between the perceptual and cognitive features and by a high degree of indeterminism. The interpretation of "objects" in this framework makes it necessary to arrange for several knowledge-sources to cooperate in an efficient manner. We have particularly emphasized the representation of knowledge and the way it can be used together with the associated control structures and search strategies. Practical examples have shown the analogy that exists between the two domains of speech and vision.

Considerable progress has been made in computer understanding during the past ten years even though the models that have been proposed still need improving. An important point is the necessity of adapted, parallel architectures for real-time implementation of these models. The different projects on new computer generation and the use of VLSI custom circuits will hopefully bring solutions to this problem.

REFERENCES

Balzer, R. et al. (1980). Hearsay III : A Domain-Independent Framework for Expert Systems. Proc. Conf. Amer. Assoc. Intell.

Barrow, H. & Tenenbaum, J. (1976). MSYS : A System for Reasoning about Scenes. SRI Techn. Note 121.

Brachman, R.J. (1978). A Structural Paradigm for Representing Knowledge. BBN Report 3605.

Brady, J.M. (1981). The Changing Shape of Computer Vision. Artificial Intelligence, 17, n° 1-3, pp. 1-15.

Brooks, R.A. (1981). Symbolic Reasoning among 3D Objects and 2D Models. Artificial Intelligence, 16, pp. 285-348.

Bush, M.A., Kopec, G.E. & Zue, V.W. (1983). Selecting Acoustic Features for Stop Consonant Identification. Proc. IEEE ICASSP, Boston.

Caelen, J. et al. (1983). Structuration des informations acoustiques dans le projet ARIAL. Speech Communication, 2, n° 2-3, pp. 219-222.

Carbonell, N., Fohr, D., Haton, J.P., Lonchamp, F. & Pierrel, J.M. (1984). An Expert System for the Automatic Reading of French Spectro-grams. Proc. IEEE ICASSP-84, San Diego.

Davis, R. & King J. (1977). An Overview of Production Systems. Machine Intelligence, 8, pp. 300-332.

De Mori, R., Laface, P. Petrone, G. & Segnan, M. (1983). Access to a Large Lexicon Using Phonetic Features. EUSIPCO, Erlangen.

Dove, W. et al. (1983). Knowledge-Based Pitch Detection. Proc. IEEE ICASSP, Boston.

Engelmore, R.E. & Terry A. (1979). Structure and Function of the CRYSALIS System. Proc. IJCAI-6, 1979.

Geschwind, N. (1980). Neurological Knowledge and Complex Behaviors. Cognitive Science, 4, n° 2, pp. 185-193.

Gillet, D. et al. (1984). SERAC : un système expert en reconnaissance
    acoustico-phonétique. 4ème congrès RF-IA, AFCET-INRIA, Paris.

Green, P.D. & Wood, A.R. (1984). Knowledge-Based Speech Understanding :
    Towards a Representational Approach, Proc. ECAI-84, pp.
    337-340.

Hanson, A.R. & Riseman, E.M. (1978). VISIONS : A Computer System for
    Interpreting Scenes. In Computer Vision Systems, Hanson,
    A.R. & Riseman, E.M., editors, Academic Press.

Haton, J.P. & Mohr, R. (1976). A New Parsing Algorithm for Imperfect
    Patterns and its Applications. Proc. ICPR, San Diego.

Haton, J.P. & Lazrek, M. (1984). Segmentation et identification des
    phonèmes dans un système de reconnaissance automatique de
    la parole continue. 4ème congrès RF-IA, AFCET-INRIA, Paris.

Haton, J.P. & Damestoy, J.P. (1985). A Frame Language for the Control
    of Phonetic Decoding in Continuous Speech Recognition. Proc.
    ICASSP, Tampa, Florida.

Jelinek, F. (1982). Self-Organized Continuous Speech Recognition. In
    Automatic Speech Analysis and Recognition, Haton, J.P.,
    editor, D. Reidel.

Kim, J.H., Payton, D.W. & Olin, K.E. (1984). An Expert System for Object
    Recognition in Natural Scenes. Proc. First COnf. on Applic.
    of AI, Denver.

Klatt, D.H. (1975). Review of the ARPA Speech Understanding System.
    In Speech Recognition, Reddy, D., editor, Academic Press.

Konolige, K. (1979). An Inference Net Compiler for the PROSPECTOR Rule-
    Based Consultation System. Proc. IJCAI-6.

Lee, H.S. & Thakor, N.V. (1984). Frame-Based Understanding of ECG Signals.
    Proc. First Conf. on Applic. of AI, Denver.

Lesser, V.R. et al. (1975). Organization of the HEARSAY II Speech Under-
    standing System, IEEE Trans. ASSP, 23, pp. 11-23.

Lowerre, B.T. (1976). The HARPY Speech Recognition System. Technical
    Report, CMU, Dept. of Computer Sciences.

Makhoul, J. (1975). Linear Prediction : A Tutorial Review. Proc. IEEE,
    63, n° 4, pp. 561-580.

Mari, J.F. & Haton, J.P. (1984). Some Experiments in Automatic Recognition
    of a Thousand Word Vocabulary. Proc. IEEE ICASSP, San Diego.

Mariani, J. (1982). ESOPE : un système de compréhension de la parole
    continue. Thèse d'Etat, Université de Paris VI, juillet.

Marr, D. (1982). Vision. Freeman.

Masini, G. (1978). Réalisation d'un système de reconnaissance structu-
    relle et d'interprétation de dessins. Thèse de 3ème cycle,
    Université de Nancy I.

Masini, G. & Zaroli, F. (1984). Présentation de TRIDENT : un système
    d'interprétation d'images tridimensionnelles. 4ème congrès
    RF-IA, AFCET-INRIA, Paris.

Mc Cracken, D.L. (1981). A Production System Version of the HEARSAY II
    Speech Understanding System. Univ. Research Press.

Mc Keown, D.M., Jr. & Mc Dermott, J. (1983). Toward Expert Systems for
    Photo Interpretation. IEEE Conf. on Trends and Applications
    83, pp. 33-39.

Meloni, H., Gispert, J. & Guizol, J. (1985). Traitement de connaissances
    pour l'identification analytique de mots dans le discours
    continu. Congrès AGCET Informatique, Paris.

Memmi, D., Eskenazi, M. & Mariani, J. (1983). Un système expert pour
    la lecture de sonagrammes. Speech Communication, 2, n° 2-3,
    pp. 234-236.

Mizoguchi, R. & Kakusho, O. (1984). Continuous Speech Recognition Based on Knowledge Engineering Techniques. Proc. 7th Int. Conf. Pattern Recognition, Montreal.

Nagao, M.T. et al. (1979). Structural Analysis of Complex Aerial Photographs. 6th IJCAI.

Nazif, A.M. & Levine, M.D. (1984). Low Level Image Segmentation : An Expert System. IEEE Tr. PAMI, 6, n° 5, pp. 555-577.

Newell, A. et al. (1973). Speech Understanding Systems : Final Report of a Study Group. North-Holland, Amsterdam.

Newell, A. (1976). Production Systems : Models of Control Structures. In Visual Information Processing, Chase, W., editor, Academic Press.

Nii, H.P. & Feigenbaum, E.A. (1983). Rule-Based Understanding of Signals. In Pattern-Directed Inference Systems, Waterman and Hayes-Roth, editors, Academic Press.

Nii, H.P. & Aiello, N. (1979). AGE (Attempt to GEneralize) : A Knowledge-Based Program for Building Knowledge-Based Programs. 6th IJCAI.

Oshika, B. (1984). Phonological Rules for Continuous Speech Recognition. In Towards Robustness in Speech Recognition, Lea, W., editor, Prentice-Hall.

Perennou, G. (1982). Lexical Access and Phonologic Processing in ARIAL II. 6th ICPR, Munich.

Pierrel, J.M. (1975). Contribution à la compréhension automatique du discours continu. Thèse de 3ème cycle, Université de Nancy I.

Prager, J. et al. (1977). Segmentation Processes in the VISIONS System. Proc. 5th IJCAI, Cambridge.

Quinton, P. (1982). Utilisation de contraintes syntaxiques pour la reconnaissance de la parole continue. TSI, 1, n° 3, pp. 233-248.

Reynolds, G. et al. (1984). Hierarchical Knowledge Directed Object Extraction Using a Combined Region and Line Representation. Proc. Workshop on Computer Vision : Representation and Control Annapolis.

Riseman, E.M. & Hanson, A.R. (1984). A Methodology for the Development of General Knowledge-Based Vision Systems. Proc. IEEE Workshop on Principles of Knowledge-Based Systems, Denver.

Rubin, S. (1978). The ARGOS Image Understanding System. Ph. D. Thesis, Carnegie-Mellon University, Pittsburgh.

Shank, R.C. (1975). Conceptual Information Processing, North-Holland.

Shirai, Y. (1973). A Context Sensitive Line Finder for Recognition of Polyhedra. Artificial Intelligence, 4, pp. 95-119.

Shoup, J.E. (1980). Phonological Aspects of Speech Recognition. In Trends in Speech Recognition, Lea, W., editor, prentice-Hall.

Waterman, J. and Hayes-Roth, F. (1978), editors. Pattern-Directed Inference Systems, Academic Press.

Woods, W.A. et al. (1976). Speech Understanding Systems. Final Technical Progress Report, Report n° 3438, Vol. I-V, BBN.

Zucker, S.W. (1976). Relaxation Labeling and the Reduction of Local Ambiguities. In Pattern Recognition and Artificial Intelligence, Chen, C.H., editor, Academic Press.

Zue, V. & Cole, R. (1979). Experiments in Spectrogram Reading. Proc. IEEE ICASSP, Washington.

Knowledge Representation: Features of Knowledge

James P. Delgrande*

Department of Computer Science, University of Toronto, Canada

John Mylopoulos**

Department of Computer Science, University of Toronto, Canada

1. Introduction

It is by now a cliché to claim that knowledge representation is a fundamental research issue in Artificial Intelligence (AI) underlying much of the research, and the progress, of the last fifteen years. And yet, it is difficult to pinpoint exactly what knowledge representation is, does, or promises to do. A thorough survey of the field by Ron Brachman and Brian Smith [Brachman & Smith 80] points out quite clearly the tremendous range in viewpoints and methodologies of researchers in knowledge representation. This paper is a further attempt to look at the field in order to examine the state of the art and provide some insights into the nature of the research methods and results. The distinctive mark of this overview is its viewpoint: that propositions encoded in knowledge bases have a number of important features, and these features serve, or ought to serve, as a basis for guiding current interest and activity in AI. Accordingly, the paper provides an account of some of the issues that arise in studying knowledge, belief, and conjecture, and discusses some of the approaches that have been adopted in formalizing and using some of these features in AI. The account is intended primarily for the computer scientist with little exposure to AI and Knowledge Representation, and who is interested in understanding some of the issues. As such, the paper concentrates on raising issues and sketching possible approaches to solutions. More technical details can be found in the work referenced throughout the paper.

Naively, and circularly, knowledge representation is concerned with the development of suitable notations for representing knowledge. The reason for its importance in AI is that the current paradigm for building "intelligent" systems assumes that such systems must have access to domain-specific knowledge and must be capable of using it in performing their intended task (hence the term **knowledge based systems**). This paradigm is in sharp contrast to the approaches used in the sixties, when the emphasis was on general-

---

* Current address: Department of Computing Science, Simon Fraser University, Burnaby, BC.
** Senior fellow, Canadian Institute for Advanced Research.

purpose search techniques. The aim of the earlier approaches, which are termed **power-oriented**, was to construct general, domain-independent problem-solving systems [Goldstein & Papert 77]. This goal was generally found to be unrealistic for nontrivial tasks since, with undirected search, the number of alternatives that needs to be explored grows exponentially with the size of the problem to be solved. Current attitudes towards "intelligent" system building can be accurately summarized by the slogan "**knowledge is power**".

According to popular wisdom, a knowledge based system includes a **knowledge base** which can be thought of as a data structure assumed to represent propositions about a **domain of discourse** (or **world**). A knowledge base is constructed in terms of a **knowledge representation scheme** which, ideally, provides a means for interpreting the data structure with respect to its intended subject matter and for manipulating it in ways which are consistent with its intended meaning. There already exist several surveys of Knowledge Representation which describe the field mostly from the point of view of current practice; these include [Hayes 74], [McDermott 78], [Barr & Davidson 80] and [Mylopoulos & Levesque 84]. In addition, there have been several fine collections of research papers focusing on Knowledge Representation, such as [McCalla & Cercone 83] and [Brachman and Levesque 85]. The newcomer to the area may also be interested in key papers such as [McCarthy & Hayes 69], [Minsky 75], [Woods 75], [Hayes 77], [Reiter 78], [Newell 81], and [Brachman & Levesque 82] which have raised fundamental research issues and have influenced the direction of research.

We already noted the difficulty of characterizing Knowledge Representation as a research area in terms of a coherent set of goals or methodologies. In preparation for the discussion, however, we need to adopt at least working definitions for the terms "knowledge" and "representation". By **knowledge** we will mean **justified true belief**, following traditional philosophical literature. While there are shortcomings to such a working definition, as [Dretske 81] points out, it is adequate for our purpose. By **representation** we will understand an encoding into a data structure. Intuitively then, **knowledge representation** means the encoding of justified true beliefs into suitable data structures. This though is a little rigid for our purposes. For example we will want to consider also encodings where the information is only thought to be true or maybe even is known to be false or inconsistent. So we will on occasion want to deal with encodings where the information may not be knowledge *per se*.

Preference for one knowledge representation scheme over another depends heavily on the nature of the formal system adopted as a formalization of knowledge. However the preference for one scheme over another depends also on the suitability of the data structures offered, i.e., on how direct the mapping is from the components of the data structures used into their intended interpretations. This paper is concerned primarily with the nature of knowledge and its formalizations, rather than its representation. A companion paper [Kramer & Mylopoulos 85] attempts to examine the knowledge *representation* issues by surveying organizational structures that have been proposed for knowledge bases.

For the purposes of the discussion in the remainder of the paper, a knowledge base KB is a pair $<KB_0, \vdash_L>$ where KB_0 is a collection of statements in the language of some logic L, for example:

$$KB_0 = \{Student(John), Supervisor(John, Mary)\}$$

and $\vdash_L$ is the derivability relation in L, i.e., specifies what can be derived from the axioms, given the rules of inference of L. Then

$$\alpha \in KB \quad \text{iff} \quad KB_0 \vdash_L \alpha$$

(Adoption of this view implies that knowledge bases are essentially treated here as theories in Mathematical Logic, with KB_0 playing the role of a set of proper axioms.) Thus the example knowledge base contains not just the statements in KB_0 but also others that can be derived from them in L. So KB may contain statements such as

$$Student(John) \lor Professor(Joe)$$

$$\neg\neg Student(John)$$

depending on our choice of L.

Statements in a knowledge base can be assigned a **truth value** (usually either true or false) given a world or domain of discourse. The assignment of truth values to statements is carried out in terms of a **semantic function**. A standard method for doing so, due to Alfred Tarski, treats a knowledge base **interpretation** as a 3-tuple $<D, R, F>$ where D is the set of individuals in the domain of discourse, and R and F are respectively the relations and functions between individuals that hold in the world. Tarskian semantics assumes the availability of semantic functions that map constant symbols in L, such as *John*, onto individuals in D, predicate symbols in L, such as *Student*, onto relations in R, and function symbols in L onto functions in F. From these functions, the notion of truth in L can be made explicit. So, for example, *Student(John)* is true (roughly) if John (the object in D) *satisfies* the property of studenthood. A consequence of *Student(John)* being true in the interpretation is that (in most logics)

$$Student(John) \lor Student(Mary)$$

will also be true. An interpretation is said to be a **model** of a knowledge base if and only if all sentences in the knowledge base come out true in the interpretation.

Of course, interpretations are only idealizations of the "real" worlds of students, ships, and bombs with respect to which *we* interpret a knowledge base. Nevertheless, a formal semantics, Tarskian or other, can be extremely valuable as long as the structure of the interpretation captures our intuitions about the world or domain in question.

The remainder of the paper consists of two parts. The first discusses the basic nature of knowledge, belief, and hypothesis, and introduces a number of important concepts and methods for their study. The second part points out a number of features that information in knowledge bases has, such as incompleteness, inconsistency, inaccuracy, and uncertainty, and provides a brief overview of methods that have been used in attempting to deal with these features within a representational framework.

2. On The Nature of Knowledge

The main concern of this section is the relationship between the information contained in a knowledge base, and the state of the world or domain of discourse which the knowledge base is intended to describe. First we discuss the commitment that is made with respect to the truth of a statement. While we have restricted ourselves so far to knowledge *per se*, many systems treat weaker notions such as belief or hypothesis. This commitment may be called the **epistemic status** of a statement. Second we consider the **assertional status** of a statement, i.e., the confidence in the assertion represented by a statement. For example, a statement may be regarded as holding absolutely and without exception, or alternatively as only being usually true. Lastly we review semantic theories that have been proposed for assigning meaning to encodings of knowledge.

2.1. Knowledge, Belief, and Hypothesis

Knowledge was defined as "true, justified, belief". In this section we develop this notion further by exploring the terms "true", "justified", and "belief". The notion of truth can be discharged by a standard Tarskian account. However we are still left with the terms "justified" and "belief". Let us look at "belief" first.

Belief can be defined in a surprisingly simple way. Given a knowledge-based system (or agent) A, A believes a sentence P, just when P appears in A's knowledge base (or "language of thought"). Belief then, so construed, consists of literally anything that can be represented. So does this make the term vacuous? Not quite: belief may be taken as distinguishing genuine cognitive systems from simple processors of information, such as television sets [Dretske 81]. However since belief is what is attributed to cognitive systems, it is clear that a general unconstrained "believing" system is unacceptable: one would also want to ensure that beliefs are coherent, consistent, and (in a nutshell) "reasonable". So, for example, given that

$Student(John)$

$(x)[Student(x) \supset HardWorker(x)]$

are believed to be true, one may want to require that

$HardWorker(John)$

also be believed to be true. Similarly it seems reasonable to stipulate that it not be the case that

$\neg Student(John)$

be believed. Typically then one would want beliefs, although possibly counterfactual, to have properties similar to knowledge.

Logical systems of knowledge and belief typically deal with only one of knowledge or belief. For such systems standard first-order logic is usually augmented with a sentential operator K, where $K\alpha$ may be read as "α is known (believed) to be true". Whether the informal interpretation of K actually corresponds to knowledge, or instead to belief, though usually depends only on whether the axiom

$K\alpha \supset \alpha$

is present. This axiom has the informal reading "if α is believed to be true, then α is true". If the axiom is present, then whatever is in the knowledge base is in fact true, and the notion corresponds to knowledge; otherwise it corresponds to belief. Any other axioms of the system apply both to knowledge and belief. The fact that a system deals with knowledge (say) rather than belief then has very little effect on the characteristics of the system. Given this, the work of Moore on reasoning about knowledge and action ([Moore 80]) and of Fagin and his co-workers on multi-agent reasoning ([Fagin et al 84]) deal with knowledge, while that of Levesque on incomplete knowledge bases ([Levesque 81]) deals with belief. Konolige, in his dissertation research [Konolige 84], examines both notions from the point of view of a set of agents. Clearly many systems of default reasoning are not knowledge-preserving and thus deal with belief. [Halpern & Moses 85] provides a general introduction to logics of knowledge and belief, while [Hughes & Cresswell 68] is an excellent introduction to Modal Logic.

However matters do not end here. For example, if a sentence is belief only, then it is possible that the sentence may later be discovered to not in fact hold. In this case, other beliefs based on the erroneous belief would have to be re-examined and perhaps modified or retracted. This leads to the question of which beliefs should be introduced or held, or, more broadly, how one may justify a belief. Let us call a justified belief that is not known to be true a **hypothesis**. [Quine & Ullian 78] is a good introduction to issues surrounding this notion, while [Scheffler 81] provides a more thorough exposition. Under this view, it is the established truth of a sentence that separates knowledge *per se* from hypothesis and belief. The justification of a sentence, on the other hand, separates knowledge and hypothesis from belief. In this latter case, a known sentence may be regarded as being *absolutely* justified.

It would be going too far afield to survey justification in any depth. It is instructive though to consider forms of reasoning that can be used to introduce justified belief into a knowledge base. For purposes of illustration we will make use of the following classical form for deductive reasoning.

$$(x)[P(x) \supset Q(x)] \tag{1}$$

$$P(a) \tag{2}$$

$$Q(a) \tag{3}$$

The inference from (1) and (2) to (3) is of course absolutely justified. However, the schema can also be used as a template for introducing justified belief. Some default logics for example may be regarded as automating a weaker form of the above deduction. Thus if one knows that most elephants are grey, and that Clyde is an elephant, then lacking information to the contrary, one may feel justified in concluding that Clyde is grey. (These considerations are discussed further in the section on nonmonotonicity.) Strictly speaking, such an inference would introduce a *hypothesis* that Clyde is grey. Justification would depend on pragmatic factors, such as the number of elephants seen, knowledge of albinoism, etc.

However, the schema may be employed in quite different ways for introducing hypotheses. Consider first situations where we have instances of (1) and (3). We can then claim that rule (1), together with conclusion (3) suggests a cause, namely (2). Thus for example if we have that "All people with colds have runny noses" and "John has a runny nose", we can propose the hypothesis "John has a cold". If we knew further that people with colds had elevated temperature, and that John had this symptom, then our faith in the hypothesis that John had a cold would be strengthened. This type of reasoning is known as *abductive inference* [Pople 73]. Abduction provides a mechanism for reasoning from effect to possible cause. It provides a model of reasoning that has been found useful in the development of medical diagnosis systems (in particular) and expert systems (in general). The inferencing components of many production rule systems, as perhaps best exemplified by MYCIN [Shortliffe 76], can be viewed as implementing particular forms of abductive reasoning. Abduction can also be associated with default reasoning. Thus if we knew that people with colds *typically* had an elevated temperature, then, again, if John had this symptom, we could propose that John had a cold. The question of how to determine one's faith in such a diagnosis in a non *ad hoc* fashion is, of course, very difficult.

Returning to our schema for reasoning, consider the third alternative where we have instances of (2) and (3) — for example, a large collection of ravens, all of which happen to be black. In this case we might hypothesise the general statement "All ravens are black". This is known as **inductive** reasoning. An inductive mechanism provides a means whereby general conjectures may be formed from simple facts or ground atomic formulas. However the general problems of justifying induction and explicating the notion of confirmation are known from philosophy to be extremely difficult [Goodman 79], [Scheffler 81]. In AI, inductive inference programs typically assume that the domain of application is governed by some underlying grammar. [Angulin & Smith 82] provides a thorough survey of efforts in this area, while [Shapiro 81] presents a particularly elegant treatment of some of the problems.

This breakdown into knowledge, hypothesis, and belief gives us a means of characterising the **epistemic status** of a statement. If a statement is considered to be knowledge, then presumably one would be unwilling to allow that it can be anything but true. Thus any mathematical or definitional statement would be treated as knowledge. There are certainly other sentences though that one would wish to treat as knowledge. For example whales, which were once regarded as fish, are now are recognised as being mammals. However, while this demonstrates that "all whales are mammals" isn't knowledge *per se*, it would be a rare knowledge base that didn't treat it as such. Knowledge then, pragmatically viewed, consists of those sentences that are taken for granted, i.e. that one is unwilling to give up. This suggests that a particular set of formulas may or may not be taken as knowledge, depending on one's viewpoint. For example, much of current astronomy is conducted under the assumption that the theory of relativity is true. Yet relativity certainly isn't knowledge as such (since the theory, like most of its predecessors, could be incorrect) and so, at a lower level, this theory itself is subject to experimentation and confirmation.

2.2. Assertional Status

The previous section dealt with the epistemic status of a statement — that is, the presumed truth of a sentence. In this section we turn to the **assertional status** of a (general) sentence, that is, the strength of the claim being made by a sentence. This notion is best introduced by means of an example. Consider the statement

"Elephants are grey".

There are at least three readings:

(1)   "All elephants are grey". While this seems intuitively reasonable, strictly speaking it is false, since there are, among other things, albino elephants.

(2)   "Typically elephants are grey". This has the related reading "an elephant is grey with confidence or probability p".

(3)   "Elephants are grey. However we acknowledge possible exceptional individuals". In this case the intention is that greyness is in some sense associated with elephanthood (although it is not clear exactly how).

These possibilities lead to three different approaches to specifying the meaning of a term. Consider the first case. The claim that a term may be exactly identified with a collection of properties has been called the **traditional theory of meaning** [Schwartz 77]. Under this theory, "all elephants have four legs" (if true) would be **analytic** (i.e. would be true purely by virtue of meaning and independently of collateral information), and the meaning of "elephant" could be laid out by specifying enough of these properties. Squares being equilateral rectangles and bachelors being unmarried males are, in most accounts, examples of analytic truths.

However, it is certainly not the case that all elephants have four legs, nor is it the case that every elephant is grey or has a trunk. In fact it seems that elephants may have no commonplace exceptionless properties, and that, barring assertions such as "all elephants are mammals" and logical truths, any general statement concerning elephants may have exceptions. Clearly a similar argument can be applied to other common nouns, such as "lemon", "gold", "water" and so on. Thus for example a lemon need not be yellow, nor bitter, nor necessarily oblong. Such terms are examples of **natural kind** terms. These terms may be characterised as being of explanatory importance, but whose normal distinguishing characteristics are explained by deep-lying mechanisms [Putman 75]. Hilary Putnam, in the reference just cited, argues persuasively that natural kind terms have *no* knowable defining conditions, and no non-trivial exceptionless properties. Thus he takes the position that a statement such as "elephants are mammals" may be falsified; this seems not unreasonable if one considers that "whales are fish" was once thought to be true.

There are of course terms that may be precisely defined or specified. For example, a square is defined to be an equilateral rectangle — a three-sided square makes no sense whatsoever. Also, if we define "uncle" to mean a brother-in-law of a parent, then someone who fulfills the latter conditions cannot fail to be an uncle, and an uncle cannot but be a brother-in-law of a parent. These definitions clearly do not allow for exceptions. The notions of definitional terms and terminology moreover are key in the design of many knowledge representation systems, and in particular semantic network formalisms such as KL-ONE [Brachman 79]. So the notions of analyticity and the traditional theory of meaning, while inapplicable to natural kind terms, are nonetheless necessary for terminology and definition.

In the second reading of "elephants are grey", where we have, "typically elephants are grey", a term is identified with a description of a typical member. This is the essence of prototype theory [Rosch 78]. In AI, prototype theory provides the foundation for many frame-based reasoning systems. Frame-based reasoning systems are commonly used for recognizing stereotypical situations. For such applications, where an individual, situation, etc. is identified on the basis of a description, prototype theory seems perfectly adequate. Thus to recognise an elephant, we might look for a trunk, grey colouring, four legs, and so on. If any of these features are missing, it doesn't mean that the object isn't an elephant, although it may make us less certain that it in fact is. For general reasoning systems however prototype theory has drawbacks. Foremost is the fact that for reasoning with prototypes, one is forced to use a probabilistic or default theory of reasoning. In contrast, standard first-order logic can be employed for reasoning with analytic (definitional) statements. Also, as is pointed out in [Israel & Brachman 81], one cannot form complex concepts strictly within prototype theory. A prototype system has to be told for example that (the concept) "four-legged elephant" subsumes both "four-legged" and "elephant". In summary then prototype theory appears too weak to be used as a medium for the general representation of knowledge. However, it has been found useful in representing *descriptions* of natural kind terms.

The third case attempts to maintain a general sentence such as "elephants have four legs" while admitting exceptions to the sentence at the same time. This approach lacks a precise and complete formalisation; however it can be motivated by means of a naive view of scientific theory formation. Consider the scientific hypothesis that water boils at 273°K. In testing this hypothesis by examining a particular sample of water, one verifies not just the statement in question, but also a host of underlying assumptions [Putnam 79], [Quine & Ullian 78]. Thus a test of the statement "water boils at 273°K" presumes that the water is pure, that atmospheric pressure is 760mm, that the thermometer is accurate, that the act of measurement does not affect the boiling point, etc. The failure of a sample to boil at 273°K then does not necessarily falsify the hypothesis, but rather falsifies the conjunction of the hypothesis and the underlying assumptions. The original conjecture can be maintained by claiming that some assumption has been falsified, even though the particular assumption may not be specified, nor even known. Similar remarks apply to four-leggedness and elephanthood: a three-legged instance may be discharged by appealing to some (possibly unknown) underlying assumption. This is not to say though that defining conditions for natural kind terms may not be hypothesised. For example we may entertain the hypothesis that water *is* H_2O. In this case no exceptions are permitted; the radical OH for example is simply not water. On the other hand, the hypothesis that water is H_2O may be used to account for (at least in principle) the notion of boiling point, and to account for any exceptions.

2.3. Semantic Theories of Knowledge

A knowledge representation scheme is usually intended as a vehicle for conveying meanings about some domain of discourse. To be at all useful there must be an external account of the way particular configurations expressed in terms of the scheme correspond to particular arrangements in the domain. That is, there must be an associated **semantic theory**. Simply put, this means that knowledge bases must be *about* something, and a formal account of this aboutness constitutes a semantic theory.

As indicated in the introduction, the standard starting point for semantic theories is Tarskian semantics, which is relatively straightforward, well understood, and well accepted by now. The question arises though as to how this treatment can be extended to deal with knowledge (or belief — since the points made in this section apply equally to both notions, we will use them interchangeably). The main difficulty in providing a semantic theory for knowledge is that the truth value of statements may or may not be known, independently of their actual truth value in the domain of discourse. Thus for example one may not know whether it is raining in North Bay at present, although it certainly either is or is not raining there now. Moreover if we allow that knowledge can be explicitly referred to, there arise questions concerning the extent to which one can have knowledge about one's own knowledge or knowledge about one's ignorance. If we introduce a new monadic operator K for "knows", then these questions concern the status of sentences such as $KK\alpha$ or $K\neg K\alpha$. In our review, we consider three semantic theories that have been proposed for knowledge and belief. Following [Levesque 84], we refer to them as the **possible worlds**, **syntactic**, and **situational** approaches.

For possible worlds semantics, [Hintikka 62] is the seminal work. Within AI, [Moore 80] and [Levesque 84] present formalisations of knowledge or belief based on a possible-worlds semantics. To illustrate this approach, consider the following knowledge base:

Teacher(*John*)

Teacher(*Bill*) ∨ *Teacher*(*Mary*)

(*x*)[*Teacher*(*x*) ⊃ *SchoolEmployee*(*x*)].

This knowledge base may be regarded as specifying what is known about the world. Thus it *constrains* the way the world is thought to be; for example, under the intended interpretation, John is a teacher and at least one of Bill and Mary are teachers. However it also *underconstrains* the world. If Lou is an individual, then according to what's known, she may or may not be a teacher. That is, the actual world may be such that Lou teaches, or it may be such that she does not. We can say then that there are, according to the knowledge base, possible worlds in which Lou does teach, and others in which she does not. On the other hand, there are no possible worlds compatible with the knowledge base in which John doesn't teach; and in each possible world compatible with the knowledge base at least one of Bill or Mary teaches.

Now each such possible world may be characterised using a Tarskian framework. Thus if *Teach*(*Lou*) is true in a possible world, so are ¬¬*Teach*(*Lou*) and *Teach*(*Lou*) ∨ ¬*Teach*(*John*). So a knowledge base can be characterised semantically as a set of possible worlds. A system knows a sentence α just when α is true in all worlds that are possible according to the system's knowledge base. Thus, from our previous example, the system knows not just that John is a teacher, but also that John is a school employee. Depending on how the notion of "possible" is defined, one can stipulate, for example, that if something is known, then it is known to be known, and that if something is not known, then it is known to be not known — that is, whether Kα implies KKα, or ¬Kα implies K¬Kα respectively. A drawback to this approach for modelling knowledge is that it implies **logical omniscience**; that is, all logical consequences of beliefs must also be believed. Thus all valid sentences must be believed. This entails for example that such a system knows the outcome of an optimal strategy in chess or the truth of Fermat's last theorem. Furthermore, if a sentence and its negation are believed, then so must be every sentence. Neither restriction seems particularly realistic. The first is computationally unreasonable and, for the second, most people would happily admit to the possibility of harbouring inconsistent beliefs, without thereby believing everything.

An alternative, which may be called the **syntactic approach**, is to have the model structure contain, or be isomorphic to, an explicit set of sentences. [Moore & Hendrix 79] and [Konolige 84] are both advocates of this approach. Given our example knowledge base then, all that would be known would be the three original sentences. It would not necessarily be known that *SchoolEmployee(John)*, since this sentence doesn't appear explicitly in the knowledge base. However this is not unreasonable: one cannot in general know all consequences of one's beliefs — this after all is the problem with logical omniscience. This alternative also has some intuitive support. Certainly when people acquire beliefs, they seem to usually do so without markedly altering their prior set of beliefs. Conceivably belief acquisition, in most instances, consists of little more than adding a belief to an existent set. The approach also avoids the problem of logical omniscience, since everything believed is explicitly represented.

However this approach seems to make too "fine grain" a distinction with respect to the *form* of a belief. The sentence

$$Teacher(Bill) \lor Teacher(Mary)$$

is in the belief set, and so is believed. However

$$Teacher(Mary) \lor Teacher(Bill)$$

is not in the belief set, and so is not believed. Yet this is counterintuitive: a disjunction, $\alpha \lor \beta$, may be informally read as "α or β (or both) are true" — a reading that is independent of any ordering on α and β. So it would seem that whenever $\alpha \lor \beta$ is believed then $\beta \lor \alpha$ should be also. In general then any knowledge representation scheme using the syntactic approach must also (presumably) specify what beliefs follow from a given set.

A third possibility, presented in [Levesque 84] generalises the notion of a possible world to that of a **situation**. The general idea is that while a possible world fixes the truth value for all sentences, a situation may support the truth of some sentences, the falsity of others, and neither the truth nor falsity of yet other sentences. Phrased slightly differently, a knowledge base is relevant to (the truth value of) some sentences and is irrelevant to others. So our example knowledge base supports the truth of John being a teacher and at least one of Bill or Mary being a teacher. On the other hand it supports neither the truth or falsity of Lou being a teacher.

The definition of a "support" relation specifies what beliefs are held, given that others are held. Roughly speaking, the definition extends the standard possible worlds model structure by replacing the notion of a possible world, where the truth value of all sentences is specified, by the notion of a situation, where the truth value of a sentence may or may not be specified. The definition of the support relation also ensures that desired relations among sentences hold. Thus a situation supports the truth of $\alpha \lor \beta$ if and only if it supports the truth of either α or β, and a situation supports the falsity of $\alpha \lor \beta$ if and only if it supports the falsity of both α and β. Thus if

$$Teacher(Bill) \vee Teacher(Mary)$$

is believed, then so is

$$Teacher(Mary) \vee Teacher(Bill).$$

In fact, in some sense these statements may be regarded as being the *same* belief. Unlike the possible worlds approach though, logical omniscience is avoided. In particular, a valid sentence need not be (explicitly) believed, beliefs need not be closed under implication, and beliefs can be inconsistent without every sentence being believed. Thus given our example knowledge base it may or may not be the case that either of

$$SchoolEmployee(John)$$

$$Teacher(Lou) \vee \neg Teacher(Lou)$$

is believed. Finally, unlike the syntactic approach, the semantics of belief are ultimately based on the (Tarskian) conception of truth, rather than on restrictions to a set of sentences.

The situational approach also permits a distinction between what may be called **explicit** belief and **implicit** belief. The former deals with what an agent actually holds to be the case, while the latter deals with the way that the world would be, assuming that the agent's beliefs are in fact true. In this view then, implicit belief is the "limiting" case of explicit belief. This fits in well with the semantic view, where a possible worlds semantics may be regarded as the "limiting" case of a situational semantics, wherein either the truth or falsity of all (rather than some) sentences is supported.

There is a second distinction, separate from semantic theories of knowledge, that may be profitably discussed at this point. This distinction concerns how knowledge is to be formulated in a knowledge representation scheme. There are at present two major approaches. The first extends a logic, typically classical propositional or predicate logic, by adding the sentential operator K mentioned previously, where a sentence Kα may be read as "α is known to be true". Thus the following statements

"John is a student and Mary is known to be a student."

"It is known that the only students are the known students."

"There is a student apart from the known students."

might be respectively represented

$$Student(John) \wedge KStudent(Mary)$$

$$K\,(x)[Student(x) \equiv KStudent(x)]$$

$$(\exists x)[Student(x) \wedge \neg KStudent(x)]$$

The operator B, for "believes", is sometimes used instead of K; [Konolige 84] uses $[S_i]\alpha$ to mean "agent S_i believes α". [Levesque 81], [Levesque 84], [Konolige 84], and [Fagin et al 84] are all examples that approach the question of knowledge by extending first-order logic.

The second approach is to formulate a theory of knowledge within first-order logic; [McCarthy 79] and [Moore 80] are both examples of this approach. The idea is that one introduces a predicate "Know", and then provides axioms to govern this predicate. Thus Moore represents the import of "Know" by reducing it to the notions of truth in possible worlds, and of worlds possible according to what is known. His "fundamental axiom of knowledge" is

$$T(w_1, \text{Know}(a, p)) \equiv (w_2)(K(a, w_1, w_2) \supset T(w_2, p))$$

which can be read as "a person a knows the facts p that are true in every world w_2 that is possible according to what he knows". Further axioms of course are required to pin down the predicates K and T; these axioms amount to encoding the object language (which talks about known facts) into expressions of first-order logic that talks about possible worlds.

So, is there any reason to favour one approach over the other? or, more to the point, is there anything that one buys you that the other does not? First of all, the second approach has the advantage that it embeds the characteristics of knowledge within a well-understood formal framework. This also means that one can take an existing, off-the-shelf theorem prover (say) for deriving sentences from a knowledge base phrased in such terms. With the first approach, inference procedures implementing the system must be developed.

However this advantage isn't conclusive. With the first approach we have, after all, encoded a language within the meta-language, first-order logic, and need to express explicitly how one may reason with knowledge. Thus for example if we have that if someone knows that $p \wedge q$ is true then it doesn't automatically follow that one knows that p is true. Thus, one way or another, one must state that something like

$$\text{Know}(a, "p \wedge q") \supset \text{Know}(a, "p")$$

holds. So it is not clear that an automatic computational advantage obtains.

A potential disadvantage to the second approach is that it posits entities that may not be directly useful or applicable to the task of representing knowledge and moreover may lead to problems of their own. Thus, taking Moore's work as an example again, possible worlds are recognised as real entities in the language (in the sense that they appear in the range of quantifiable variables). The first approach doesn't have to make this explicit commitment. However once we allow possible worlds into our language, one is forced to deal with these entities. Questions arise as to how one possible world differs from another, how individuals may differ across worlds, and how, given an individual in one world, it can be identified in another. For these reasons the first approach, where an existing logic is extended, is generally favoured for reasoning with knowledge.

3. The "Ins", "Uns" and "Nons" of Knowledge

To understand a phenomenon, such as cars, hearts, or knowledge, one needs to study more than just its textbook definition. In particular, one needs to examine dimensions in terms of which the phenomenon can be characterized, and to study the allowable variations of the phenomena along each dimension. This section surveys some such dimensions for encodings of knowledge and describes relevant research issues and results.

3.1. Incompleteness

When a query is evaluated with respect to a database to find out for example if John Smith is a student, it is customary to assume that the database contains complete information about students. Thus failure to find information in the database is interpreted as negative information. In this case if John Smith's status was not found in the database, it would be concluded not that his status was unknown, but that he was not a student. This hidden assumption was pointed out and examined in [Reiter 78] and has been labelled the **closed world assumption**. In general, however, this assumption is not justified and cannot be used. For anything but idealized microworlds, a knowledge base will have to be an incomplete account of the domain of discourse. Given this state of affairs, we want to be able to first, express our lack of information, and second, ask questions about it.

Before discussing some proposals for dealing with incompleteness, it is instructive to examine some of its sources. The most obvious source is lack of information about the domain of discourse. Thus, an incomplete knowledge base may only know two students when in fact there are many more. Moreover, it may be the case that the knowledge base *knows* that there are other, unknown students. A second important source of incompleteness has to do with the derivability relation $\vdash_L$ which defines what can be derived from given facts in the knowledge base. In particular, this relation may be "weak" in the sense that there are statements whose truth would seem to be implicit in the given facts (the set KB_0 discussed in the introduction), and yet are not in the knowledge base because they are not derivable through $\vdash_L$. For example, a knowledge base may contain

$$Student(John) \tag{4}$$

$$Student(Mary) \tag{5}$$

and use the empty derivability relation (i.e., there are no inference rules). Such a knowledge base does not contain

$Student(John) \lor Student(Joe)$

even though this is clearly true in every possible world described by the knowledge base.

It may seem to the reader that this is a pathological example and that, in fact, "reasonable" knowledge bases will always have a sufficiently strong derivability relation to eliminate such examples. It turns out, however, that there are several reasons why a derivability relation may be weak either by necessity or design [Lakemeyer 84]. Firstly, weak derivability relations may make much smaller demands on computational resources, and thus may be desirable from a computational point of view (see [Brachman & Levesque 84] for a discussion of such issues). In addition, Gödel's incompleteness theorem establishes that there are inherent limits to the completeness of a knowledge base when the knowledge representation scheme is sufficiently powerful.

Expressing incompleteness involves a number of capabilities, including saying that something has a property without identifying the thing with that property, saying that everything in a class has a property without saying what is in the class, and allowing the possibility that two nonidentical expressions name the same object [Moore 80]. First-order logic provides facilities for handling these situations through the use of logical connectives, quantifiers, and terms. Thus, easily and trivially, we can state:

$(\exists x)[Teach(x) \land PlaceOfResidence(x, Paris)]$

$(x)[Teacher(x) \supset Erudite(x)]$

$MorningStar = EveningStar.$

However difficulties arise in a first-order logic setting when one attempts to deal with the closed world assumption or its converse, the open world assumption. Suppose for example that we want to state that there is an unknown student in a knowledge base which includes statements (4) and (5). Thus:

$(\exists x)[Student(x) \land \neg(x=John) \land \neg(x=Mary)]$ \hfill (6)

One drawback of this formulation is that the length of such formulas could be proportional to the size of the knowledge base (for example, in the case where the knowledge base initially consists only of a lengthy list of students). A more important drawback of (6) comes into the picture if we try to use it as a query, asking of the knowledge base whether there exists an unknown student. To express such a query the user will have to know *all* the known students. An alternative, explored in [Levesque 84], is to use the modal operator K where $K\alpha$ means α is known. Then, stating that there is an unknown student can be expressed by

$$(\exists x)[Student(x) \wedge \neg KStudent(x)]$$

and a similar formulation can be used to ask if the knowledge base knows all students. Note that this statement, unlike (4), (5), or (6) is a statement about the knowledge of the knowledge base (or lack of it) rather than about the domain of discourse (students).

A complementary approach to Levesque's is proposed in [Moore 80] which focuses on a knowledge base's knowledge about other agents, rather than on self-knowledge. To say that John knows a French-speaking teacher might be expressed as

$$Know(John, "(\exists x)[Teacher(x) \wedge FrenchSpeaking(x)]")$$

whereas the statement that there is a French-speaking individual that John knows is a teacher might be represented as

$$(\exists x)[FrenchSpeaking(x) \wedge Know(John, "Teacher(x)")]$$

As discussed earlier, Moore's work is also distinguished by the fact that it formulates its theory within first-order logic. In both Levesque's and Moore's approaches, possible world semantics serve as the basis for a semantic theory.

An alternative approach to those described so far is presented in [Konolige 84] where each agent in a multi-agent environment is assumed to have its own set of facts and its own (possibly weak) derivability relation. Thus, stating that John knows that Sue is a teacher is expressed as

$$[John]\,Teacher(Sue)$$

and the facts derivable from this are determined by the derivability relation associated with agent John. A similar proposal is outlined in [Bibel 83].

Yet another treatment to incompleteness is described in [Belnap 75] which proposes a four-valued logic where the extra two values can be read as "unknown" and "inconsistent". This approach has been used by [Shapiro & Bechtel 76] in the development of a semantics for a semantic network formalism and by [Vassiliou 80] in accounting for "null values" in databases.

3.2. Nonmonotonity

If we view a knowledge base as a first-order theory, additional facts invariably lead to additional knowledge. For instance, if we have a knowledge base which is given (4) and (5), and add

$$Student(Jane)$$

we now know — in addition to everything that logically follows from (4) and (5) — formulas such as

$$Student(John) \wedge Student(Jane)$$

$$Student(Jane) \vee Married(Bill)$$

that were not known previously. More formally, if KB and KB′ are knowledge bases and

$$KB = <KB_0, \vdash_L>$$

$$KB' = <KB_0 \cup \alpha, \vdash_L>$$

then

$$KB \subseteq KB'.$$

This property makes first-order and most other "conventional logics" **monotonic**. Unfortunately, monotonicity is not a property of commonsense knowledge and reasoning with respect to such knowledge [Minsky 75]. Indeed, there are many situations where monotonicity leads to problems. Here are some, noted in [Reiter 78]:

Default assignments. Default rules are used to assign values to properties in the absence of specific information. Two examples are:

"Unless you know otherwise, assume that a person's city of residence is Toronto."

"Unless you know otherwise, assume that an elephant is grey."

Knowledge Incompleteness. The closed world assumption discussed in the previous section can be expressed with statements of the form

"Unless you know otherwise, assume that an object is not a student."

which amounts to saying that all students are assumed to be known.

Default Inheritance. Consider a prototypical description of birds which states that birds fly. Of course, this can be false, either for particular birds (Tweety) or classes of birds (penguins). It can then be understood as a rule of the form

"Unless you know otherwise, assume that a bird flies."

This is a classical example of "default inheritance" used in semantic networks (e.g., [Fahlman 79]) where a "flies" attribute is associated with the concept of bird, and is then inherited by instances or specializations of the concept if there isn't information to the contrary.

So far we have seen the need to introduce assumptions into the knowledge base while reasoning in order to deal with ignorance (incompleteness) or with knowledge that only provides an approximate account of the world (e.g., prototypical descriptions). Nonmonotonic reasoning is brought about by the introduction of such assumptions. If at some time an assumption is introduced in the knowledge base, say

$\neg Student(Sue)$

because of lack of information, and it is later discovered that Sue is in fact a student, we must remove the assumption concerning Sue's student status, or face the prospect of an inconsistent knowledge base. Thus in this situation, the addition of facts to the knowledge base leads to some (former) conclusions no longer being derivable. This is the feature that renders reasoning systems that use "unless otherwise" rules nonmonotonic.

Versions of nonmonotonic reasoning were used in semantic network and procedural representation languages such as PLANNER [Hewitt 71] before any attempts were made within AI to formalize and study it. [Reiter 78] and subsequently [Reiter 80] offered a formalization based on **default logics**. These are logics which include first-order logic, but in addition can have domain-specific inference rules of the form

$$\frac{\alpha(x_1, \ldots, x_n): M\beta(x_1, \ldots, x_n)}{\gamma(x_1, \ldots, x_n)}.$$

These rules can be read informally as "If for particular values of $x_1, \ldots, x_n$, α is true and β can be assumed consistently, then assume γ". For example,

$$\frac{Person(x): MLives(x, Toronto)}{Lives(x, Toronto)}$$

states that if someone is a person and it can be consistently assumed that he lives in Toronto (i.e. it cannot be derived from the knowledge base that this someone doesn't live in Toronto) then assume that he lives in Toronto. Likewise, the closed world assumption for students can be approximated by the inference rule

$$\frac{Person(x): M\neg Student(x)}{\neg Student(x)}.$$

With this machinery, a default theory consists of a set of axioms and a set of default inference rules. Its theorems include those that logically follow from the axioms using not only first-order logic inference rules, but also "assumptions" generated by the default inference rules. It proves to be the case that a default theory can have more than one possible set of theorems, depending on the order of application of its default inference rules [Reiter 80]. Each of these sets can be viewed as an acceptable set of beliefs that one can entertain with respect to a default theory.

Another approach to default reasoning, first proposed in [McCarthy 80], is the notion of circumscription. Intuitively, circumscription can be thought of as a rule of conjecture that allows one to jump to certain conclusions in the absence of knowledge. This is achieved by stating that all objects that can be shown to have property P, given some set of facts, are in fact the only objects that satisfy P. Consider, for example, a blocks world situation with two (known) blocks A and B:

$Block(A)$

$Block(B)$.

One way of circumscribing with respect to the predicate $Block$ amounts to saying that the known blocks are the only blocks. To achieve this we pick the following as the circumscription of $Block$, written $C(Block)$:

$$C(Block) \equiv Block(A) \wedge Block(B)$$

and substitute this in the formula schema

$$C(\Phi) \wedge (x)[\Phi(x) \supset P(x)] \supset (x)[P(x) \supset \Phi(x)]$$

(from [McCarthy 80]). This schema can be regarded as stating that the only objects that satisfy P are those that have to, assuming the sentence C. $C(\Phi)$ is the result of replacing all occurrences of P (here $Block$) in C by some predicate expression Φ. Thus it states that Φ satisfies the conditions satisfied by P. The second conjunct, $(x)[\Phi(x) \supset P(x)]$ states that entities satisfying Φ also satisfy P, while the conclusion states that Φ and P are then equivalent. In our example, if we then pick

$$\Phi(x) \equiv (x{=}A \vee x{=}B)$$

and we substitute back in the circumscriptive schema and simplify, we end up with the circumscriptive inference

$$(Block(A) \wedge Block(B)) \vdash_C (x)[Block(x) \supset (x{=}A \vee x{=}B)].$$

Note that not every possible choice of a circumscription for $Block$ leads to reasonable conclusions (see, for example, discussion in [Papalaskaris & Bundy 84]). [Etherington et al 85] study the power and limitations of circumscription, while [McCarthy 84] provides a more recent account of circumscription, including a more general formulation of this important method of nonmonotonic reasoning.

3.3. Inconsistency

In principle, one of the advantages of "conventional" logics (e.g., standard first-order predicate calculus) is the availability of a notion of consistency which determines, for example, that the knowledge base

$Canadian(John) \lor Canadian(Mary)$

$\neg Canadian(John)$

$\neg Canadian(Mary)$

is inconsistent, i.e., there is no interpretation that is a model for this knowledge base. Unfortunately, however, it is a fact of life that large knowledge bases are inherently inconsistent, in the same way large programs are inherently buggy. Moreover, within a conventional logic, the inconsistency of a knowledge base has the catastrophic consequence that *everything* is derivable from the knowledge base.

From the point of view of knowledge representation, dealing with inconsistency involves two issues. The first concerns the *assimilation* of inconsistent information, i.e., the ability to include in a knowledge base inconsistent information without rendering the knowledge base useless. The second issue concerns the *accommodation* of inconsistent knowledge, i.e., the modification of the knowledge base to restore consistency. It must be stressed that both issues are important and should be seen as opposite sides of the same coin. Indeed, a knowledge base should be able to behave like a body of scientific knowledge consisting of observations and general laws. Inconsistencies can exist at any time, but there are also mechanisms for rationalising inconsistencies and for introducing new general laws that account for observational knowledge and at the same time eliminate or reduce the inconsistencies.

Consider assimilation first. The source of catastrophe in conventional logics can be traced to the so-called **paradoxes of implication**, such as

$A \supset (B \supset A)$

which can be paraphrased as "anything implies a true proposition", or

$(A \land \neg A) \supset B,$

"a contradiction implies anything". One way to eliminate these undesirables is to modify the axiom set and revise the notion of proof so that a proof of B from hypotheses A_1, $A_2, \ldots, A_n$ is well-formed only if it actually *uses* each hypothesis in some step. Thus proofs are well-formed, according to this proposal, only if each hypothesis is *relevant* to the conclusion of the proof. [Anderson & Belnap 75] provide a thorough study of such

relevance logics. As mentioned earlier, Levesque's formulation of a situational semantics for belief uses similar ideas and ends up with a notion of entailment that is the same as one of the relevance logics.

A novel proposal for treating inconsistency is described in [Borgida & Imielinski 84]. A knowledge base is treated as a collection of viewpoints held by members of a committee, where each viewpoint includes a consistent collection of facts. Derivability with respect to the knowledge base is then determined by means of a committee decision rule. Some examples of alternative derivation rules are:

$KB \vdash_L p$ if in each viewpoint V, $V \vdash p$

$KB \vdash_L p$ if in at least one viewpoint V, $V \vdash p$ and in no viewpoint V, $V \vdash \neg p$

Note that the first is a very conservative definition of derivability. Both definitions allow conflicting viewpoints among committee members without leading to contradictory knowledge bases. The proposal is shown to be capable of handling a variety of nonmonotonic phenomena, including default rules and database updates.

Turning to the issue of accommodation, one way to resolve the problem, indeed eliminate it altogether, is to treat "suspect" formulas (i.e. formulas that might be contradicted) as hypotheses. This point of view is adopted by [Delgrande 85] where it is assumed that facts in a knowledge base are of three different kinds: ground atomic formulas such as

Student(John)

Supervisor(John, Mary)

hypothesized general statements such as

"Elephants are hypothesized to be mammals"

"An uncle is hypothesised to be a brother or husband of a sibling of a parent"

and arbitrary sentences presumed to be beyond refutation. Given this assumption, three issues are explored: first, how to generate and maintain the consistency among the hypothesised general statements, given ground atomic formulas and other statements; second, how to formally prescribe the set of general statements that may be hypothesised; and last, how such a hypothesis formation system might interact with a system for deductively reasoning with hypothesis and knowledge.

The problem of forming conjectures and maintaining consistency is treated less as an inductive inference problem and more as a deductive, consistency-restoration problem. Simplistic criteria are used to form general hypotheses on the basis of the ground facts; these criteria however are not strong enough to ensure that standard relations hold among hypotheses. However it is shown how consistency may be deductively restored by the means of determining the truth value of knowable but unknown ground instances, and reapplying the simplistic criteria to the expanded set of ground instances.

Thus for example if it was known that instructors in some university department with their Master's degree could supervise M.Sc. students, we might hypothesise that these groups are equivalent, say

$$H(x)[HasMSc(x) \equiv MScSup(x)]. \tag{7}$$

In another department it may turn out that it is not inconsistent with what is known that supervisors of M.Sc. students can also supervise Ph.D. students:

$$H(x)[MScSup(x) \equiv PhDSup(x)]. \tag{8}$$

However there is, as yet, no reason (i.e. common satisfying individuals) to conjecture the transitive equivalence

$$H(x)[HasMSc(x) \equiv PhDSup(x)]. \tag{9}$$

Clearly though if the individuals known to satisfy (7) were determined to satisfy $PhDSup(x)$, then we would have reason to hypothesise (9). If one of these individuals was determined to not satisfy $PhDSup(x)$, then this individual would also falsify (8), and so we would obtain

$$H(x)[PhDSup(x) \supset MScSup(x)]$$

$$H(x)[PhDSup(x) \supset HasMSc(x)]$$

and so in any case consistency would be restored.

Another approach to the issue of accommodation due to [Borgida 85] takes the view that general laws are useful and should be available in a knowledge representation framework, along with a mechanism for accommodating exceptions. Consider, for example, a statement such as

"Before admission to the hospital, a person must present his hospital insurance number"

This statement cannot be treated as a default rule because then it has no force. At the same time, it cannot be treated as a universally quantified constraint because it is obvious that it will be violated in individual cases (e.g., during the admission of a VIP to the hospital) as well as in whole classes of cases (e.g., in emergency situations where the person being admitted is in no position to worry about his hospital insurance number). Borgida's proposal treats the introduction of an exception as a composite operation which includes a modification of the general statement. Thus if John is admitted to the hospital under emergency conditions and it is decided to delay enforcement of the constraint specified above, the constraint is revised to read

"Before admission to the hospital, a person must present his hospital insurance number
or the person is John"

Thus at any one time, a general formula is thought of as having a given number of exceptions which were introduced in the knowledge base after permission was granted. One
desirable feature of this mechanism is that reasoning can be done in first-order logic.

The previously-cited four-valued logic described in [Belnap 75] presents an explicit
recognition of, and thus an ability to reason with, inconsistency. So if a system was told
from one source that *Student(John)* was true, and later informed by another source that
¬*Student(John)* was true, the system could assign "inconsistent" as the truth value of the
statement. As well, the work described in [Etherington & Reiter 83] and [Touretsky 84]
which treats the particular problem of general statements and inconsistent instances by
means of default rules is also relevant here.

3.4. Inaccuracy

A knowledge base may contain information which is assumed to be true when in fact
it is not. For instance, we may have

Student(John)

Supervisor(John, Mary)

when actually John isn't a student (he was last year) and/or he is not supervised by Mary
(the data entry clerk make a typing error in entering this fact in the knowledge base). We
call such a knowledge base **inaccurate** since it does not provide an accurate description of
the world being modelled. Inaccuracy, like incompleteness and inconsistency, has to be
treated as a fact of life in any large knowledge base, either because external sources of
information may be incorrect, or because unintended coding errors may occur in adding the
information to the knowledge base, or because the knowledge base isn't updated properly. It
is important to note that inaccuracy is a different notion from inconsistency. Thus if a
knowledge base knows that a person's age is between 0 and 120, and it is asserted that
John's age is 134, when in fact it is 34, then the resultant knowledge base will be both
inconsistent and inaccurate. But claiming that John's age was 43, when in fact it is 34,
leads to an inaccurate but consistent knowledge base.

What can be done about inaccuracy? Well, as with other features of knowledge, at
the very least we would like to be able to *talk* about it. We would like to be able to state,
for instance,

(1) "An entity asserted to be a student in the knowledge base is, in fact, a student in the
     domain of discourse",

which asserts that the knowledge base has accurate knowledge with respect to studenthood,
or

(2) "A person's age as recorded in the knowledge base may be off by up to two years".

One way to achieve this is through the use of a modal operator, such as the operator K discussed earlier. Thus, to assert (1) we can write

$$(x)[KStudent(x) \supset Student(x)]$$

while (2) can be asserted with

$$(x)(y)[K(age(x)=y) \supset |real\_age(x)-y| \leqslant 2].$$

Note that if we further assume that

(3) $K\alpha \supset \alpha$

then an inaccurate knowledge base must also be inconsistent. Thus (3) has the undesirable
consequence that accuracy of the knowledge base is legislated, and so cannot be discussed,
constrained, or asserted — in contrast to (1). This point is discussed further in [Levesque
81, pp 2-5].

The careful reader will note that there is nothing about the K operator that is specific
to (in)accuracy. This operator simply allows us to talk about statements in the knowledge
base, and this capability makes it useful in the treatment of incompleteness, inaccuracy,
and other features of encodings of knowledge. This suggests that other mechanisms which
allow one to talk about statements in the knowledge base should also be suitable for talking
about inaccuracy. This is indeed the case, and we'll discuss one such mechanism due to
[McCarthy 79], which provides capabilities comparable to those provided by the K operator,
but in a first-order logical setting.

McCarthy's point of departure is to treat concepts such as that of John or Mary as
objects in a first-order theory, thus bringing them into the domain of discourse. In order to
relate a concept (e.g., John) to the entity denoted by the concept (e.g., the real person john)
McCarthy uses a **denotation function** *denot* so that

$$denot(John)=john.$$

Assuming that symbols beginning with a capital letter denote concepts, or functions or
predicates over concepts, while symbols beginning with lower case letters denote entities, or
functions or predicates over entities, in the domain of discourse, we can now write

$$(X)[Student(X) \supset student(denot(X))]$$

to assert that student concepts in the knowledge base denote students in the domain of discourse, while

$$(X)(Y)[Age(X)=Y \supset |real\_age(denot(X))-denot(Y)| \leqslant 2]$$

asserts that the age of a person stored in the knowledge base may be inaccurate by up to two years.

A comparable approach is used in [Konolige 81] to describe the contents of a relational database. Here the role of the knowledge base is played by the relational database and Konolige uses a predicate DB which takes as arguments encodings of statements with respect to the database, and returns true or false depending on whether the statement is true or false with respect to the database. For example, if f is the encoding of the statement

$$(t/SHIPR)[sname(t)=LAFAYETTE \lor length(t)>300]$$

then DB(f) is true if and only if every tuple in the relation $SHIPR$ has sname attribute equal to 'LAFAYETTE' or its length attribute is greater than 300. Of course, since DB represents truth in the database, it has to satisfy axioms such as

$$(f)[DB(\neg f) = \neg DB(f)]$$

$$(f)(g)[DB(f \land g) = DB(f) \land DB(g)]$$

etc. In addition, a denotation function comparable to McCarthy's is used to talk about the denotations of database terms. It is shown that this machinery is adequate for answering questions about the domain of discourse, given a database and a set of axioms that describe its semantics, and also for the expression of incompleteness in the database.

3.5. Relativity

Yet another important feature of knowledge and belief is that it is **relative to an agent**. Different agents have different, possibly inconsistent beliefs about a domain of discourse. Moreover, they have beliefs about each others' knowledge and belief as well as their own. Consider, for example, the situation in which John is to meet Mary at a restaurant for dinner, and where John knows the location of the restaurant, and Mary believes that she knows the location, but is mistaken in her belief. If John realises that Mary is mistaken in her belief he may either telephone her beforehand, with the intention of altering the erroneous belief, or go to where he believes Mary believes that the restaurant is located. In any case his reasoning and actions are based not just on external factors and his own knowledge, but also on his knowledge of others' beliefs.

Fagin and his co-workers presents a general model for reasoning about this sort of knowledge for a set of agents [Fagin et al 84]. Instead of an extension to possible world semantics for an agent's beliefs, they present a model based on a notion of "knowledge levels". Each level corresponds to an iteration of the "knows" operator, or to a level of meta-knowledge. For example, assume that level zero, where the domain itself is described, contains just the sentence

$$Student(Bill) \tag{10}$$

The first level gives each agent's knowledge about the domain. So perhaps John knows that (10) is true while Mary does not:

$$K_{John}Student(Bill)$$

$$\neg K_{Mary}Student(Bill) \wedge \neg K_{Mary}\neg Student(Bill).$$

The second level tells each agent's knowledge about the other agent's knowledge about the domain. So Mary may know that John knows the truth value of (10), while John may not know whether Mary knows whether (10) is true or false:

$$K_{Mary}(K_{John}Student(Bill) \vee K_{John}\neg Student(Bill))$$

$$\neg K_{John}(K_{Mary}Student(Bill) \vee K_{Mary}\neg Student(Bill))$$

Since an agent's self-knowledge is complete and accurate, we also obtain sentences such as

$$K_{John}K_{John}Student(Bill),$$

stating that John knows that he knows that Bill is a student.

Konolige presents a complementary approach based on the syntactic approach to semantics. With respect to reasoning about other agents' beliefs, his approach allows a certain flexibility in representing nested beliefs and belief systems. For example, John may have a set of beliefs B_{John} and deduction rules R_{John}, while Mary has B_{Mary} and R_{Mary}. John's beliefs about Mary's though are given in $B_{John/Mary}$ and his beliefs concerning her rules of inference in $R_{John/Mary}$. All such belief systems and belief subsystems may be of varying power and capabilities. So if John is reasoning about Mary's beliefs, his reasoning is "filtered" through Mary's *perceived* beliefs and deduction rules.

McCarthy's proposal for treating knowledge, belief, and related concepts from within first order logic, discussed in the previous section, also applies to reasoning about other agents' beliefs. So,

$$Know(A,P)$$

is a proposition meaning that agent A knows the value of concept P, while

$true$ Know(A,P)

asserts the truth of the proposition. Thus we can assert that John knows whether Mary knows Bill's telephone number by:

$true$ Know$(John,$ Know$(Mary, Telephone\ Bill))$.

It may seem to the reader that knowledge about other agents is simply a generalisation of self-knowledge. Surprisingly, this is not quite true. Consider an example (paraphrased from [Levesque 81]):

$(\exists x)$Know$(John, "Teacher(x)")$

which asserts that there is an individual known by John to be a teacher. Replacing John by the agent itself, we have

$(\exists x)$Know$(KB, "Teacher(x)")$

which is either trivially true (if there is, in fact, a teacher in the knowledge base) or meaningless (if there isn't one because it is claimed that the agent knows a teacher when, in fact, none is known). The conclusion that can be drawn from this example is that there are statements about an agent's knowledge which make sense as long as they are not statements of self knowledge.

Adoption of a relativist viewpoint means that it is no longer possible to assume that every statement about the domain of discourse is either true or false. Indeed, the notion that there is a unique domain of discourse ("God's point of view", if you like) is abandoned in favour of a subjective reality. It is interesting that "useful" knowledge bases developed so far ignore relativism and assume that for a particular application one can construct an objective account by piecing together personal viewpoints.

3.6. Uncertainty

The next feature of knowledge we will examine is concerned with the degree of confidence an agent has in the truth of a particular fact in its knowledge base. Each fact then has associated **certainty information** which indicates the degree of this confidence. The notions of "certainty" and "confidence" however have proved very difficult to formalise and consequently most of the measures that have been used for measuring the degree of this confidence have been quantitative (rather than qualitative).

The basic idea behind such measures is to provide a function *unc* from propositions to reals such that $unc(p)$ indicates the certainty of proposition p. Hence if p is more certain than q then

$unc(p) \geqslant unc(q).$

The inspiration for such measures comes from probability theory which, until recently, had provided the best-developed mathematical framework for dealing with uncertainty. Let Π be a finite set of propositions, closed under negation and conjunction, and assume that $\varnothing$ and $\mathbf{I}$ denote respectively the inconsistent and true propositions in the set Π. A probability measure P defined over Π, intended to represent the certainty (or probability or plausibility or credibility) of a proposition, is a function from Π to $[0,1]$ such that

(1) $\quad P(\varnothing) = 0$
(2) $\quad P(\mathbf{I}) = 1$
(3) $\quad P(p \lor q) = P(p) + P(q)$ if $p \land q = \varnothing$

One drawback to such measures is that it is very difficult in general to establish a P function for a particular set of propositions. A second perceived drawback is that the above formulation of uncertainty has the property that

$$P(q) + P(\neg q) = 1 \tag{11}$$

which means that whatever uncertainty is missing with respect to a proposition q must be attached to its complement $\neg q$. It follows that there is no room in this framework for ignorance in the certainty of a proposition *and* its complement. Thus, even if we know nothing about John being or not being a millionaire, for

$q \equiv John\ is\ a\ millionaire,$

we are forced to have (11) hold.

A fundamental issue that needs to be addressed in selecting an uncertainty function for a set of propositions is how the uncertainty function should be constrained by propositions that are logically or probabilistically related. An answer to this issue is provided by Bayes's rule:

$$P(H \mid E_1, E_2 \cdots E_n) = \frac{P(H) \times P(E_1, E_2, \ldots, E_n \mid H)}{P(E_1, E_2, \ldots, E_n)}$$

where $P(H \mid E_1, \cdots)$ is the conditional probability of H given $E_1, E_2, \ldots, E_n$, i.e., the probability that H is true given that $E_1, E_2, \ldots, E_n$ are all true. Unfortunately, this formula is highly impractical to use in a realistic setting because $P(E_1,E_2,\ldots,E_n)$ and $P(E_1,E_2,\ldots,E_n\,|H)$ are usually very difficult to determine; moreover the formula leads to severe combinatorial problems. (Consider for example the number of P values that would have to be calculated, somehow, for $n=10$ and each E taking two possible values.) In order to overcome these problems, two simplifying assumptions are usually made. Firstly, the events E_i are assumed to be **statistically independent**, in which case

$$P(E_1,E_2,\ldots,E_n) = P(E_1) \times P(E_2) \times \cdots \times P(E_n).$$

This drastically reduces the number of P values that needs to be estimated. Unfortunately however the assumption of statistical independence is usually false. Secondly, it is assumed that statistical independence between E_i continues to hold given H, i.e.,

$$P(E_1,E_2,\ldots,E_n\,|H) = P(E_1\,|H) \times \cdots \times P(E_n\,|H).$$

An appealing result of these simplifications is that the conditional certainty in H, given i pieces of evidence, is a linear function of the certainty in H given $(i-1)$ pieces of evidence and the certainty in the ith piece of evidence:

$$P(H\,|E_1,\ldots,E_n) = P(H\,|E_1,\ldots,E_{(n-1)}) \times [P(E_n\,|H)\,/\,P(E_n)]$$

This method of calculating uncertainty forms the basis of the reasoning component for PROSPECTOR [Duda et al 78] and provides evidence that simplifying assumptions can sometimes be a positive step towards building practical systems.

Many alternatives to the above formulation of uncertainty relax condition (3) so that

(3') $P(p)+P(\neg p) \leqslant 1$.

The Dempster-Shafer theory ([Dempster 68]) proposes such an alternative. Here, the **support** of a proposition p is defined by

$$sup(p) \equiv P(p)$$

while the **plausibility** of p is defined by

$$pls(p) \equiv 1-P(\neg p)$$

The **confidence** in a proposition p, $conf(p)$ then is defined by the belief interval $[sup(p), pls(p)]$. Thus the proposition p denoting "John is a millionaire" and its negation might be assigned confidence $[0,0]$ if nothing is known about the matter. If, on the other hand, it is certain that John is not a millionaire, then

$$conf(p) = [0,1]$$

while

$$conf(\neg p) = [1,1].$$

The Dempster-Shafer theory provides for a method of calculating $P(p)$ from a so-called "basic probability assignment" which specifies for each proposition the probability that the known state of affairs is exactly and completely described by the proposition. The theory has also been extended to allow for the calculation of the confidence of logical combinations of propositions [Lowrence 82]. For example, if $p \rightarrow q$ then

$$conf(p) \equiv [0, pls(q)]$$

$$conf(q) \equiv [sup(p), 1]$$

Such rules offer an alternative to the Bayes' rule and essentially replace statistical dependence concerns with logical dependence ones among the evidence and the conceivable hypotheses for a given setting.

3.7. Imprecision

Apart from uncertainty in the truth value of a proposition, there is also the issue of the *contents* of a proposition being imprecise. For instance, asserting that

"John was born in 1956"

is imprecise in that we are not told exactly when in 1956 John was born. Likewise,

"John is very young"

"Most Swedes are blond"

"George is bald"

are imprecise with respect to the age of John, the proportion of blond Swedes [Prade 85], and the degree of George's baldness. It is important to emphasize that imprecision and uncertainty are orthogonal notions. We may be absolutely certain that John is young but only have imprecise information about how young he is. Conversely, we may be uncertain about very precise propositions such as "the area of a circle is π times the square of its radius".

A popular way of dealing with imprecision involves the notion of **fuzzy sets** [Zadeh 75]. These are sets defined by a membership function μ which ranges over the full interval [0, 1] instead of being just binary. A proposition of the form

"X is A"

(e.g., "George is bald") is thought as describing X's membership in a fuzzy set S_A. For example, the fuzzy set S_{BALD} may have a membership function μ_{BALD} such that

$$\mu_{BALD}(George) = 0.9$$

$\mu_{BALD}(Mary) = 0.05.$

In [Zadeh 83], this simple account is extended to show how one can represent the meaning of statements such as "Most Swedes are blond", given a (fuzzy) world which includes information on the hair colour of Swedes, the nature of blondness as a function of hair colour, and the ratio of true instances of "Swedes are blond" which would satisfy the quantifier "Most". Zadeh calls his method **test score semantics** and argues that it constitutes a generalization of other types of semantics such as the Tarskian and possible worlds semantics discussed earlier.

In addition to fuzzy sets, probability functions (or probability distributions) can also be used to represent imprecision. For instance, we can think of

"John is very young"

as defining a probability function, π, for the age of John. Then if S_{AGE} is the set of all age values, $\pi(s)$ specifies the probability of John's age being s. Presumably, π must assign larger values to younger ages and in addition,

$$\sum \pi(s) = 1 \text{ for all } s \epsilon S_{AGE}.$$

[Prade 85] provides a thorough account of the use of this machinery for the representation of imprecision. The methods of fuzzy sets have been extended in a number of directions and attempts have been made to apply them in other ways in representing common sense knowledge. Despite these attempts, there doesn't appear strong support for the use of fuzzy sets in the representation of anything but imprecision in measure spaces [Hayes 79]. [Osherson & Smith 81] also is a critique of accepted views of imprecision as they bear on intuitions concerned with the combination of concepts to form complex concepts.

4. Conclusions

Clearly there is no single, complete set of features of knowledge. In this paper we have attempted to identify some features that are of interest to researchers in Knowledge Representation and to sketch some of the approaches that have been used to formalize and study them. There are other features one may want to examine. We know, for example, that **informal specifications**, including comments attached to a program, graphical sketches of the overall structure of a system, and natural language accounts of requirements for a piece of software, are all time-honoured and accepted practices for representing knowledge about a program. Would we have a more powerful knowledge representational framework if it could handle **informality**? Likewise, we may want to be able to talk about the **significance** or **insignificance** of an item in a knowledge base, or its **relevance** or **irrelevance** to the knowledge base. The reader may want to add his own list of features of knowledge to what has been presented or mentioned so far.

If there is a common direction or theme to the work reviewed here, it is the continuing concern with formality. This is indicated by the emphasis on formal logics, both as a tool for representing knowledge and as a tool for the analysis of knowledge. While the paper itself has emphasised formal approaches, it nonetheless appears that many researchers are concerned with investigating the fundamental, foundational properties of knowledge. This certainly is to be expected, given that many of the issues are only now beginning to be fully understood and explored in AI.

It is interesting that in the discussion of mechanisms for handling the different features of knowledge, we turned several times to the same mechanisms for help. Non-monotonic reasoning, modal operators, and the availability of a metalanguage that allows one to treat propositions in the knowledge base as entities within the domain of discourse, are three such mechanisms. It is significant that by and large there has been little interest in embedding such mechanisms in a representational framework, but understandably so since these mechanisms are still under development.

This paper provides an admittedly brief and subjective overview of some issues concerning the nature of knowledge. There is no claim that either the list of issues or the list of references given for each one is exhaustive. We do hope however, that we have helped the reader with background in Computer Science but little in Artificial Intelligence appreciate some of the deeper issues that need to be addressed if one is to call the information handled by his system "knowledge" and the data structures storing this information "knowledge bases".

References

A.R. Anderson and N.D. Belnap Jr., *Entailment: The Logic of Relevance and Necessity, Vol. I*, Princeton University Press, 1975.

D. Angluin and C.H. Smith, "A Survey of Inductive Inference: Theory and Methods", Technical Report 250, Department of Computer Science, Yale University, 1982.

A. Barr and J. Davidson, "Representation of Knowledge", Stanford Heuristic Programming Project, Memo HPP-80-3, Stanford University, 1980.

N.D. Belnap, "A Useful Four-Valued Logic" in *Modern Uses of Multiple-Valued Logic*, J.M. Dunn and G. Epstein eds., D. Reidel Pub. Co., 1975.

W. Bibel, "First-Order Reasoning About Knowledge and Belief", ATP-21-IX-83, Technical University of Munich, 1983.

A. Borgida and T. Imielinski, "Decision Making in Committees — A Framework for Dealing with Inconsistency and Non-Monotonicity", *Workshop on Non-Monotonic Reasoning*, New Paltz, 1984.

A. Borgida, "Language Features For Flexible Handling Of Exceptions In Information Systems", Transactions on Database Systems, to appear.

R.J. Brachman, "On the Epistemological Status of Semantic Networks", in *Associative Networks: Representation and Use of Knowledge by Computers*, N.V. Findler (ed.), Academic Press, 1979, pp 3-50.

R.J. Brachman and H.J. Levesque, "Competence in Knowledge Representation" *Proc. AAAI-82*, Pittsburgh, 1982, pp 189-192.

R.J. Brachman and H.J. Levesque, "The Tractability of Subsumption in Frame-Based Description Languages" *Proc. AAAI-84*, Austin, 1984, pp 34-37.

R.J. Brachman and H.J. Levesque (eds.), *Readings in Knowledge Representation*, Morgan Kaufmann Publishers, Inc., 1985

R.J. Brachman and B.C. Smith (eds.), *Special Issue on Knowledge Representation, SIGART Newsletter No. 70*, Feb. 1980.

J.P. Delgrande, "A Foundational Approach to Conjecture and Knowledge in Knowledge Bases", Ph.D. Thesis, Department of Computer Science, University of Toronto, 1985.

A. P. Dempster, "A Generalization Of Bayesian Inference", *Journal of the Royal Statistical Society*, Vol. 30, pp 205-247, 1968.

F.I. Dretske, *Knowledge and the Flow of Information*, Bradford Books, the MIT Press, 1981.

R.O. Duda, P.E. Hart, N.J. Nilsson, and G.L. Sutherland, "Semantic Network Representations in Rule-Based Inference Systems", in *Pattern-Directed Inference Systems*, D.A. Waterman and F. Hayes-Roth eds., Academic Press, 1978.

D.W. Etherington, R.E. Mercer, and R. Reiter, "On the Adequacy of Predicate Circumscription for Closed-World Reasoning", *Computational Intelligence*, Vol. 1, No. 1, 1985, pp 11-15.

D.W. Etherington and R. Reiter, "On Inheritance Hierarchies with Exceptions", *Proc. AAAI-83*, 1983, pp 104-108.

R. Fagin, J.Y. Halpern, and M.Y. Vardi, "A Model-Theoretic Analysis of Knowledge: Preliminary Report", *Proceedings of the Twenty-Fifth IEEE Symposium on Foundations of Computer Science*, Florida, 1984.

S.E. Fahlman, *NETL: A System for Representing and Using Real-World Knowledge*, MIT Press, 1979.

I. Goldstein and S. Papert, "Artificial Intelligence, Language, and the Study of Knowledge", *Cognitive Science*, Vol. 1, No. 1, 1977.

N. Goodman, *Fact, Fiction and Forecast, 3rd ed.*, Hackett Publishing Co., 1979.

J.Y. Halpern and Y.O. Moses, "A Guide to the Modal Logics of Knowledge and Belief: Preliminary Draft", *Proc IJCAI-85*, Los Angeles, 1985.

P. J. Hayes, "Some problems and Non-Problems in Representation Theory", *Proceedings AISB Summer Conference*, 1974, pp 63-79.

P.J. Hayes, "In Defense of Logic", *Proc. IJCAI-77*, Cambridge, 1977, pp 559-565.

P. J. Hayes, "The Naive Physics Manifesto", *Machine Intelligence 9*, D. Michie (ed.), Edinburgh University Press, 1979, pp 243-270.

C. Hewitt, "PLANNER: A Language for Proving Theorems in Robots", *Proceedings IJCAI-71*, London, 1971.

J. Hintikka, *Knowledge and Belief: An Introduction to the Logic of the Two Notions*, Cornell University Press, 1962.

G.E. Hughes and M.J. Cresswell, *An Introduction to Modal Logic*, Methuen and Co., 1968.

D.J. Israel and R.J. Brachman, "Distinctions and Confusions: A Catalogue Raisonne", *Proceedings of the Seventh International Conference on Artificial Intelligence*, Vancouver, B.C., 1981, pp 252-259.

K. Konolige, "A Metalanguage Representation of Relational Databases for Deductive Question-Answering Systems", *Proceedings of the Seventh International Conference on Artificial Intelligence*, Vancouver, B.C., 1981, pp 496-503.

K. Konolige, "A Deductive Model of Belief", Ph.D. Thesis, Department of Computer Science, Stanford University, 1984.

B. Kramer and J. Mylopoulos, "Knowledge Representation: Knowledge Organization", to appear.

G. Lakemeyer, Internal Memo, Department of Computer Science, University of Toronto, 1984.

H.J. Levesque, "A Formal Treatment of Incomplete Knowledge Bases", Ph.D. thesis, Department of Computer Science, University of Toronto, 1981.

H.J. Levesque, "A Logic of Implicit and Explicit Belief", *Proc. AAAI-84*, Austin, 1984.

J. D. Lowrence, "Dependency-Graph Models of Evidence Support", COINS technical report 82-26, University of Massachusetts at Amherst, 1982.

G. McCalla and N. Cercone (eds.), *IEEE Computer (Special Issue on Knowledge Representation)* Vol. 16, No. 10, October 1983.

J. McCarthy, "First Order Theories of Individual Concepts and Propositions", in *Machine Intelligence 9*, D. Michie (ed.), Edinburgh University Press, 1979, pp 129-147.

J. McCarthy, "Circumscription -- A Form of Non-Monotonic Reasoning", *Artificial Intelligence 13*, pp 27-39, 1980.

J. McCarthy, "Applications of Circumscription to Formalizing Common Sense Knowledge", in *Non-Monotonic Reasoning Workshop*, New Paltz, New York, 1984, pp 295-324.

J. McCarthy and P.J. Hayes, "Some Philosophical Problems from the Standpoint of Artificial Intelligence", in *Machine Intelligence 4*, D. Michie and B. Meltzer (eds.), Edinburgh University Press, 1969, pp 463-502.

J.P. Martins and S.C. Shapiro, "A Model for Belief Revision", *Non-Monotonic Reasoning Workshop*, New Paltz, 1984.

D. McDermott, "The Last Survey of Representation of Knowledge", *Proceedings AISB/GI Conference*, 1978, 206-221.

M. Minsky, "A Framework for Representing Knowledge" in *The Psychology of Computer Vision*, P.H. Winston (ed.), McGraw-Hill, 1975, pp 211-277.

R.C. Moore, "Reasoning About Knowledge and Action", Technical Note 284, Artificial Intelligence Centre, SRI International, 1980.

R.C. Moore, "Semantical Considerations on Nonmonotonic Logic", *Proc. IJCAI-83*, Karlsruhe, 1983, pp 272-279.

R.C. Moore and G. Hendrix, "Computational Models of Beliefs and the Semantics of Belief-Sentences", Technical Note 187, SRI International, Menlo Park, 1979.

J. Mylopoulos and H.J. Levesque, "An Overview of Knowledge Representation" in *On Conceptual Modelling*, M.L. Brodie, J. Mylopoulos, and J.W. Schmidt (eds.), Springer-Verlag, 1984.

A. Newell, "The Knowledge Level", *AI Magazine 2(2)*, 1981, pp 1-20.

D.N. Osherson and E.E. Smith, "On the Adequacy of Prototype Theory as a Theory of Concepts", *Cognition 9*, 1981, pp 35-58.

M. Papalaskaris and A. Bundy, "Topics for Circumscription", *Non-Monotonic Reasoning Workshop*, New Paltz, New York, 1984, pp 355-362.

H.E. Pople, "On the Mechanisation of Abductive Logic", *Proceedings of the Third International Conference on Artificial Intelligence*, Stanford, Ca., 1973, pp 147-152.

H. Prade, "A Computational Approach to Approximate and Plausible Reasoning with Applications to Expert Systems", *IEEE Transactions on Pattern Analysis and Machine Intelligence*, Vol. 7, No. 3, May 1985.

H. Putnam, "Is Semantics Possible?" in *Mind, Language and Reality: Philosophical Papers Volume II*, Cambridge University Press, 1975, pp 215-271.

H. Putnam, "The 'Corroboration' of Theories", in *Mathematics, Matter, and Method: Philosophical Papers Volume I, 2nd ed.*, Cambridge University Press, 1979, pp 250-269.

W.V.O. Quine and J.S. Ullian, *The Web of Belief*, 2nd ed., Random House, 1978.

R. Reiter, "On Closed World Data Bases", in *Logic and Databases*, H. Gallaire and J. Minker eds., Plenum Press, 1978.

R. Reiter, "A Logic for Default Reasoning", *Artificial Intelligence 13*, 1980, pp 81-132.

E. Rosch, "Principles of Categorisation" in *Cognition and Categorisation*, E. Rosch and B.B. Lloyds eds., Lawrence Erlbaum Associates, 1978.

I. Scheffler, *The Anatomy of Inquiry: Philosophical Studies in the Theory of Science*, Hackett Publishing Co., 1981.

S.P. Schwartz (ed.), *Naming, Necessity, and Natural Kinds*, Cornell University Press, 1977.

E.Y. Shapiro, "Inductive Inference of Theories from Facts", Research Report 192, Department of Computer Science, Yale University, 1981.

S. Shapiro and R. Bechtel, "The Logic of Semantic Networks", TR-47, Department of Computer Science, Indiana University, 1976.

E.H. Shortliffe, *Computer-Based Medical Consultation: MYCIN*, American Elsevier, 1976.

D.S. Touretzky, "Implicit Ordering of Defaults in Inheritance Systems" in *Proc. AAAI-84*, Austin, Texas, 1984, pp 322-325.

Y. Vassiliou, "A Formal Treatment of Imperfect Information in Database Management", Ph.D. Thesis, Department of Computer Science, University of Toronto, 1980.

W.A. Woods, "What's in a Link: Foundations for Semantic Networks" in *Representation and Understanding*, D.G. Bobrow and A. Collins eds., Academic Press, 1975.

L.A. Zadeh, "Fuzzy Logic and Approximate Reasoning", *Synthese 30*, 1975, pp 407-428.

L.A. Zadeh, "Commonsense Knowledge Representation Based on Fuzzy Logic", *IEEE Computer*, Vol. 16, No. 10, October 1983, 61-66.

Some Considerations on Computer Architectures for Artificial Intelligence

Roberto Bisiani

Computer Science Department
Carnegie-Mellon University
Pittsburgh, PA 15213

Abstract

Problems in Artificial Intelligence are characterized by the need to use heuristic methods for their solution. Heuristic methods are necessary because exhaustive search through the solution space is usually computationally expensive, if not impossible. Heuristic methods have computational requirements that are very different from the requirements of scientific computation. The object of this paper is to give an indication of how Artificial Intelligence task requirements and computer architecture capabilities interact. First, a number of Artificial Intelligence tasks will be examined and their computational characteristics compared. Then, some architectural features that are crucial for Artificial Intelligence applications will be examined.

1. Introduction

Problems in Artificial Intelligence (AI) are often characterized by the need to use heuristic methods for their solution. Heuristic methods are required because exhaustive search through the solution space is usually computationally expensive, if not impossible. AI heuristic methods have computational requirements that are very different from the requirements of "scientific" computation, namely:

-their flow of control is data dependent;
-they access large amount of data in a data dependent pattern;
-they manipulate complex structures that are not part of the basic data types of a

---

This research is sponsored by the Defense Advanced Research Project Agency, DoD, through DARPA order N00039-84-PR-DX051, and monitored by the Naval Electronic Systems Command under contract N00039-85-C-0163. Views and conclusions contained in this document are those of the authors and should not be interpreted as representing official policies, either expressed or implied, of the Defense Research Projects Agency or of the United States Government.

general purpose architecture;

-they are more easily programmed in languages that are not very suitable to conventional general purpose machines.

With AI systems becoming more and more sophisticated (and demanding) the inefficiency of conventional general purpose architectures becomes too large and more suitable architectures have to be designed.

This paper analyzes the field of computer architecture from different angles and points out the characteristics that are going to be more important for AI: *multiprocessing, specialized architectures and custom architectures.*

2. AI Problems and Solutions: A Few Examples

Artificial Intelligence encompasses a large number of very different applications and needs. Although AI systems are all "intelligence amplifiers" enhancing the problem solving capabilities of human beings, their computational characteristics vary widely because their algorithms are, in most cases, tightly connected to the specific characteristics of the problem to be solved (unlike our brain).

Often, AI systems not only have to deal with difficult (e.g. exponential) problems, but also must operate in real time, tolerate errorful and noisy input, tolerate ambiguous input, use a large amount of knowledge and increase their knowledge base automatically.

Different AI problems exhibit a wide variation in knowledge content, amount of data processed and required response time. Tasks go from knowledge poor to knowledge rich, from low to high data rates and from slow response to instantaneous response. This leads to a large variation in memory capacity and bandwidth requirements, processor functionality and processor speed.

Let us look at some "typical" problems to see what the task characteristics and current solutions are. The examples that are presented do not represent the whole spectrum of AI applications and are not necessarily the only representative of a particular AI application. Nevertheless, they illustrate the most common kinds of computational characteristics in AI systems. Some of these examples were taken from a talk by Reddy [13].

2.1. Vision

Vision is perhaps the most difficult problem currently being studied. Vision requires the instantaneous solution of knowledge rich, high data rate problems. For example, take stereo image registration, the task of finding common points in two images taken from two cameras close one to another. If the images require high resolution, say 1000 x 1000 points, 10^{12} convolutions are necessary to find corresponding image points by using the exhaustive matching approach, leading to a computational requirement of 10^{14} to 10^{15} operations. If both cameras are in a plane the amount of computation can be reduced by a factor of 10^3. A similar improvement can be obtained by using an analysis technique that uses lower resolution images, information learned from previous images and table lookup.

The amount of algorithmic improvements that can be used in this task is impressive. However, after applying all the algorithmic improvements, we are still left with 10^9 operations per image. Fortunately, custom architectures as the one designed by Berger and Thibadeau [18] can speed up this kind of computations by a few orders of magnitude (in this case by a factor of 10^4).

2.2. Natural Language

Natural language is often necessary in order to improve the effectiveness of man-machine interactions, especially when the task being controlled is very complicated. Natural language is particularly expensive because of ambiguity. Sources of ambiguity can be the multiple meanings of words (lexical ambiguity), the inability to avoid different meanings at the grammar level (syntactic ambiguity), the omission of words (ellipsis), etc.

In the English language, each word can have, on the average, 17 different meanings, a sentence can be parsed in 3 different ways, and 3 different interpretations can be caused by ellipsis or similar phenomena. This causes a sentence with 7 content words to have over 10 billion potential interpretations.

The performance of natural language systems depends heavily on the particular task at hand and it is hard to characterize the improvements that can be obtained with proper algorithmic techniques.

Natural language is an example of an application where a specialized machine (e.g. Symbolics 3600) can be usefully applied. Such a machine can provide an improvement of about a factor of 10 over general purpose architectural solutions. Still, the computational complexity of some real life natural understanding tasks seem to be more than algorithmic improvements and specialized machines can tackle.

2.3. Chess

Chess is interesting because it is unsolvable through exhaustive techniques. Selection of a possible move is an exponential process and it has been estimated that 10^{120} moves would have to be explored in an exhaustive search. Current solutions limit the burden of the search by using clever algorithmic solutions. Still, a 12-ply search requires about one billion nodes to be searched.

A state-of-the-art chess system (based on a multi-million dollar Cray X-MP) can examine about 5 million nodes in 3 minutes using the equivalent of a 25 million-instruction-per-second (MIPS) machine. A system based on a custom device designed by Ebeling and Berliner [6] promises to improve this performance by a factor of 10 at a fraction of the cost (10^2 to 10^3 less than a Cray). The system is based on a set of 64 custom chips (one for each sqare on the board) that compute in parallel the best move to a square. The custom architecture used in this case represents a radical departure from the classical chess algorithms.

2.4. Expert Systems

Depending on the size of the rule knowledge base, the computational cost of an expert system can become substantial. For example, if there are 10,000 rules in the knowledge base, each with 10 conditions to be executed where each of these conditions is matched with 1000 facts in the working memory, a system has to perform 100 million matches at each cycle. If it costs about 10^2 instructions to perform a match, it will take 10^8 instructions to select and execute a production.

A number of algorithmic considerations can be used to make the problem easier: only 3 or 4 facts change in the working memory at every cycle, and knowledge can be pre-compiled in a form that minimizes the search effort. This reduces the computation by about 3 orders of magnitude.

Still, a 1 MIPS machine will only be able to execute about 50 productions per second while one could devise useful production systems that require two orders of magnitude more computation. A mixture of parallelism, specialized and custom architectures has been proposed to improve the speed of production systems [16, 11].

In some applications, speed can be improved by taking advantage of the fact that knowledge can be divided among a number of highly specialized experts which cooperate to find a solution. In this case it is the intrinsic parallelism of the solution (the fact that the experts are independent) that suggests the architecture: a multiprocessor. For example the Agora system [1], that is being developed at Carnegie-Mellon University to support the development of speech recognition systems, takes advantage of a number of parallel decompositions that are possible in a hypothesize-and-test system and maps them on various multiprocessor structures.

2.5. Knowledge Access

Selective knowledge access is performed very quickly by humans. On the contrary, when recognizing, for instance, a building in a picture, "computer solutions" use time consuming algorithms, e.g. they perform a template matching of a large number of objects, including all the variations generated by shades, occlusions, etc.

Although some algorithmic problem reductions can be used in specific cases, there is no general technique to reduce the computational load. Interesting architectural solutions that are unbuildable for lack of proper technology have been proposed. These solutions mimic the structure of the human brain: parallelism, rather than raw speed, seems the way the brain gets most jobs done. These machines, called massively parallel architectures, are machines with a very large number of (perhaps small) processing elements connected by some ad-hoc network. The computation consists in sending information to other elements and combining the incoming information. The connections between the elements are part of the "program" or the "knowledge" present in the machine.

These kinds of machines can be classified by the type of information that is passed among the elements: some simply exchange a marker [9], some exchange values [12], some exchange arbitrary messages [7].

Only the Connection Machine has currently a hardware implementation. The machine has 64,000 processors (16 processors per chip). The processors are interconnected by a Boolean n-Cube direct network. The machine is about 10^4 times faster than a general purpose engine on some tasks.

2.6. Speech Recognition

Speech recognition is another task that can require a very large amount of computation. Take a 10,000 word vocabulary with about 7 words per sentence. In this case, the total number of possible alternative word sequences would be $10,000^7$ or 10^{28}. Knowledge, in the form of grammar, semantics, etc. can reduce this number to 10^{24}. Using a graph representation, the number decreases to 10^{10}. The use of heuristic search techniques like beam search reduces the number of possible word matches to around 10^8. Since a word match takes about 1000 instructions, it will take about 100 billion operations for a 7 word sentence, more than 10^{10} instructions per second.

Not only a lot of computation is necessary but, no matter what kind of system is being considered, the computation required varies widely among the different components of the same system (e.g. signal processing vs. word hypothesization). For instance, although numeric computation is usually a significant part of the computation, as the complexity of the task increases, memory access operations become prevalent. The computation required is also influenced by the recognition task (number of words, grammar, etc.) that a system can deal with.

In order to tackle some of the problems in speech recognition, Anantharaman and Bisiani have designed a VLSI device that speeds up the execution of beam search [2]. A machine that uses this device can speed up search by two orders of magnitude.

The kind of operations that this device performs is best understood when looking at a real system that would benefit from such a chip. A good example of such a system is the Harpy system. The Harpy system relies on a graph search to establish an optimal path through the candidate data. This procedure is usually referred to as *beam* search. The graph embodies the syntactic and vocabulary constraints of the language. Given an unknown utterance, Harpy segments the signal and assigns probabilistic labels. The sequence of labeled segments is compared to each of the alternative paths in the graph that represent acceptable phoneme sequences in the target language. At each stage of the comparative process, the Harpy algorithm examines each promising (i.e. remaining) candidate, accesses potential successor information from the syntatic and vocabulary constraints, compares each successor to the unknown signal, rank orders the resulting candidates, eliminates the least promising, and repeats the process until a match is achieved. The Harpy algorithm is discussed in detail by Lowerre and Reddy [15]. The custom device described in [2] achieves a two order of magnitude improvement over a large mainframe by means of pipeling, parallelism, high memory bandwidth and tailored data paths. This device will be described in more detail in the following section .

2.7. What can we learn from these examples?

TASKS (sample task)	Instr./sec	Algorithmic improvement	Architectural improvement
VISION	10^{15}	10^5	10^4
NATURAL LANGUAGE	10^{10}	?	10
CHESS	10^{11}	10^6	10 (10^3 cost)
EXPERT SYSTEMS	10^{10}	10^3	10^4
KNOWLEDGE ACCESS	?	?	10^2
SPEECH	10^{28}	10^{10}	10^2

Table 2-1: Summary of the Examples

Table 2-1 is a summary of the characteristics of the examples presented in this section. What can we infer from these examples? First, there is no way that any of the tasks outlined could be solved by straight, brute force architectural solutions. In all cases at least half of the possible improvements are algorithmic improvements. Secondly, specialized machines, i.e. machines tailored to a class of computations, can only provide about one order of magnitude improvement. Thirdly, custom machines, i.e. machines tailored to a specific task and algorithm, are potentially very effective but require a non-trivial effort to be designed and built.

3. Key Architectural Features

In the second part of this paper I will examine three key features that will have an impact in the future on the performance of AI systems: multiprocessing, specialized machines and custom machines.

Although electronic technology will not be explicitly dealt with, one should remember that computer architecture is often driven by technology improvements but not vice-versa. Computer systems are based on a number of different technologies that do not improve at the same pace. For example, bus technology has improved very little in the last ten years, while processors and memory have dramatically increased their speed. This means that custom architecture solutions must be examined in the context of the technology in which they were designed. It also means that driving the development of algorithms on the basis of their feasibility with current technology could not be the best strategy.

3.1. Multiprocessors

Multiprocessors are often the only way to get more computing power. The problem with multiprocessors is that in most cases some restructuring of the algorithms has to be done in order to take advantage of the parallelism.

In the near future, technology will make readily available three kinds of multiprocessors:

-loosely connected processors on a local area network;
-tightly connected processors connected by shared memory (*transparent multiprocessors*);
-tightly connected processors interconnected by direct networks, e.g. hypercube networks (*non-transparent multiprocessors*).

Loosely connected processors are quite useful in AI applications in which non homogeneous computational requirements need different kinds of machines in different parts of the system and in applications where geographic distribution of processing is necessary [8].

Tightly connected processors linked by shared memory have a good chance of becoming the most common multiprocessors, since it is particularly easy to take a single-processor operating system and modify it to execute user jobs concurrently on a shared memory multiprocessor. Such multiprocessors could be called "transparent" multiprocessors since the user does not have to be aware to be executing on a multiprocessor instead of a uniprcessor. Transparent multiprocessors will probably be very popular with vendors since they are the easiest mean to improve the computing power (i.e. the number of users supported) of a time-shared system. Transparent multiprocessors can be used very easily if the task exhibits a natural partitioning in multiple processes, e.g. see [1].

Non-transparent multiprocessors are at this point less attractive for all AI tasks but the lower level ones (e.g. vision pre-processing). Algorithms have to be rearranged to take advantage of these multiprocessors because of their constrained communication structure.

As an example of how various kinds of parallel systems could be used for an AI task, I will describe some of the alternatives that are being considered in designing the C-MU distributed speech recognition system.

3.1.1. Loosely Connected Systems for Speech Recognition

Different techniques exist for word recognition, each representing an independent recognition strategy. Multiple techniques are desirable when the deficiencies of a particular technique are covered by exactly the strengths of another technique. For example, alternative techniques are: analyzing the fine-phonetic information in the signal, and performing prosodic analysis. Although each technique produces the same result--a word hypothesis--there is no necessary connection between them since they typically do not share either representations or intermediate results. The following diagram, taken from the CMU connected-word system, summarizes this design:

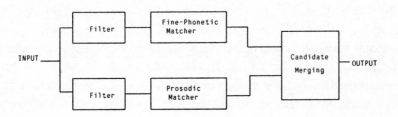

Fine-phonetic analysis is a two-stage process: The selection of portions of the segment lattice over which to hypothesize a word (the *Filter* stage) and the actual matching. Prosodic analysis is similar in structure, but operates on suprasegmental data rather than fine-phonetic data. An output stage merges the hypotheses produced by each analyzer into a single candidate list that is placed in the word lattice.

On a loosely connected multiprocesssor, a number of strategies suggest themselves: The system can rely primarily on the Fine-Phonetic matcher to produce word hypotheses, using the Prosodic analysis only in cases of ambiguity (e.g., *proDUCE* vs *PROduce*). It can be used to weigh hypotheses on the basis of their conformance to sentential attributes (e.g., the stress pattern), and so on.

Computation that would not be justified in a uniprocessor system because of its high risk of being unuseful, could be effective in this case because it could run in the background and use resources that would otherwise go unused. Therefore scheduling strategies, less conservative than the opportunistic strategy, could be used to control a background activity. One possibility would be to spread this extra processing power over a large number of competitive hypotheses while still pursuing the best or a few good ones as the main activity in the system. Such a "breadth-first" policy would have a chance to increase the accuracy of the system when no hypothesis or set of hypotheses is really better than others, as it often happens with noisy data or "bad" speakers.

3.1.2. Tightly Connected Systems for Speech Recognition

Although a loosely connected system offers the maximum flexibility when implementing a number of different parallel processing strategies, certain parallel decomposition strategies, that can be useful for applications like speech recognition, are only effective in terms of performance if applied in the context of a tightly connected multiprocessor. For example, word matching can be very expensive if performed exhaustively, and heuristics that dynamically "prune" part of the search space must be used. If the computation load is shared among different processors, these heuristics require frequent communication between the processors to keep a common view of the status of the search. Moreover, depending on the behavior of the search on a particular set of data, partially expanded paths will have to be redistributed among the processors to even out the load. Two characteristics of tightly connected systems are important in this case: *the higher speed of communication* and the fact that the *memory can be shared among processors.*

In tightly connected systems, when housekeeping operations (e.g. synchronization) can be minimized because of the characteristics of the application (e.g. no need to have perfectly consistent data across the whole system), data can be moved *between* processors almost as quickly as *within* processors. Given the current hardware and software technology, this means a difference in speed of two orders of magnitude (10msec to 100μsec) between the time it takes to send a message in a distributed system and the time it takes to send a message in a tightly coupled system. Fast communication opens a number of possibilities for speech recognition systems: *it makes small granularity possible,* it potentially *reduces the amount of information that has to be kept locally* and (as a consequence of small granularity) it *makes redundant computation schemes possible.*

The cost of scheduling is related to the cost of the mechanisms (e.g. synchronization primitives) and to the cost of the policies (e.g. demons that observe the status and decide what is the best course of action). A tightly coupled system gives the possibility of rescheduling a computation very often, while causing a limited amount of overhead. For example, at the word level, a large number of contrasting "islands of reliability" could be expanded in parallel. The status of these searches could be evaluated very often (something that would not be possible in a loosely connected system) and some of the searches pruned or "slowed down" according to their likelyhood to succeed.

Memory sharing can be used effectively to perform indirect control and scheduling of computation. For example, in the Harpy machine, memory sharing mechanisms were used to dynamically schedule computations on available processors with almost no overhead, very high utilization of the processors and close to linear speed-up [4].

3.1.3. Fine Grain Parallelism in Speech Recognition
A distributed hypothesize-and-test system has few chances to take advantage of a large number of parallel processors unless a large number of knowledge sources is used and all the knowledge sources use a comparable amount of computation. Given the current knowledge in speech recognition, it is hard to identify more than 20 knowledge sources, some of which are only used when special situations arise, e.g. to resolve conflicting evidence by applying very specialized knowledge. Thus, different decompositions must be tried in order to make the most of more than about twenty parallel processors.

Word hypothesization is an example of a subsystem that could be configured to take advantage of a large number of processors if the vocabulary is large enough: all the algorithms relative to word hypothesization could be clustered into a single processor, and each processor could be assigned a small number of words (for example 200, if the vocabulary is 10,000 and there are 50 processors). In principle, such a scheme could allow a speed-up that is very close to the number of processors. In practice, a naive scheme that statically partitions the vocabulary across the processors could have a bad performance because different sets of words, depending on the input data, could require radically different amounts of computation. If static partitioning strategies (like distributing similar words that are likely to be closely investigated at the same time to different sets of processors) do not perform well, a tightly coupled system provides the opportunity to perform some dynamic reallocation of the load. This can be achieved by making partial results available to idle processors and by allowing all the processors to access the word descriptions (e.g. networks) without having to physically redistribute static knowledge every time a word migrates from one processor to another.

Another possibility would be to assign "time intervals" to a small pool of processors, where the processors are completely responsible and have to perform all the computation. Such time intervals could span roughly a word and be overlapped. If a new time interval is started at each segment (about every 150ms), and assuming that an interval will span about a second of speech, there will be about 7 active time intervals, each interval using a pool of processors. Such a partition could be combined with the previous one by partitioning the vocabulary among the pool of processors, for example a 10,000 word vocabulary could be partitioned among nine processors to form a pool and seven pools could be used, if 64 processors were available.

3.2. Specialized Machines

When executing a given algorithm, the easiest, most cost-effective way to increase the performance of a machine is to tailor the instruction set and data paths to the task at hand. This generates a new "general-purpose" machine that behaves much better for some kinds of algorithms but can still be programmed to execute almost any kind of algorithm. This is at the basis of the current breed of LISP machines [10] or some proposed Prolog machines [19]. Such machines are often referred to as "specialized machines".

LISP machines make it reasonable to run large, sequential, LISP based systems that require a lot of computation. For example, Boley [5] reports 3 to 12 fold improvement in speed by using a LISP machine instead of a "typical" LISP mainframe like the DECSystem-10.

However, the success of LISP machines might in part be due to other features like their "window " system and their user interface. For example, in speech recognition, LISP machines can be very good at executing some of the algorithms that might arise at the Word and Sentence Level (and sometimes at the Phonetic Analyzer Level), but their current value is more in the possibility to implement and test algorithms very quickly. This is possible with a language like LISP when executed in a rich environment.

Therefore, specialized machines are likely to have an impact on AI research not as the ultimate engine for a given task but rather as a very effective research tool, especially if integrated with custom machines.

3.3. Custom Machines

It is in custom machines that most of the hope for the future should lie. Custom machines are machines that have been designed for a specific task and cannot execute any other task, even if similar. Custom machines ought to be considered at the same level as software modules:

-their design ought to be supported by non-trivial tools (e.g. compilers);
-their interface with the rest of the system should be specifiable at high level;
-the turn-around time to design, build and integrate a custom machine in a system should be less than a month;

Custom machines are very important because they can obtain large improvements in cost-effectiveness. The problem, though, is that a large effort is necessary to design such machines and most of the design cannot be easily re-used.

The validity of custom machines can be illustrated by describing the steps that have been taken between the first implementation of the Harpy algorithm on a mainframe and the design of a custom architecture.

A substantial amount of work was done in order to understand the best way to partition the Harpy algorithm among parallel processors. Initially, the amount of memory required to execute the algorithm was the main problem [3]; later, partitioning of the task for general purpose multiprocessors (C.mmp and Cm*) to some extent failed to attain satisfactory speed-up because of poor load balancing, synchronization overhead [17] or memory partitioning problems [14]. Most of these problems were overcome in the Harpy Machine [4] which, for the first time, partitioned the algorithm in very small processes and efficiently distributed them on the available resources. The Harpy Machine was an efficient structure when implemented with multiple general purpose, off-the-shelf microprocessors but it was not suitable for a custom VLSI implementation. Moreover, the Harpy Machine had a central resource (called data structure machine) that could have created a bottleneck had the system been scaled up to tackle substantially bigger tasks.

The solution that was most advantageous with the available technology and for the task at hand was to exploit the parallelism within the various steps of the likelihood computation and of the pruning. This led to a pipelined architecture that strongly resembles the *maximum parallelism*, data flow description of the task. Due to the characteristics of the algorithm, the computation can be split into many pipeline stages that contain only a few basic functional units (e.g add and multiply) in series. Therefore, a large throughput can be potentially achieved.

Figure 1 shows the structure of the device (search chip) and how it interfaces with a host and with its two memories. The *knowledge network memory* contains the information associated with each node in the network and the topology of the network. This memory is addressed by a *node identifier* and returns the information associated with all the successors of that node, one node at a time. This information is 40 bits wide and is multiplexed on a 20-bit input port. The *backpointer memory* stores enough information to allow the retrieval of the best path at the end of the computation. The *candidates memory* stores the identifier and the score of the nodes that have been evaluated. This memory is organized as a 40-bit wide FIFO and interfaces with the search chip by means of a multiplexed, 20-bit wide input/output port. A third input/output port, 8-bit wide, is used to output the node address (16 bits multiplexed) and input a number of parameters that are necessary for the computation (e.g. the length of a segment of speech or one of the pruning thresholds). As mentioned before, this custom machine improves the search speed by two orders of magnitude.

4. Conclusions

Computer architecture will become more and more interconnected with every-day AI research and with end-user AI systems. The time is not very far when the performance of general-purpose or specialized engines will not be enough and the only way of improving performance will be with custom architectures.

On the other hand, it would be foolish to count on computer architecture as the only mean to tackle the complexity of problems since architecture cannot beat exponentially exploding problems.

Multiprocessors and custom systems will be the two architectural features that will allow an AI researcher to build AI systems that perform their task in a reasonable amount of time.

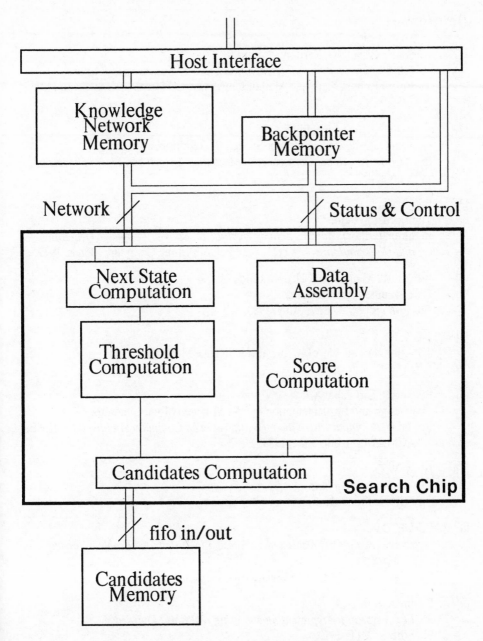

Figure 1: The *search chip* and its environment.

References

[1]   Alleva,F., Bisiani,R., Forin,A., Lerner,R.
       AGORA Distributed Speech Recognition System. Design Specifications.
       Technical Report, Carnegie-Mellon University, CS Dept., Speech Group, May,
       1985.

[2]   Anantharaman, T., Bisiani, R.
       Custom Data-flow Machines for Speech Recognition.
       In *IEEE International Conference on Acoustics, Speech and Signal Processing.*
       March, 85.

[3]   Bisiani, R.
       The Locust System.
       In Simon (editor), *Advanced Study Institute on Spoken Language Generation
       and Understanding.* NATO, D. Reidel Publishing Company, Bonas, 1979.

[4]   Bisiani, R., Mauersberg, H. and Reddy, R.
       Task-Oriented Architectures.
       Proceedings of the IEEE , July, 1983.

[5]   Boley, H.
       A Preliminary Survey of Artificial Intelligence Machines.
       SIGART (72), July, 80.

[6]   Ebeling,C. and Palay,A.
       The Design and Implementation of a VLSI Chess Move Generator.
       In *The 11th Annual International Symposium on Computer Architecture.* IEEE,
       ACM, Ann Arbor, June, 1984.

[7]   Hillis, W.D.
       The connection machine.
       T.R. 646, MIT, 1981.

[8]   Corkill, D.A.
       *A Framework for Organizational Self-design in Distributed Problem Solving
       Networks.*
       PhD thesis, University of Massachusetts, February, 1983.

[9]   Fahlman, S.E.
       NETL: A system for representing and using real world knowledge.
       PhD thesis, MIT, 1979.

[10]   Greenblatt, R. and Knight, T. and Holloway, J.
       A LISP Machine.
       In *Fifth Workshop on Architectures for Non-numeric Processing*. Asilomar,
          March, 1980.

[11]   Gupta, A. and Forgy, C.L.
       Measurements on Production Systems.
       Technical Report, Carnegie-Mellon University, 1983.

[12]   Fahlman, S.E, Hinton, G.E., Sejnowski, T.J.
       Massively Parallel Architectures for AI: NETL, THISTLE and Boltzmann
          Machines.
       In *AAAI-83*. AAAI, Washington, DC, 1983.

[13]   Reddy, D.R.
       Superchips and AI.
       In *32nd ISSCC Digest of Technical Papers*. IEEE, 1985.

[14]   Jones, A.K. et al.
       Programming Issues Raised by a Multiprocessor.
       Proceedings of the IEEE 66(2):229-237, February, 1978.

[15]   Lowerre, B.T. and R.D. Reddy.
       The Harpy Speech Understanding System.
       In Wayne A. Lea (editor), *Trends in Speech Recognition*. Prentice-Hall, 1980.

[16]   Oflazer, K.
       Partitioning in Parallel Processing of Production Systems.
       Computer Science Dept., Carnegie-Mellon University, Thesis Proposal 1984.

[17]   Oleinick, P.N.
       The Implementation and Evaluation of Parallel Algorithms on C.mmp.
       PhD thesis, Carnegie-Mellon University, Computer Science Department, 1978.

[18]   Berger, W.R. and Thibadeau, R.
       A High Speed Processor for Binary Images.
       Technical Report, Robotics Institute, Carnegie-Mellon University, February,
          1984.

[19]   Warren, D.H.D.
       A View of the Fifth Generation and its Impact.
       The AI Magazine, Fall, 82.

ERGONOMICS ASPECTS OF MAN-MACHINE COMMUNICATIONS

J.C.Sperandio
Université Paris V, 28 rue Serpente, 75006 Paris, France

D.L.Scapin
INRIA, B.P. 105, 78153 Le Chesnay, France

Abstract. This paper provides an overview of ergonomics in man-machine communications. The first part of the paper concerns the characterization of ergonomics and of its relationship with other scientific domains. Also a brief review is provided concerning aspects such as information theory, theory of operativity, and alternative sensory modes.
The second part of the paper is focused on the human-computer communications. Several design criteria and critical issues are mentionned about the design process itself, the dialogue, the inputs, the outputs, with a particuliar emphasis on the pre-requisites of the design, i.e. the users and the task.

ERGONOMICS

There are several academic definitions of ergonomics, but they all agree on the major issue : ergonomics is an applied science that incorporates the theories, methods and results from other sciences. Ergonomics gathers, develops and consolidates the scientific knowledge necessary to the design of machines compatible with the aim of improving the working (or use) conditions and environment, i.e., increasing the safety, the reliability, the performance and the satisfaction, while decreasing the stress and discomfort.

The concept of Machine refers here not only to the equipment, the workplace, the production tools for goods and services, the systems of information storage, processing and retrieval, but also to the physical environment, to the work schedules and rythms, to the sociotechnical organization, etc. Obviously, the field of ergonomics is very wide. Therefore, no single science can be specialized in all these aspects,which by virtue of interacting, complexify the relationship between the operator and his work. The interdisciplinarity of ergonomics is an obvious requirement. What is specific to ergonomics is to sollicit other sciences while focusing on the operational aspects of the man-machine interface, to consolidate the various contributions from other fields (theories, models, experimental data, methods, etc.) in a common knowledge base, always ultimately characterized by the requirement of a better adaptation of the Machine to the human operator.

As for any science at the crossroads of other sciences, it is always difficult to define precisely the field of ergonomics and the boundaries between ergonomics and all the sciences ergonomics borrows from (physiology, anthropology, psychology, sociology, linguistics, etc.).

According to the social and technological evolutions, the topics of interest and the fields of application of ergonomics change, as well as the relationships of ergonomics with the other sciences.   At its begining, several decades before this label 'ergonomics' was chosen (in 1949), ergonomics was characterized by a major influence of physiology and medicine. The topics investigated were mainly the difficult, stressful and hazardous conditions at work. The increase in number and complexity of the situations in which the human operator was involved resulted in an increasing influence of other sciences.   The human operator started more and more to rely on perceiving, processing, and regulating information, on controlling and making decisions, rather than relying on physical strength. Therefore, ergonomics became more and more influenced by domains such as sensory psychophysiology, physiology of vigilance, and more recently cognitive psychology. As a matter of fact, it is the booming of computers in the last decades that increased the influence of the latter domain.

The contributions of psychosociology have been increasing as well in the last few years. The reason is that ergonomists place a greater importance than before on the social factors in the analysis and organization of work.

Finally, linguistics and psycholinguistics, that were ignored until now in ergonomics, are becoming a scientific asset to ergonomics because the man-machine communications, or man-to-man communications through a device (often a computer) are begining to utilize means of interaction based on natural language.

Knowing the intimate relationships between ergonomics and the other sciences mentionned before, one can wonder why the specialists of these domains do not attempt to perform ergonomics studies ? There are at least two reasons.

First of all, this approach is not possible without being interdisciplinary. Second, and most important, the scientific aim of each specialist is to develop his/her own science, even in his/her limited domain, rather than attempting to improve the conditions at work. For instance, the specialist of vision or visual perception, or the specialist of audition or auditory perception, tell us everything they know about these topics, which is very interesting for ergonomist. However, these specialists are not interested per se in comparing (for exemple) visual versus auditory perception, using performance criteria such as operative cost. Furthermore, they are not interested in studying specifically a particuliar operator, while performing a particuliar task, in a particuliar environment.

There is a similar situation in the use of natural language for man-machine communications. The ergonomist can believe that natural language is an appropriate communication tool since everyone knows more or less how to use it. Nevertheless, this communication tool needs to be evaluated. The advantages and disadvantages of natural language have to be analysed and measured according to various criteria such as learning, speed, reliability, stress, satisfaction, etc. The ultimate aim should be to find out in which conditions natural language can be a communication mode either superior or inferior to other communication modes used in the human-computer interface.

Also, it appears most necessary to find and to describe the rules underlying normal human communication, particularly spoken language. It is not sufficient to conduct linguistic studies of "pure and perfect" written language. As a matter of fact, the two important facts about natural language communications are first its unruliness, and second that, despite that apparent lack of rules, people understand each other quite easily, solve problems together, etc. This is why real progress in natural language-based human-computer communication will mainly result from identifying these rules in order to make the software more forgiving, tolerant to human errors; in other words, a little smarter.

MAN-MACHINE COMMUNICATIONS IN TERMS OF SIGNAL-RESPONSE

Each type of work, even the most simple or the most physical one, can be analysed through the communications between the human operator and his/her work. However, such an approach is only accurate if the task involves a sufficient amount of information to be processed. With this perspective, ergonomics has been defined as "the technology of communications in man-machine systems". Directly inherited from behaviorism, this concept of "man-machine system" has become the main model of Human Engineering, defining a comprehensive framework for the analysis of each and every human bahavior, -including the operator-, as a simple exchange of quantifiable information between a source sending a signal and a receptor supplying a response. With this framework (now obsolete, because too reducing), ergonomics has nevertheless gathered a robust amount of data which remain valid for the art of setting up efficiently work positions and environments. In this case, efficiently means the most accurate and most performant way to display information, and to supply means a response. The strength of this orientation is to use accurately the information theory, which allows quantifying the communication by its uncertainty, rather than by its content or its aim. Based on experimental studies on the human operator, characterized by a limited and stable ability to process information, the aim has been to look for conditions optimizing the signal/response relationship, mainly for visual and auditory modes, under criteria such as precision and speed of the response. A good example of such an approach can be found in the American handbooks of Human Engineering.

It is very fashionable, among researchers, particularly in France, to consider Human Engineering with a certain amount of contempt, usually because of a lack of knowledge of what Human Engineering really is. Let's not forget that Human Engineering contains an essential component which is the search for general models about basic behavioral mechanisms, and cannot be reduced only to practical recommendations. Let's not forget either that this applied aspect for ergonomics is the one that answers to the engineers who can find in this field what they need for the design and installation of the workspace : e.g., choice of the best "displays and controls", under performance criteria. On the other hand, the risk is to consider as general recipes the data or recommendations which validity can be reduced to particuliar conditions. As a matter of fact, the optimization of displays and controls has been studied most often under very strong time constraints, which is not necessarily the case in real life situations. Besides, many results have been established with samples of very selected subjects (for instance, young male subjects, selected according to technical tests, for military tasks), which make them often not suited for a generalization to larger populations, for instance to applications concerning the large public of consumers, the elderly, or the children. Finally, to consider the operator only as a passive information handler (receiver) leads to investigating the human sensory/perceptive limitations and reduces the role of other factors that correspond to what is called "operativity".

INFORMATION PROCESSING AND OPERATIVITY

It is obvious to say that among all the information sent by the environment at a particular time, only part of it is accessible to the operator. The data that are beyong the scope of the human perceptive abilities are unavailable and psychophysics identifies, for each sense, its boundaries. It is similar for the human response. However, all the data within these perceptual limits are not necessarily processed. The operator selects the available information according to a large variety of variables that relate to the individual, to the situation, and to the task. This selection, which is required because the human operator only has a limited capability of perception and processing, is conditionned for example by the attention, the training, and the task goals. What is called "theory of operativity", to which several trends in cognitive psychology have contributed, explains the organizing role of the operational goals on the selection of the information relevant for the operator, as a function of his/her knowledge. For instance, in visual perception, using eye movement recordings, it has been discovered that the subjects extract information preferentially on the information useful to them, rather than the information not directly relevant to the task, as soon as a quantitative competition occurs. Likewise, the storage of this relevant information follows organization rules related to the task structure.

Mental images also conforms to such a model, in terms of action goals and previous knowledge. The typical experimental paradigm consists in comparing the perception, the memorization or the mental image between experienced operators and inexperienced ones. The behavior of the former is characterized by an increased efficiency due to a more operative information selection. The ergonomics application of these results consists in designing information displays so that the information most useful for the task and for a particular type of users is displayed at the best location and with the best format.

CHOICE OF THE MOST EFFICIENT SENSORY-MOTOR CHANNELS

At first, it is possible to look, for each sensory and motor mode, at the conditions for an optimal performance. This leads to reject the inappropriate devices and to choose the best ones. However, sometimes, several techniques (for displays or for controls) are available, which correspond to different sensory modes. For instance, a message can be displayed on a CRT, solliciting visual perception, or the message can be provided auditorily.

Similarly, one can choose between allowing control entries with a keyboard or in spoken language. Assuming that the machine capabilities are equivalent, the problem is to decide which modes are the most efficient for the user, in terms of speed, reliability, learning, vigilance, resistance to stress, such as fatigue, fear, lack of motivation, etc. More generally, the problem is to select the mode or format which should be used to display information so that it is processed in the best fashion by the human operator. Indeed, even if in some cases, there is no significant difference between visual and auditory perception, under criteria of speed and accuracy, there can be differences that appear later in the use of the information perceived.

At this time, there are very few experimental data that address such operational comparisons. For example, recent work on the display of messages to automobile drivers, either in a visual mode or an auditory mode, has shown that the question is complex. The perceptive performance does not differ significantly, but the efficiency differs according to the way the driver will later use the information, which depends on the type of message.

In the same way, speaking to a machine in natural language may seem more "natural" that to use a keyboard. It is certainly more natural, but not necessarily faster nor safer. First of all today's machines recognize spoken words only within boundaries that are much more restricted that man to man communication. This technological constraint requires the operator to speak in a more stereotypical way than in everyday life, and to use a reduced language. Therefore, the user has a greater risk to violate these boundaries, these rules, than if he/she was using a more classical entry mode, such as a keyboard. Of course, this does not mean that Man-Machine dialogue based on speech recognition is not recommended, but that its usage must be limited to the situations where other devices cannot be used or are less performant. Also, this means improving the speech technology to extend these boundaries. (Other considerations about speech technology are presented in another section).

HUMAN-COMPUTER COMMUNICATIONS

The optimization of Human-Computer dialogues concerns both the design process, particularly the software design process, and the choice and installation of hardware.

The Design of software

Design deficiencies result from several different misconceptions, as well as from design organization and timing. For example, there are still people that believe improvements for the user can result mainly from using new technologies or common sense. It is of course inaccurate since new problems arise with new technologies and because common sense does not apply to the complexity of the human cognitive processes. Also, systems that are implemented by people that do not share the same view of design is established independently for several systems or features that will interact, the result might be to impose a burden of incompatible habits to the users. In the absence of effective ergonomics guidance, the design of software may become the responsability of programmers unfamiliar with operational requirements. Software design may be produced slowly, while detection and correction of design flaws occur after initial system implementation, when software changes are difficult and costly to make.

Current software design can sometimes be described as an art rather than a science, depending more on individual judgement than systematic application of knowledge. It is that knowledge, both in terms of methods and existing results that software ergonomics can provide.

There are some common errors or deficiencies that characterize the design. Here are some examples : lack of knowledge in various areas, such as the tasks and the users to be supported by the software; the impact of the transactions when interacting; lack of user-oriented design methodology; etc.

Also, the design is characterized by a lack of consistency, of good human error forecasting, by being oriented only toward the computer performance rather than toward the task and the user. For instance, it is not unusual to see designs where all imaginable functions are provided rather than a carefully selected set of functions, or designs where all information available is provided rather than only that needed to perform the task.

The software is a tool. It should be judged in terms of how well it helps the users to accomplish their goals, not in terms of how sophisticated or how fast it is.

From an ergonomist point of view, some aspects of the design are better known than others; some problems are common to many applications, whereas others are specific to almost each application and require additional analysis. However, there are a few general criteria that should be followed when designing software :
- respect the users objectives, methods, and knowledge representations,
- reduce the users memory load,
- ensure that the user is in control and that his/her actions are explicit,
- minimize the users actions and processing time,
- provide always good user prompting and feed-back,
- adapt the system to the users experience,
- adapt wording to users needs,
- provide ways for the users to correct their own errors.

Considering these simple criteria, many recommendations can be made, concerning the various components of the users interface : the dialogue, the inputs and the outputs.

The dialogue.
Among the various dialogue properties :

Initiative : for naive users, computer-initiated dialogues are preferable, whereas it is very disruptive for the frequent, experienced user. It should be possible for the user to select either mode.

Flexibility (ways to accomplish a function) : low flexibility should be preferred for naive users, whereas highly flexible dialogues are more desirable for experienced users.

Other properties concern the complexity, the power, the information load.

The choice of a dialogue mode can also be made according to the above criteria. For instance, question/answer mode is probably the most error-free dialogue type for inexperienced users. Of course, this requires the data to be well known and their ordering constrained. Form-filling is often best when user input is dominated by parameter values, rather than commands.

For the menu selection mode, which is very convenient when response time criteria are satisfied and efficient pointing devices are used, there are several requirements to be taken into consideration, for instance : only one selection for each menu display; logical ordering of options; appropriate grouping; consistant organization of displayed menus; compatibility between different menus; consistent wording; etc.

Choosing a <u>function-keys</u> based dialogue type versus other types refers to the ease of learning, the potential for errors, and the number of functions. For instance, function keys are particularly suited when the task requires a limited number of control entries, and/or for frequently used entries, as a ready means to accomplish quickly critical entries that should be error-free.

<u>Command language</u> is recommended for well-trained users that have fully internalized the system functions and the language syntax. Otherwise, it is error prone and sometimes frustrating. Many important issues concern the coding, the command naming and the abbreviations.

The Inputs.

Many guidelines can be identified concerning the entry of data and the sequence control.

For <u>data entry</u>, they concern the display of keyed entries, the prompting, the editing, the lenght of entry items, the display protection, the sequential organization of the entry items, the use of special delimiters, the identification of data fields, the management of errors, etc.

For <u>sequence control</u>, they are related to the complexity, the frequency or the case of urgent versus destructive actions, the implicits, the keyboard lock, the consistency, the prompting. Also they concern the dialogue interrupts, the control sequence feed-back, the avoidance of errors, etc.

The Outputs.

Other guidelines can be identified for topics such as the response time, the general characteristics (legibility, readibility, consistency, conciseness, usability). Other more specific recommmendations concern the messages, the data grouping (frequency, sequencial, functional, by importance), the standardization, the labeling, and other display considerations.

Without going into detail, suggested display design steps would be : choose the most appropriate grouping (on the basis of data collection), develop headings and labels for groups and items names, determine media to be used, attempt several alternative layouts, and choose the one that will produce the best human performance.

Inputs/Outputs with Speech Technology

Very little work has been done on the ergonomics aspects of speech technology. However, several issues should be mentionned. One is the need for the investigation of the effect of vocabulary size, user experience and type of task on the speech input performance. It is known that there is no significant difference in speed and accuracy between keyboard and speech input, for simple tasks, but that for more complex tasks, voice-entry performance deteriorates less than with manual entry. Also, spatial and analog tasks require visual inputs and manual responses, whereas verbal tasks require auditory inputs and speech responses. However, complexity and time sharing of the task affect the performance. It is a very difficult situation to compare voice and manual inputs because the units of measurements are not strictly similar. Most other ergonomics studies actually do not concern directly the speech technology, but rather the communication modes (comparisons between different modes, workload effects, operative languages).

Concerning synthetic speech, it appears that people differ considerably in their reaction, e.g., some subjects recognize the sounds, others do not. The two main critics from an aesthetic point of view that can be pointed out concerning synthetic speech are the lack of natural prosody and the very "nasal" sound. However, a current experiment with naive users demonstrates that the users accept a synthetic voice, even with a poor prosody, as long as the words are recognizable. It is interesting to observe also that these users tend to speak very slowly, with long pauses when the synthetized speech is itself slow.

Other ergonomics issues concern aspects such as : the speaker training, the microphone placement, the microphone on/off control, the control of the speech amplitude and of the input level, the control of the rejection level, the speech sampling, the prompting, the language design (which is not specific to speech synthesis), the error correction and the feed-back, etc. A general comment is that current technology places a heavy burden on the user to comply with speech constraints. In other words, the users accept to speak to the computer, but they may not accept the constraints attached to that communication mode (e.g., slowness, restricted vocabulary, low reliability).

It is only superficially true to consider that speech generation is very advanced relative to speech recognition technology : it is still limited to highly structured and invariant messages within a limited conceptual and lexical domain. In other words, a lot remains to be done, which actually is not strickly speaking, specific to speech technology.

As a matter of fact, what is most needed is work on the upstream aspects of speech technology, i.e. concerning the characteristics of user created natural language for the recognition and accuracy of the messages toward the task for the synthesis. A major step will be taken when computer systems will produce synthesized messages or instructions that make sense, that are flexible and usable.

Prerequisites for the Design

Before designing sofware, or improve existing software, two elements of the systems have to be well known : the users and the task.

The users.

First of all, the designer must be aware that a new system cannot elicit an acceptable level of human performance from all people in the world. Therefore, the designer must know in advance the design related characteristics of the user group. Indeed, individual differences among users involving variables such as abilities, acquired skills, general background, etc., may affect performance in tasks involving interactive systems. Designing computer-based systems becomes even more difficult : any given system will have users with various characteristics, and as each user gains experience with the system, there will probably be changes in some of his/her original characteristics. Ideally, as people change, the systems should also change. One design objective should be to build the interface where the critical elements change as the users become more experienced in the human-computer relationship, and to provide different levels of interface for different levels of user experience.

When designing the specific requirements for a system, designers should be fully aware of the needs of potential users. In fact, the users can also help define the system requirements, as long as appropriate methods are used, eventhough many users are not familiar with the state of the art of computer technology and may not think of the best ways to meet their requirements. The more experienced users can ensure that all requirements are being met, via interviews and walkthroughs, eventhough they are not fully aware of all that is required to accomplish certain goals of the systems. Also, there is some evidence that potential users are more likely to give a new system a fair trial if they have been involved in its requirement definition and if they see the implementation of some of their suggestions. In other words, use users, but be aware of their limitations.

Novice or inexperienced users are probably the largest population of potential computer users. These users should be required to think of a computer as a tool that obeys commands expressed in strict accordance with a set of rules, rather than consider it as a "magic" device. Often, users assume more intelligence from the computer's part than it generally has.

It is not necessary for most users to know anything at all about the nature of the machine, just as for driving a car, it is not necessary to understand the detailed workings of the engine.

The task.

Knowing precisely the task to be supported is essential to proper design of sofware. Many techniques are readily available to improve our knowledge of existing tools with or without computers, with the aim of establishing user requirements or evaluating systems. It is not our purpose here to present these techniques, which can be found elsewhere. However, it is important to keep in mind what these techniques are used for.

Basically task analysis techniques are ways of providing data necessary to the decision making processes in designing the interface. The objective is to define, from a user point of view, the requirements to which the software must conform. It concerns the gathering of information and functions involved in the task as well as the operational sequence : events, data, decisions, and actions. The analysis allows the description of task flows and scenarios that will support the design decisions and the simulation or evaluation of alternative design decisions. The data gathered concern topics such as inputs/outputs, allocation of functions between the user and the computer, the sequence of operations, the characteristics and organization of the data, the level of training required, etc.

These analyses are part of a on-going process at the different stages of system development and implementation. These analyses should be an integral part of the design process in order to avoid design errors mentionned earlier : lack of knowledge of the users and of the task, and lack of methodology in the design of the interface.

Choice and installation of equipments

To choose the equipment, there are several ways : trust the computer manufacturer and monitor his/her catalogues; visit the computer fairs; buy the last up and coming gadgets; require the usual brand of equipment used in-house; establish the system requirements after an analysis conducted according to a systematic methodology.

Obviously, the latter is by far the best one. However, at certain stages of the analysis, it may be necessary to select alternative solutions that are contradictory on various different criteria (i.e. to make choices according to trade-offs, priorities). This is a main difficulty. As long as the criteria remain stable, the classical experimental approach always provides a good answer. Between several keyboards, screens, speech recognition devices, it will be always possible to select the best one, from the point of view of speed, or ease of use, or ease of learning, or compatibility with other uses, prior habits, other applications, or cost, etc.

As a matter of fact, it will not be always necessary to conduct in each case experimental comparisons. The literature in ergonomics is very rich in this area. The keyboards, for instance, are very well known (advantages, disadvantages, engineering of the keys, dimensions, spatial location, etc.). Many different types of keyboards have been designed and evaluated under various criteria, and on various tasks. Displays are also well known. Many precise recommendations have been presented, including recommendations on the work organization and the work schedules, and on the physiological and physiopathological aspects of vision.

All this is supported by strong scientific evidence. In addition to classical keyboards, more or less derived from typewriter keyboards, studies have concern various pointing devices, such as mouse, light pen, touch-screens, etc. Very little is yet known about the speech based conducted both on speech synthesis and speech recognition. Some evaluation criteria and some illusions to be avoided concerning the "natural" characteristics of this communications mode have been mentioned earlier. However, carefulness does not mean skepticism.

CONCLUSION

First, task analysis techniques, which were mentionned as a necessary step for the design, require a certain amount of training to be accurate. For instance, there is sometimes the temptation for the novice analyst to describe in detail certain events or task features that are either unimportant or out of focus, whereas important matters are left out. There is also the temptation to please the potential readers rather than bring to light critical issues, or to attempt quantifying data without the proper statistical methodology.

Second, ergonomics recommendations, such as the ones provided here, are not sufficient to solve all users problems. The reasons are that most systems are somewhat unique, which prevents using the knowledge obtained on other systems, some design questions are more complex than others, which requires additional studies, including experimental ones, and finally, many design questions are trade-offs between alternatives.

In other words, optimizing design decisions with the user in mind requires the expertise of the ergonomist, in much the same way it is not always sufficient to use a medical encyclopedia to cure one's diseases, or to use a cookbook to prepare an elaborate gourmet dish.

There are areas in which ergonomics can help to improve the user-computer interface, which in any case, require the use of the proper data and methodologies. However, the ultimate and most needed contribution of ergonomics will be in the future to provide grounds for the design of "smarter" systems.

ADVANCED DATABASES

MULTI - MEDIA INTERFACE

CHRISMENT C.Y.
Laboratoire CERFIA-CSI - UA CNRS 824 Toulouse - FRANCE

ZURFLUH G.
Laboratoire CERFIA-CSI - UA CNRS 824 Toulouse - FRANCE

This paper presents some aspects of work in generalized data bases :

- integration of data, image, text, voice... using AGREGATIVE MODEL for information modelling. This model is derived from extended entity-relationship model and includes abstract data type.

- manipulation language AS issued from ADA and SEQUEL,

- multi media interface supporting AS language.

Concepts of Document Structure, Navigational Structure are presented. We show how it is possible to search information contained in a complex document which includes data, text, image. Search can be realized by using references, and/or image.

A general study on functionalities, applications and technologies of future databases has been recently realized by the BD3 group (see BD3.84). The report established by the group specifies advanced data base research topics. The concept of Generalized Data Base (GDB) has been introduced (see CHRISMENT & al. 84, SCHEK & LUM.83, VELEZ.84).

A GDB integrates various types of information in a unique set (data, text, image, digitized pictures, graphics, voice,...).

The three major points are :
- information modelling,
- information manipulation,
- user-system communication and multi-media interface.

In this paper, we present a multi-media interface supporting manipulation language AS. An application using this interface concerns technical document production. System hardware architecture includes document composition system as shown in next figure.

HARDWARE ARCHITECTURE

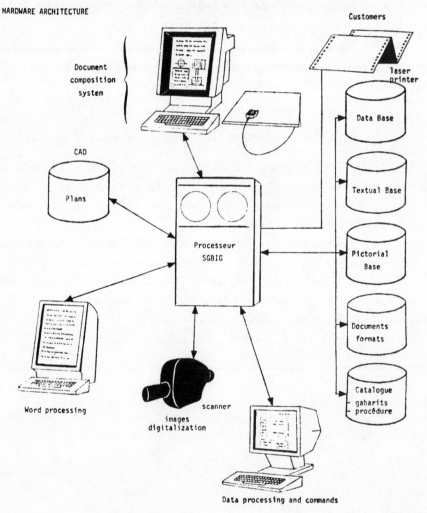

Document composition system

Customers

laser printer

Data Base

CAD

Plans

Textual Base

Processeur SGBIG

Pictorial Base

Documents formats

Word processing

scanner
images digitalization

Catalogue
- gabarits
- procédure

Data processing and commands

1   MULTI-MEDIA INTERFACE

Interface implementation necessits the use of personal workstation with cursor design (tactile screen, mouse, joystick, lightpen,... (Bolt.
83)) and multiple viewing. Fundamental aspects of man-machine communication
with such a workstation are described in (JOLOBOFF.84).

1.1   DISPLAY SCREEN

A display screen (420 × 300 mm) is divided into two major windows :

- S window to visualize GDB schema,
- V window used to display the values of a given type.

A window size is not a limit for the object displaying. A system allows the scrolling of any truncated, in selected window, object representation. It is also possible to overlap several windows.

S WINDOW   V WINDOW

STRUCTURE		VALUES	
OPERATORS		OPERATORS	

Schema
operation

Schema

Value
operation

Messages (man-
machine) dialog

values

Overlapping windows is handled automatically. The displaying of
temporary windows is user-controlled.

1.2 POINTING DEVICE

A vital workstation component is a tablet with a pointing device
this tablet is used to point any part of the display. A software cursor appears in the screen to indicate the pointed place. Pointing device is a
joystick with a four-button cursor. Two buttons are frequently used :

- RED button to select operators and values,
- GREEN button which realizes inverted operations of button-ones.

A software cursor coupled with a hardware cursor indicates the po
sition on the screen corresponding to the current position of the tablet's
pointing. The moving of the hardware cursor is accompagnated by the moving of
the software corsor. In the next display screens, this cursor is materialized
by an arrow (↖).

1.3 RUNNING PRINCIPLE

When a user wishes to access to a GDB, he gives a GDB name to the
system. The diagram of GDB schema is then displayed in S window. Schema operators are showed in the left column of S window :

- SELECT

- CREATE

- DELETE

- MODIFY

It is the SELECT operation, implicity selected by the system,
which cames GDB schema displaying. This schema is the startpoint of all operations realized on GDB.

For example, creating a letter necessits to select, in the schema
a document class in which the created letter must be inserted. This selection
allows the system to retrieve and display :

- document type description,
- applicable operators on this document type.

Object selection is realized with a cursor by using the following
rules :

- a leaf of schema (array [⬤], class [☐], structure element) can be directly selected,
- non terminal node of schema can be selected, and then depending nodes (or qualified nodes - in the hierarchy are implicitly selected.

Object selecting necessits :

    - to select his representation in the schema,
    - to select a value in the object value set.
For this, the user must :
    - point (↖) at the object representation in S window, with a
cursor,
    - press the joystick red button.
In the screen window V, the system displays :
    - all or part of set selected values,
    - the operators list allowed on this object type.

    A standard display format is associated to every non structured
type.

STRUCTURE		VALUES		
OPERATORS		OPERATORS	NAMES	
☐ SELECT	EMPLOYEE	• >	DUPONT	TOUVIER
☐ CREATE		• <	DENIS	DURAND
☐ DELETE		• =	RAZIN	RENAULT
☐ MODIFY		• &	MARTIN	LALANNE
	INSEE NO	• • •	VERGET	POTIER
	(STRING) NAMES		ERNEST	VIDAL
	(STRING)		CARTIER	DUPOND
			DUCROC	DUVAL
			DUPUY	LACASE
			BERTRAND	BOULIER
			LAURENT	TOURETTE
			BOUCHER	CHARBON
				☐ NEXT

Defined operators
on type STRING

    In case of display of only a part of the set value, operator NEXT
appears in V window, in right down corner. To obtain remaining values this
operators is selected with joystick red button. With the green button prior
values are selected.

    For volumineous object such as image or text, only one occurence
can be visualized in V window.

When window size is smaller than image size, this one is automatically adapted by using functions INCREASE, REDUCE and possibly TRUNC.

For a text, such adaptation is not possible for readibility reason. An the right corner of V window then appears a two-color scrolling bar (black and white) used to control text scrolling. This bar represents the whole text, the white area indicates size and position of displayed text part

STRUCTURE		VALUES	
OPERATORS		OPERATORS	BODY
☐ SELECT ☐ CREATE ☐ DELETE ☐ MODIFY	LETTERS BODY (text)	. INSERT . REPLACE . ERASE . FIND . DELETE . COPY . MODIFY	plages entre la presqu'île du Coter tin de l'embouchure de l'Orne. Cet épisode, un des plus glorieux de la Deuxième Guerre mor diale, devait force ment inspirer les cinéastes. Ce qui est intéressant c'e l'esprit dans leque ☐ NEXT

Scrolling bar

When positionning the cursor on the black area of the scrolling bar white area is increasing and corresponding part of text is displayed in V window.

This bar controls electronic browsing of class element pages. Pointing NEXT operator in the right corner of V window allows to continue display of other elements. Only the first page of each element is displayed. This operation is the same as to manual search to retrieve documents in a set of folders.

• Selection refinement

When selection concerns a relation (list or agregate), what is a non terminal node of schema, hierarchic depending objects of the relation are also selected. Consider, for example, following schema :

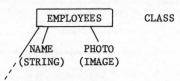

                                              CLASS

When selecting EMPLOYEES class and PHOTO attribute in this order, the system displays only photo of employees.

This selection can be refined by using agregate concept. If we suppose one user wants to display photo of an employee named CARTIER, in term of AS language, the resquest will be the following :

Select EMPLOYEES → PHOTO
    where EMPLOYEES → NOM = 'CARTIER' ;

Selection is first to EMPLOYEES class and NAME attribute. The effect of this operation is to display employees names in window V. After visual research in this window, "CARTIER" value must be selected.

STRUCTURE		VALUES	
OPERATORS		OPERATORS	EMPLOYEES > NAMES
☐ SELECT ☐ CREATE ☐ DELETE ☐ MODIFY	EMPLOYEES ◄—— (1) NAME PHOTO (STRING) (IMAGE) (2)	•.= • > •••	DUPONT POTIER CARTIER ◄—— (3) TOURETTE BOULIER VIDAL LACAZE

Only employees names appears

Selecting "CARTIER" value makes other values of V window disappear. Moving afterwards the cursor in S windox and then selecting attribute PHOTO, cause display in V window of PHOTO objects associated to "CARTIER".

In our example, two photos are associated to "CARTIER". These photos can be displayed by using NEXT operator.

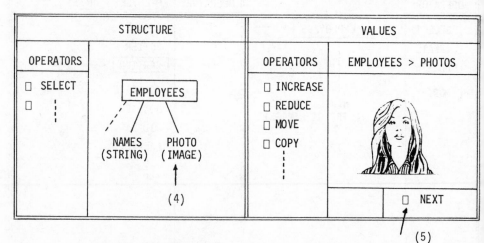

2 COMPLEX OBJECTS LAYOUT

2.1 General features

In this section, we describe layout principles for structured and volumineous objects such as technic documents (see CALDERARA.84). Mixed information (data, text, image,...) is displayed in the screen.

We illustrate this kind of consultation with documents without using paper manipulation.

Scrolling of all the document chapters is possible but not realistic for a partial search. This scrolling is analageous of browsing (BOLT. 83).

A first level selection is possible by using document structure. It is necessary for this to point with cursor the selected chapter document.

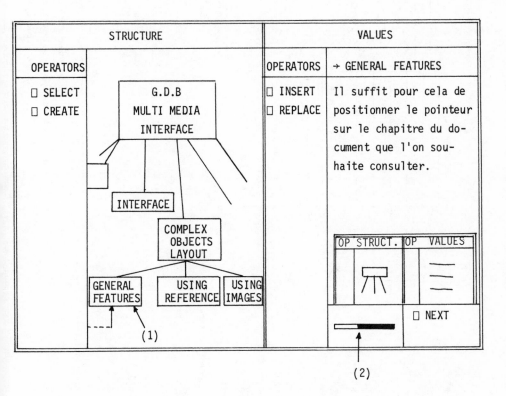

(1)

(2)

The formatted content of selected chapter is displayed in V window by the system. This chapter can be divided into subchapters (sections...) which are displayed in sequence mode, according to the specified structure, and using layout structure (see CHRISMENT & al. 83).

Display can be realized :

- in scrolling mode (2)
- page after page (using function ☐ next)

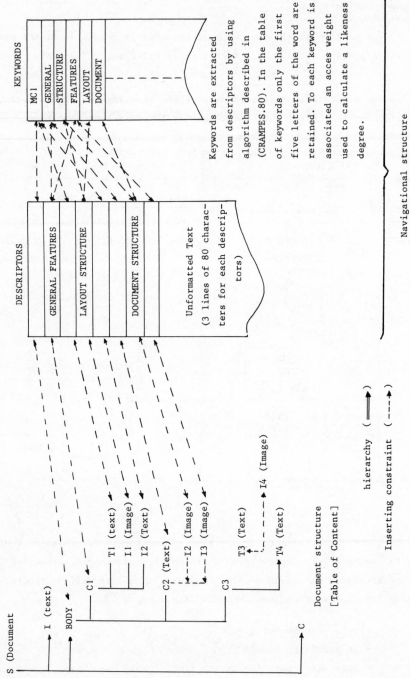

KEYWORDS

| MC1 |
| GENERAL |
| STRUCTURE |
| FEATURES |
| LAYOUT |
| DOCUMENT |

Keywords are extracted from descriptors by using algorithm described in (CRAMPES.80). In the table of keywords only the first five letters of the word are retained. To each keyword is associated an acces weight used to calculate a likeness degree.

DESCRIPTORS

| GENERAL FEATURES |
| LAYOUT STRUCTURE |
| DOCUMENT STRUCTURE |
| Unformatted Text (3 lines of 80 characters for each descriptors) |

Document structure
[Table of Content]

S (Document

I (text)

BODY

C1

T1 (text)
I1 (Image)
I2 (Text)

C2 (Text)
I2 (Image)
I3 (Image)

C3

T3 (Text)
I4 (Image)

T4 (Text)

C

hierarchy (===>)

Inserting constraint (--->)

Navigational structure

It is possible to associate a descriptor to every node of document structure

To refine NAVIGATION the document structure can be extended to construct a NAVIGATIONAL STRUCTURE with index system.

To every node (chapter for one document), it is possible to associate an abstract (three lines of 80 characters). An algorithm automatically extracts key words and integrates then in a table (index). System architecture restricted to navigational structure is visualized in the previous figure.

In this case, navigation within document necessits the use of this structure which is a whole part of the generalized data base. We can obtain schema identifiers as a request result.

Use of navigational structure is realized by mean of a request :

```
    SPECIFY D.U. ASSOCIATED-WITH  < Text >
    _____/      

             (Document Unit)
 D.U.     : Document Units (CHRISMENT.83)
                 {identifiers, titles of chapters...)
 < text > : list of keywords
 SPECIFY  : indicate a request on the schema
```

With multi-media interface we select, in S window ; the function "SCHEMA-INQUIRY" and we specify in a temporary window a selection criterion (text or list of keywords). All selected chapters appear in reverse video in the structure displayed in S window.

Thus the request :
               SPECIFY D.U ASSOCIETED-WITH "FEATURES"
           return : → C1
                    → I3
We can then :
           - display C1 using scrolling,
           - visualize I3,
           - point the beginning of the chapter which contains I3 (that is C2).

Processing a request by the system requires the next steps :

1 DESCRIPTORS SELECTION : Every descriptors which has one
keyword in commun with text of the request is selected.

2 CALCULATION of likeness degree for every descriptor according to text request.

3 DESCRIPTORS SORTING : sorting on descriptors is realized
in descending order according to the likeness degree.
This technic is used in systems such as AGINDA, BURHAU,
ETOILE, MICROBURO,... (see CRAMPES.83, ZOHOUN.84,...)

4 DISPLAY IDENTIFIERS and types of document units (structure nodes) associated to descriptors selected.

5 REFINEMENT SELECTION : The user can display (by using
scrolling) the whole list of descriptors and complete
his selection by manual process.

6 DISPLAY CONTENT of document unit. The system - user
can navigate within document from a point selected
with navigational structure (beginning of selected chapter)

The major interest of this system are :
- ability to associate descriptors to multitype information
(image, graphics, voice,...),
- restricted index area which limits noise during search and can
be very efficient if descriptors are structured,
- simplicity of request formulation, because there is no syntactic constraint.

Systems using same principles without distinguish document structure and navigational structure exists. They allow direct indewing text
without use of abstract. This kind of architecture is convenient for small
information (see Office Message Filling System (TSICHRITRIS.83) with mixed
data, text, image, voice...) but it is not the case for technic document
(100.000 pages).

2.2 Navigation using references

Prior navigational structure permits only navigation using tree
document structure. This navigation can be enhanced bu using various kind
of references inside the document.

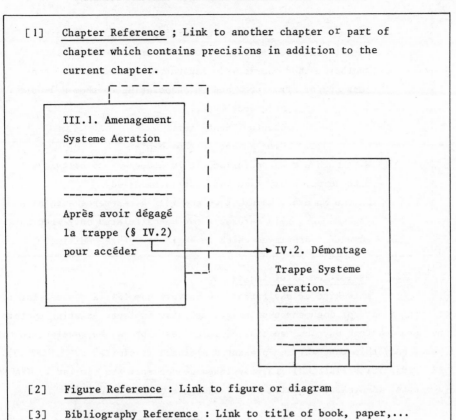

[1] Chapter Reference ; Link to another chapter or part of
     chapter which contains precisions in addition to the
     current chapter.

[2] Figure Reference : Link to figure or diagram

[3] Bibliography Reference : Link to title of book, paper,...
     in bibliography.

The role of reference is to indicate to the document reader, another complementary part of it. Reference managing is then fundamental for navigation in the document and then navigational structure is not a tree but a network.

Reference managing necessits :

[1] Various types of references.

[2] Distinction between reference use and reference definition.
     The reference Manager must able to know where references are
     defined and to identify after or before references.

[3] Reference coding : references can be defined by using struc-
     ture or by using document content.

A simple method consists in defining reference by using
structure supposing very precise document structure.
Another method consists in separating reference from content and/or structure, and in associating to them a 3-uple :
> < Reference Type,
>
>   Chapter Identifier,
>
>   Line Number in the chapter >

With such a represantation, it is necessary to calculate
line number every time the text is modified.
On the in other hand, if we consider a reference such as a
page number, this reference can be calculated only when document is displayed which necessits two-phase editing.

2.3 Navigation using images

This kind of navigation can be very complex if request for identifying a part of document uses image analysis. In fact, existing systems do
not proceed this way but use coupled image descriptors. We consider in this
paper only this context. The presented approach is similar to (CHANG.81),
ERNST.85, TSICHRITZIS.83). Inquiry language concepts are similar to TRAIMA
concepts, (ARGILAS.84), which is a language embedded in PASCAL.

Agregative model permits to consider image class with attributes.
For example, in cartographical application, we can construct images class
for all the countries. A map is associated to every country (see below) with
its name, its flag,...

We can then define virtual images on every image by using window
and grouping them in classes.

In the next figure, basic image IM1 is associated to the window
$A(1,1)$ and $B(m,n)$ when m (and n) is the count of pixels a column (and line).

On basic image IM1, two virtual images are defined :

IV1 : $A1[a_{11}, a_{12}]$, $B1[b_{11}, b_{12}]$

$1 \le a_{11} \le b_{11} \le n$ et $1 \le a_{12} \le b_{12} \le m$

IV2 : $A2[a_{21}, a_{22}]$, $B2[b_{21}, b_{22}]$

$1 \le a_{21} \le b_{21} \le n$ et $1 \le a_{22} \le b_{22} \le m$

A(1,1)

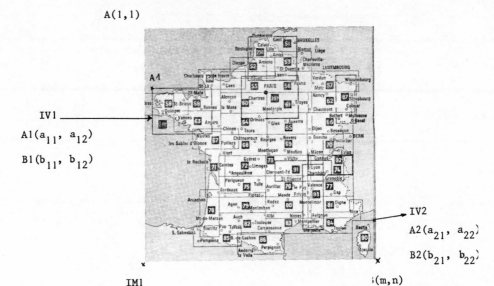

IV1

$A1(a_{11}, a_{12})$

$B1(b_{11}, b_{12})$

IV2

$A2(a_{21}, a_{22})$

$B2(b_{21}, b_{22})$

IM1 (m,n)

In this case, we consider derived domain value from other domain (we do not consider atomic value such as defined in relational model).

To each image, we can associate one or more descriptors, and one or more windows.

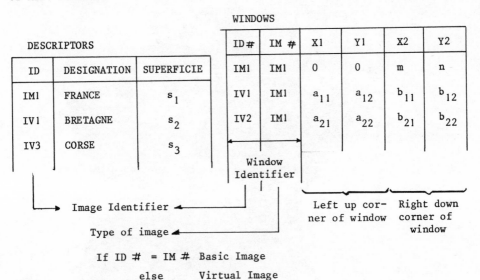

DESCRIPTORS

ID	DESIGNATION	SUPERFICIE
IM1	FRANCE	s_1
IV1	BRETAGNE	s_2
IV3	CORSE	s_3

WINDOWS

ID #	IM #	X1	Y1	X2	Y2
IM1	IM1	0	0	m	n
IV1	IM1	a_{11}	a_{12}	b_{11}	b_{12}
IV2	IM1	a_{21}	a_{22}	b_{21}	b_{22}

Window Identifier

Image Identifier

Type of image

Left up corner of window

Right down corner of window

If ID # = IM # Basic Image
else   Virtual Image

If we have overlapping basic images, a virtual image can be defined in several basic images.

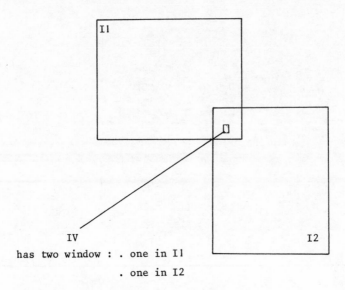

IV   has two window : . one in I1

                    . one in I2

Descriptors permit classical inquiry, but language power can be increased by using deduce process.

Consider the previous cartographical data base. We can define virtual images for cities :

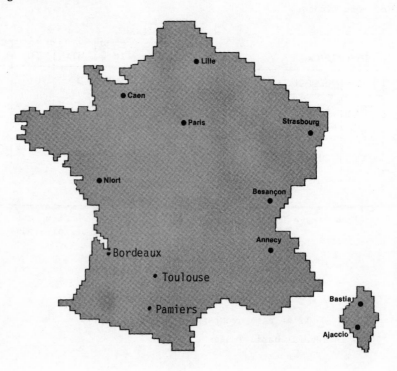

CITITES

ID #	NAME
V1	BORDEAUX
V2	TOULOUSE
V3	PAMIERS

WINDOWS

ID #	IM#	X1	Y1	X2	Y2
V1	F	800	300	802	302
V2	F	870	410	872	412
V3	F	920	400	922	402

We can define relation IS-STRICTLY-NORTH-ØF as such :

V1 IS-STRICTLY-NORTH-ØF V2

If and only if :

V1 $\in$ CITIES

V2 $\in$ CITIES

and WINDOW (V1) < WINDOW (V2)

that is if ($[a_{11}, b_{11}]$, $[a_{12}, b_{12}]$) is V1 window

and ($[a_{21}, b_{21}]$, $[a_{22}, b_{22}]$) is V2 window

[windows defined on the same image]

then $a_{12} < a_{21}$

(or WINDOW·X2 (V1) < WINDOW X1 (V2))

The relation IS-STRICTLY-NORTH-ØF is transitive.

Above definition can be generalized :

VA   IS-STRICTLY-NORTH-NORTH-ØF VB

iff : VA $\in$ CITIES

VB $\in$ CITIES

and   V1, ..., VN

WINDOW (VA) < WINDOW (V1) .... < WINDOW (VN) < WINDOW (VB)

Selecting cities located in the north of Toulouse is expressed by a request :

RANGE X Y CITIES

SELECT X·NAME WHERE X·IS-STRICTLY-NORTH-ØF Y

AND Y·NAME = 'TOULOUSE'

Applied to managing documents, figures can serve to construct an index associated with a document image class (an image can be shared by several documents). To each figure corresponds a descriptor TYPE-FIGURE, TITLE, CHARACTERISTICS... specified with document structure. This index permits to retrieve figure of any kind with such or such characteristics. Figure displaying can be associated with displaying the chapter in which the figure is included.

Other navigational technic presented in (TSICHRITZIS.83) uses miniatures. We can display reduced figure by using browsing :

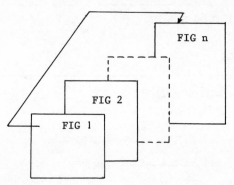

This technic is also used with smalltalk in messagerie system. For each message with voice segment, an voice abstract can be head by the system user which can select the message.

3 CONCLUSION

Presented concepts concern advanced data base domain. This permit :
- information modelling by using types,
- universal management of information without distinction between data base schema and information,
- information description and manipulation with a high level non procedural language.

Particularly, agregative model with associated manipulation language allows :
- with type concept to define static and dynamic aspects of electronic objects,
- with multi-media interface, to manage, in natural form, and at the same level, information and schema.

BIBLIOGRAPHY

ARGILAS F.C., POCQUET A.M. (1984)
Langage spécialisé dans le traitement d'images : TRAIMA II. RR CER-
FIA. Juin.

BD3 (1984) GROUPE BASES DE DONNEES TROISIEME GENERATION
Proposition pour un programme de recherches coordonnées (PRC) en bases de données troisième génération (BD3). Rapport du groupe BD3.
15/2/1984.

BELTRAN X., CHRISMENT C. (1982)
Modèle conceptuel dans les bases d'informations généralisées. Séminaire Bases de Données. Toulouse, 3-4-5 Novembre, pp. 230-249.

BOLT R.A. (1983)
Les images interactives. La recherche N° 144 - Spécial "La Révolution
des images", pp. 678-686.

CALDERARA Y., CHRISMENT C., CRAMPES J.B., ZURFLUH G. (1984)
Un système de documentation électronique. Actes de la Convention Informatique. Paris, Septembre.

CELLIER A., CHRISMENT C., ZURFLUH G. (1985)
Le système GIM : Gestion d'Informations Multitype. Actes de la Convention Informatique Latine. Barcelone, Avril.

CHANG N.S., FU K.S. (1981)
Picture Query Language for Pictorial Data Bases Systems. IEEE Transac-
tion Computer. pp. 23-33, Novembre.

CHAMBERLIN D.D., ASTRAHAM M.H., ESWARAN K.P., GRIFFITHS P.P., LORIE R.A.,
MEHL J.W., REISNER P., WADE D.W. (1976)
SEQUEL 2 : A unified approach for data definition, manipulation and
control. IBM, J, R & D, 20, n° 6, Novembre.

CHAMBERLIN D.D., BERTRAND O.P., GOODFELLOW M.J., KING J.C., SLUTZ D.R.,
TODD J.P., BLADE B.W. (1982).
JANUS : An interactive document formalter based on declarative tags.
IBM SYST. J., Vol 21, N° 3, pp. 250-271.

CHEN P.P.S. (1976)
The entity-relationship model : Toward a unified view of data. ACM
TODS. Vol 1, 1.

CHRISMENT C., CRAMPES J.B., ZURFLUH G. (1983)
    The BIG project. ICOD-2, Proceedings of the Second International Con
    ference on Databases edited by S.M. DEEN and P. HAMMERSLEY, Septembe

CHRISMENT C., PUJOLLE G., ZURFLUH G. (1985a)
    Bases d'informations généralisées : La modélisation des documents.
    L'interface de manipulation. Papier Invite - Les systèmes d'informa-
    tion pour la gestion - Developpements actuels et futurs. Montpellier
    7-8 Mars.

CHRISMENT C., ZURFLUH G. (1985b)
    Bases d'informations généralisées : Modèle agrégatif, langage de
    manipulation et interface multi-media. Journées Bases de Données
    Avancées - St Pierre de Chartreuse, 7-8 Mars.

CHRISMENT C., CRAMPES J.B., ZURFLUH G. (1985c)
    Bases d'informations généralisées. Monographie AFCET - DUNOD, Juin.

CRAMPES J.B. (1980)
    Aide à l'interrogation d'un dictionnaire de données. RAIRO Informa-
    tique, N° 1, 80, Janvier.

MC.DONALD N. (1975)
    CUPID : a graphics oriented facility for support of non programmer
    interactions with the database. PH.D Thesis, Memo N. ERL-M563, UC
    Berkeley, 12 Novembre 1985.

MC.DONALD N. (1982)
    Video graphic query facility. Data Bases : Improving usability and
    responsiveness. Jerusalem, 22-24 juin 1982, pp. 205-218.

ERNST C., MIRANDA S. (1985)
    GIRL : Un SGBD d'Images Relationnelles Logiques sur micro-ordinateur
    Projet BAOU - RR, Février 1985. Laboratoire Informatique, Nice.

HEROT C.F. (1980)
    Spatial Management of Data. ACM TODS, December 1980, Vol 5, N° 4,
    pp. 493-513.

HORAK W. (1983)
    Interchanging mixed text image documents in the office environment
    Computer & Graphics, Vol 7, N° 1, pp. 13-29.

JOLOBOFF V. (1984)
    Aspects logiciels de la communication homme-machine sur les postes
    de travail individuels. Rapport TIGRE N° 17 - IMAG, Juin.

KLUG A. (1981)
    ABE : A query language for constructing aggregates by example. Re-
    search Report, Univ. Wisconsin, TR 474.

MAC LEOD Y. (1983)
    A model for Integrated Information Systems. VLDB, Florence, 31 Oc-
    tobre-2 Novembre 1983, pp. 280-289.

MIRANDA S., NSONDE J. (1982)
    LAGRIF : A pictorial non-programmer - oriented request language for
    relational DBMS. Proceedings Second International Conference on Data-
    bases improving usability and responsiveness. Jerusalem, 22-24 Juin,
    pp. 173-204.

MIRANDA S., OUEDRAGO S., NSONDE J., LE THANN N., LASSON J., BUSTA J. (1984)
    REBU : A casual - user oriented relational DBMS on microcomputers.
    1st International Conference on Computers and Applications. Beijing,
    June 20-22.

SCHIFFNER G., SCHEUERMANN P. (1979)
    Multiple views and abstractions with an extended Entity - Relation-
    ship Model. Computer Language, Vol. 4.

SCHEUERMANN P., SCHIFFNER G., WEBER H. (1980)
    Abstractions capabilities and Invariant Modelling Properties within
    the Entity- Relationship Approach. In Entity Relationship Approach
    to System Analysis and Design. P.P. CHEN Editor.

SCHEK H.J., PISTOR P. (1982)
    Data structures for an Integrated Data Base Management ans Informa-
    tion Retrieval System. Proceedings of the 8th International Confe-
    rence on VLDB MEXICO CITY, September, pp. 197-207.

SCHEK H.J., LUM V. (1983)
    Complex data objects : Text, Voice, Image. Can DBMS manage them.
    VLDB, Florence, 31 Octobre-2 Novembre, Session 13.

SMITH J.M., SMITH D.C.P. (1977)
    Database Abstractions : Agregation. CACM, Vol 20,   6

SMITH J.M., SMITH D.C.P. (1977)
    Database Abstractions : Agregation and Generalization. ACM TODS,
    Vol 2,   2.

SOMERVILLE P.J. (1984)
    Use of images in commercial and office systems. IBM SJ, Vol 3, N° 3,
    pp. 281-296.

TSICHRITZIS D., CHRISTODOULAKIS S., ECONOMOPOULOS P., FALOUTSOS C., LEE A.,
LEE D., VANDERBROECH J., WOO G. (1983)
    A multi-media office filling system. VLDB, Florence, 31 Octobre-
    2 Novembre, pp. 2-7.

VELEZ F. (1984)
    Un modèle et un langage pour les bases de données généralisées : pro-
    jet TIGRE. Thèse de docteur-ingénieur, INP Grenoble, 5 Septembre.

ZLOOF M.M. (1975)
    Query by Example : A data base language. IBM system Journal, 16, 4,
    pp. 324-343.

ZLOOF M.M., PETER DE JONG (1977)
    The system for Business Automation (SBA) : Programming Language.
    CACM, Vol 20,   6.

ZLOOF M.M. (1982)
Office by Example : A business language that unifies data and word processing and electronic mail. IBM System Journal, Vol 21, N° 3, pp. 272-304.

ZOHOUN F. (1983)
AGINDA : Aide à la Gestion d'Informations pour la Décision et l'Administration. Convention Informatique Latine, Barcelone, pp. 521-532, Juin.

ZURFLUH G. (1985)
Bases d'Informations Généralisées : Le modèle agrégatif et son langage de manipulation. Application à la gestion de documents. Thèse d'Etat, UPS Toulouse III, 3 Janvier 1985.

PRINCIPLES OF (Low-Level) COMPUTER VISION

H.-H. Nagel
Fraunhofer-Institut für Informations- und Datenverarbeitung (IITB),
Sebastian-Kneipp-Str. 12-14, D-7500 Karlsruhe 1
and
Fakultät für Informatik der Universität Karlsruhe

1 INTRODUCTION

The title of this chapter would be more appropriate for a two-volume book. Even a terse survey which attempts to allocate appropriate attention to the numerous developments in this active area would require more space than available. The following contribution concentrates on two aspects:

- the emerging conceptual links between algorithmic approaches to image and language understanding;
- the need to explicate the notions about local variations of the image signal underlying all approaches to infer information about a depicted scene from a digitized image.

The second aspect implies a concentration on 'low-level computer vision'. The considerations outlined here are illustrated by references to selected individual approaches. These topics are treated in greater depth by recent introductory textbooks, for example Ballard & Brown (1982), Marr (1982), Rosenfeld & Kak (1982), or in advanced course books such as Faugeras (1983).

The word **vision** is used to denote the ability of a living creature - a 'biological system' (!?) - to exploit the light emitted or reflected by its environment in order to improve its chance for survival. Since most human beings employ vision daily and - it is tempting to assume - thus know what it is, **computer vision** is customarily introduced to mean the same capacity exercised by a computer. The trouble with such an often encountered definition of computer vision consists in the fact that humans have or perform vision, but they don't know - yet - in detail what is going on in their brain. It is thus rather difficult - to say the least - to simulate this capacity in every shade of meaning one might potentially attribute to vision in a colloquial expression. A somewhat related problem has been identified earlier for natural language understanding by computers, as witnessed by T. Winograd in Bobrow and Hayes (1985, p.380):

"I recognized the depth of the difficulties in getting a machine to understand language in any but a superficial and misleading way, and am convinced that people will be much better served by machines that do well-defined and understandable things than those that appear to be like a person until something goes wrong (which won't take long), at which point there is only confusion."

In an attempt to avoid a similar trap, computer vision is considered here to be a new technical term which has to be defined in such a way that it can be converted into an algorithm. The price paid for such a definition consists in a severe restriction: computer vision excludes many of the shades of meaning naturally associated with human vision.

2   DEFINITION OF COMPUTER VISION

Computer vision is defined as a capability of a **technical** system. The two essential components in the first step of the definition - image interpretation and its relation to action - are elaborated subsequently in a top-down fashion:

> Step 1:   **Computer vision** denotes the process which **interprets** an **image** and **relates** the **result** of this analysis **to** some **action**.

We study a section of the real world during a finite period of time. This section of the world should comprise at least a technical system - endowed with computer vision - and its environment. In general, some fraction of the three-dimensional environment is projected onto a transducer which yields a digitized image (see Section 2.3). That fraction of the environment which has been depicted in the image is called the **scene**. Sometimes, the depicted fraction of the environment does not exhibit a three-dimensional structure of its own, for example documents or essentially planar surfaces to be inspected like sheets of wall paper, glas or steel. The remainder of this contribution will concentrate, however, on scenes with three-dimensional (3-D) structure and will not enter into a discussion of special situations where the entire scene is planar.

2.1   The 'discourse world'

The technical system has been designed to pursue some **goals** within its environment. This overall task can be broken down into several subtasks. The system has to **estimate the current state** of itself, of its environment and of its relation to the environment. This is the subtask where **machine vision** is employed as one of several possible sensing processes. Based on this state estimation, a **planning** subsystem has to determine an action or an entire series of actions which are expected to change the current overall state into a desired goal state. Additional subsystems then have to perform the selected actions, for example **manipulation** of the environment or **locomotion** of the technical system.

Resulting changes in the overall state may be **monitored** by the machine vision subsystem.

It thus appears to be essential that the machine vision, the planning, and the acting **subsystems** can **communicate** with each other about the states of the scene, about the system's own states, and about the relations between the system and the scene. As a basis for this communication between the subsystems, the entire technical system has to have a **system-internal representation** for its goals as well as for the states of the scene, for the system's own states, and for the relations between the system and the scene.

Step 2:   The section of the real world which is covered by the system-
            internal representation will be called the **discourse world**.
This notion has been coined in the context of natural language understanding by machines. Only those aspects of the real world which are covered by the system-internal representation can be

- exploited for the estimation of the actual state of system and scene,
- communicated to other components of the technical system,
- exploited for the planning of actions,
- exploited for the execution and monitoring of actions.

Obviously, the discourse world can and should be restricted to those aspects of the real world which are relevant to the goals the technical system has been charged to pursue. In view of the fact that the system-internal representation of the discourse world is of central importance for the performance of the technical system and thus needs to be easily inspected, assessed, and modified, it is postulated that this representation has to be formulated explicitly.

2.2   Relation to natural language or the need to represent concepts

Extending the notion of discourse world to machine vision can be justified not only by reference to the fact that this notion circumscribes the possible form and content of the communication between the various subsystems which realize machine vision. A frequently desired action would like to have the technical system answer questions about the scene - see, e.g., v. Hahn et al. (1980) - or to generate a scene description in the form of a natural language text as discussed, for example, by Waltz (1979 + 1981). Such a description of an image can comprise only those assertions about the scene which have been included in the discourse world. This incapacity to formulate anything not covered by the system-internal representation of the discourse world has to be distinguished from the situation where insufficient corroborating evidence for an assertion has been extracted from an image. Although in the latter alternative a statement about the scene could be potentially formulated according to the system-internal representation, it must be either left open or considered to be false, depending on the amount of counter-evidence available.

The discourse world thus determines, too, the possibilities for communication between the developer as well as the operator of the system on the one hand and the subsystems for machine vision, planning, and plan execution on the other hand. The more complicated the images which have to be analyzed, the more important will be the ability to couch the resulting description into natural language terms: this facilitates the man-machine communication which is necessary for the debugging and extension of the entire technical system.

It should be noted that the representation of the discourse world has a quantitative as well as a qualitative aspect. The former relates to the number and types of different objects etc. which can be represented. The latter aspect relates to the richness of **concepts** for which representational means have been included. This latter aspect largely determines whether the communication about the actual state of the discourse world and its temporal development - see, e.g., Neumann (1982 + 1984) - can be organized at the appropriate level of abstraction.

2.3   A digitized image and its interpretation

In order to obtain a **digitized image**, the image plane of a transducer is tesselated, usually into a square raster. The radiation intensity received by the transducer within each raster square is averaged and quantized, yielding a **gray value**. The three-tuple consisting of the x and y coordinates of a specific raster square together with the associated gray value is called a picture element or **pixel**. A matrix of gray values ordered according to increasing x and y coordinates is called a digitized image - see Figure 1 for an example.

Step 3:   **Image interpretation** establishes a relation between each pixel and the system-internal representation of the discourse world for the depicted scene.

These three steps of the definition for computer vision emphasize three aspects which are considered to be crucial for progress in this area:

- Computer vision must not be separated from the context within which it is intended to be used.
- Since there appear to be no natural limits for what might have to be taken into account, the discourse world has to be delimited by deliberate decision.
- All relevant aspects of the discourse world have to be represented explicitly in order to make them amenable to analysis.

The representational structure of the discourse world is usually considered to be a topic of high level vision which is treated, for example, in Faugeras (1985).

Figure 1a:　A digitized image

Figure 1b:　Enlarged subimage from Figure 1a. It allows to recognize the gray values of individual pixels.

2.4　Low level vision

Many experimental approaches to machine vision just transform the input image into some kind of display which has to be judged by humans in order to assess the suitability of the result as an input to potential action routines. These approaches lack a clearly defined discourse world. Examples can be frequently found in connection with segmentation approaches:

- Segmentation is understood to mean the decomposition of an image into regions which can be uniquely associated with a single object in the depicted scene.
- A segment is the largest possible region which complies with some given homogeneity criterion.
- Segments must not overlap.
- The set of all segments has to cover an image completely.

In such an approach - see Pavlidis (1977) - the entire knowledge about the depicted scene is contained implicitly in the homogeneity criterion. There are only few situations where such a criterion is really sufficient to capture the immense variability of appearance for real world scenes.

Other approaches proceed a step further and link the result of image evaluation to - mostly rather primitive - action routines, thereby including at least fragments of a discourse world. However, relevant aspects of their discourse worlds are often represented only implicitly by special formulation of the algorithms which plan and execute actions. Such approaches are difficult to debug and cumbersome to adapt to situations even slightly different from those for which the original approach had been developed. It is usually impossible, moreover, to assess the range of applicability for such solution approaches.

Recognizing these difficulties, Kanade (1978) suggested to discuss machine vision as a process iterating between six major process-states - see Figure 2. The generic description from Figure 2 represents a parameterized model for the

Figure 2 : Machine vision according to Kanade (1978), with modifications by Nagel (1979)

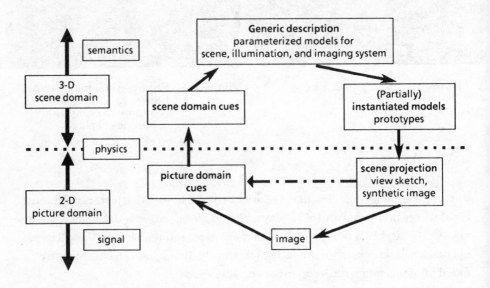

scene, complemented by parameterized models for the scene illumination and the imaging system as suggested by Nagel (1979). This generic description corresponds to the representation of the discourse world.

The initial step of a **top-down** or **model-based approach** to machine vision according to Kanade has to generate a-priori hypotheses about a scene depicted by an image to be analyzed. This step generates - at least partially - instantiated models or prototypes by restricting parameters to a subrange or a fixed value within the range of variability provided in the generic description. This instantiation subprocess comprises, too, the fixing of parameters defining the properties of the imaging system, including its position and attitude relative to the scene. The next step employs this knowledge to generate a scene projection in the form of a synthetic image which can be compared subsequently to the image of the depicted scene obtained by the transducer. Significant differences between the observed and the synthetic image are converted to picture domain cues which are combined with knowledge about the physics of image generation in order to derive cues in the three-dimensional scene domain. The scene domain cues are in turn exploited to select more appropriate models or parameter subranges from the generic description for the scene under investigation in order to improve the prototypes to be used during the next iteration around this loop. This iterative search for appropriate model instantiations can be terminated as soon as no significant differences remain between the scene projection and the original digitized image.

Instead of generating a synthetic image, one might generate some abstraction thereof, the view sketch, which represents the depicted scene only by certain features such as points - associated with gray value extrema, line intersections or corners -, line segments, straight or curved lines, blobs, regions, etc. These are to be compared directly to picture domain cues or features extracted from the original image.

The extraction of features may be considered, too, as the initial step in a **bottom-up or data-driven** approach to machine vision if not enough a-priori knowledge about the depicted scene is available to generate at least partially appropriate prototypes right from the beginning. Only a severely restricted discourse world, however, allows to jump directly from simple picture domain cues to correct conclusions about an object in the scene: 'verification vision' investigated, e.g., by Bolles (1977) in connection with the fast inspection of parts or assemblies may serve as an example.

The concepts associated with high and low level vision, respectively, may be indicated by reference to the diagram of Figure 2. The fraction of the iteration circle extending from scene domain cues via generic descriptions and instantiated models through the scene projection is attributed to **high level vision**. Since the scene projection has been generated from the generic description, the relation between each pixel of the scene projection and the representation of the discourse world is known explicitly. **Low level vision** can be considered as the group of subprocesses connecting the image via picture domain cues to scene domain cues. It can be summarily defined as the process which infers the

a) position,
b) orientation,
c) shape,
d) painting,
e) possibly the fine structure (i.e. non-painted texture), and
f) illumination

of surfaces in 3-D space from their digitized images. The remainder of this contribution will be concerned with low level vision.

Picture domain cues are only useful to the extent that the physics of the image generation process allows to relate them reliably to scene domain cues and hence to the three-dimensional representation of the scene. As a consequence, the discourse world has to include a representation at the signal level for the set of acceptable picture domain cues, specifying the conditions which control the association between each picture domain cue and components for the 3-D representation of a scene or its illumination.

3   REPRESENTATIONS FOR LOCAL GRAY VALUE VARIATIONS

The spatial variation of surfaces, of their properties and their illumination in a 3-D scene results in 2-D spatial variations of the gray values in an image of the scene. We may consider a digitized image as a set of discrete samples from a continuous bivariate picture function $g(x,y)$. In view of the enormous variability in the appearance of scenes and thus of images, it does not appear possible to find a closed form characterization for the global picture function of an entire image. We have to look for descriptors which characterize local variations of the picture function. Such local characterizations have then to be assembled into more global ones which serve as picture domain cues.

If we inspect sample gray value distributions from a digitized image - see Figure 3 - we recognize that part of the observable variation does not reflect any relevant structure in the scene or its illumination. This contribution to the observed variation can be attributed to noise associated with the light transmission between scene and transducer, with the transducer itself, and with the digitization process. As a consequence, our model for a local section of the picture function has to account for two contributions to the observed variation, one contribution associated with noise and another - structural - one associated with variations in the scene. It is usually assumed that the noise contribution is normally distributed with zero mean.

Local descriptors for the picture function will be discussed according to whether the structural contribution varies along only one dimension or inherently along both dimensions of the image plane.

3.1   One-dimensional structural gray value variation

If the picture function is locally constant along one direction - apart from noise contributions - it is sufficient to categorize the remaining structural variation along the other direction. Figures 4 through 6 show examples for local

Figure 3 : Digital representation of gray values from all but the last two columns of Figure 1b. Large numbers represent bright intensities, small numbers dark ones. One can easily recognize, e.g., the hood of the car as the area in the center with three-digit gray values.

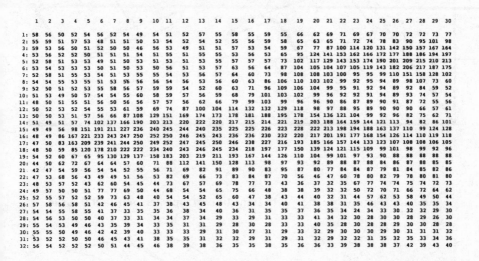

	1	2	3	4	5	6	7	8	9	10	11	12	13	14	15	16	17	18	19	20	21	22	23	24	25	26	27	28	29	30
1:	58	56	50	52	54	56	52	54	49	54	51	52	57	55	58	55	59	55	66	62	69	71	69	67	70	70	72	72	73	77
2:	55	59	51	57	53	48	51	51	50	53	54	52	54	52	55	56	59	58	65	63	65	71	72	74	78	83	90	95	101	98
3:	59	53	56	50	51	52	50	50	46	56	53	49	51	51	57	53	54	59	67	77	87	100	114	120	131	142	150	157	167	164
4:	53	56	52	52	50	51	51	51	54	51	55	51	55	55	53	56	53	65	95	124	141	153	162	166	172	177	188	186	194	197
5:	52	58	51	53	53	49	51	50	53	51	53	51	53	55	57	57	57	73	102	117	129	143	153	174	190	201	209	215	210	213
6:	53	54	53	53	53	50	51	50	53	50	56	51	53	57	63	56	64	87	104	105	104	107	105	119	143	182	206	217	187	175
7:	52	58	51	55	53	54	51	53	55	55	54	53	56	57	64	60	73	98	108	108	103	100	95	95	99	110	151	158	128	102
8:	54	54	55	53	55	51	53	56	56	56	54	54	56	53	56	60	63	86	106	110	103	102	99	92	95	94	89	98	107	73
9:	52	50	51	52	53	55	58	56	57	59	59	54	52	60	63	71	96	109	106	104	99	95	91	92	94	89	92	84	59	52
10:	51	53	49	50	57	54	54	55	60	58	59	57	56	59	68	79	101	103	102	99	96	92	92	91	94	89	93	74	57	54
11:	48	50	51	55	51	56	50	56	56	57	57	56	62	66	79	99	103	99	96	96	90	86	87	89	90	91	87	72	55	56
12:	50	52	53	52	54	55	53	61	59	69	74	87	100	104	114	132	132	129	118	98	97	88	95	89	90	90	90	66	57	61
13:	50	50	53	51	57	56	66	87	108	129	151	169	174	173	178	181	188	195	178	154	136	121	104	99	92	96	82	75	62	71
14:	51	49	51	57	74	102	137	166	190	203	213	220	222	220	217	215	214	221	219	203	188	164	159	144	121	113	94	82	86	101
15:	49	49	56	98	151	191	211	227	236	240	245	244	240	235	225	225	226	223	228	222	213	198	194	188	163	137	110	99	124	128
16:	48	49	86	167	221	233	243	247	250	252	250	246	245	243	236	230	232	220	217	201	191	177	168	154	126	114	110	119	118	
17:	47	50	83	163	209	239	241	244	250	249	252	247	245	250	246	238	227	216	193	185	166	157	144	133	123	107	108	108	106	105
18:	48	50	59	85	120	178	210	222	222	234	240	243	246	245	234	218	197	177	150	139	124	121	115	109	99	101	98	99	92	96
19:	54	52	60	67	65	95	130	129	137	158	183	203	219	211	193	167	144	126	110	104	99	101	97	93	90	88	88	88	88	88
20:	44	50	62	72	67	64	64	57	60	71	88	112	141	150	128	113	98	97	93	92	89	88	87	88	84	86	87	88	85	85
21:	42	47	54	59	56	54	54	52	55	56	71	69	82	91	89	90	83	95	87	80	77	84	84	87	79	81	84	85	82	86
22:	47	53	68	56	43	49	49	51	56	53	82	69	66	73	83	84	87	70	56	46	47	60	78	80	82	79	78	80	81	80
23:	48	53	57	52	43	62	60	54	45	44	73	67	57	69	78	77	73	43	36	37	32	35	67	77	74	74	75	74	72	73
24:	49	57	50	50	51	77	77	69	50	44	68	54	54	65	75	66	48	38	38	39	32	32	50	72	70	71	66	72	64	62
25:	52	55	57	52	52	59	73	63	48	40	54	54	52	65	60	47	38	43	44	40	32	31	44	57	62	53	58	49	50	44
26:	57	58	56	58	51	42	46	45	41	37	38	43	45	48	43	34	34	40	41	38	38	31	35	46	43	43	40	35	35	34
27:	54	54	55	58	55	41	37	33	35	35	36	38	34	40	36	31	35	35	37	36	35	34	24	34	33	30	32	32	29	30
28:	54	56	53	50	50	40	37	33	31	34	34	37	34	29	33	29	31	33	33	41	34	32	30	28	30	30	28	29	26	30
29:	55	54	53	49	46	43	35	39	34	33	35	31	31	29	28	30	28	33	33	40	35	28	30	28	28	29	30	30	28	28
30:	55	55	50	49	46	42	42	39	40	33	33	33	29	31	30	27	31	29	33	32	29	30	30	29	30	31	31	31	32	
31:	53	52	52	50	50	46	45	43	41	38	35	35	31	32	32	29	31	29	31	32	29	32	32	31	35	32	35	33	34	36
32:	56	54	52	52	52	50	51	44	45	46	38	39	38	36	35	35	38	35	36	36	33	39	38	38	38	37	42	39	43	40

variations of the picture function in one dimension. Continuously differentiable

Figure 4a : **Constant** picture function

Figure 4b : **Linearly sloping** picture function

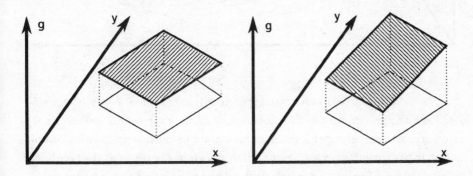

variations are given in Figure 4a-d, continuous but not everywhere differentiable variations in Figure 5a-c, and discontinuous variations in Figure 6a + b.

Figure 4c : **Cylindric** picture functions

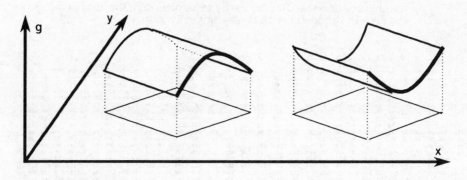

Figure 4d : Picture function with transition of type **'error integral curve'**

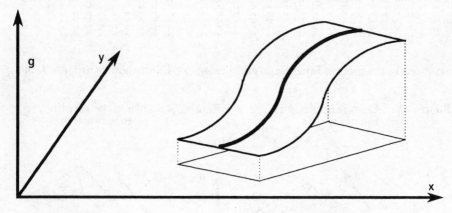

The discontinuous step type transition of Figure 6a could be considered as an approximation to the continuous, but not everywhere differentiable 'ramp' transition of Figure 5b which in turn could be considered to be an approximation to the smooth gray value transition shown in Figure 4d as the type 'error integral curve'. This latter denotation should be understood as a qualitative characterization rather than a quantitative one. Similarly, one could consider the 'bar' type transition as a discontinuous approximation to the continuous, but not differentiable 'peak' type transition shown in Figure 5c. The cylindric transition

Figure 5a : **'Roof** type' picture   Figure 5b : **'Ramp** type' picture
           function   function

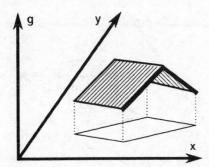   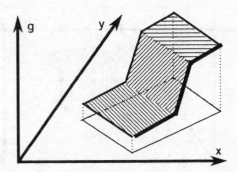

Figure 5c : **'Peak** type' picture function

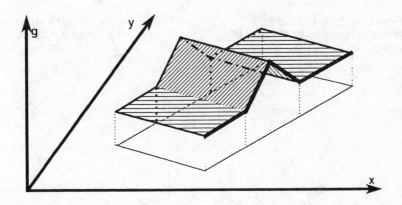

types of Figure 4c share the property of having a linearly extending gray value extremum with both the 'bar' and the 'peak' type transition. This cylindric model for the picture function, however, does not reflect the transition from a significant slope to essentially constant gray values as in the outer zones of the 'bar' and 'peak' type. In this sense, the 'bar' and 'peak' type transitions can not be considered as discrete approximations of the cylindric transition types.

Figure 6a : ' **Step** type' picture
function

Figure 6b : ' **Bar** type' picture
function

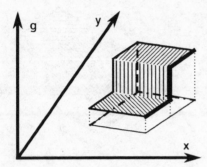
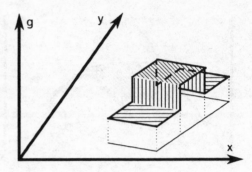

3.2   Inherently two-dimensional structural gray value variations

We may align a local coordinate system with the directions of principal curvature of the gray value transition as shown in Figure 7a. Referring to this

Figure 7a : Local coordinate
system aligned with **straight** line
gray value transition

Figure 7b : Local coordinate
system aligned with **curved** line
gray value transition

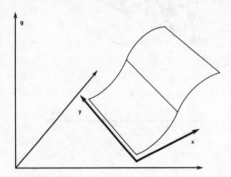
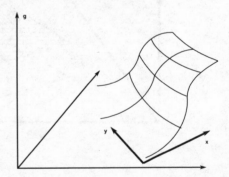

local coordinate system, the gray value transition of Figure 7a can be characterized by a non-vanishing partial derivative g_x of the picture function $g(x,y)$ with respect to x, whereas the partial derivative g_y with respect to y vanishes identically. If we 'bend' such a straight line gray value transition, we obtain a simple example for the category of inherently two-dimensional structural gray value variations , see

Figure 7b. In this case, both first partial derivatives g_x as well as g_y will be different from zero.

Increasing the curvature transforms such a 'curved line' gray value transition into a gray value 'corner' shown in Figure 8. Kitchen and Rosenfeld

Figure 8 :   Gray value 'corner', defined as the point of maximum planar curvature for the line of steepest slope.

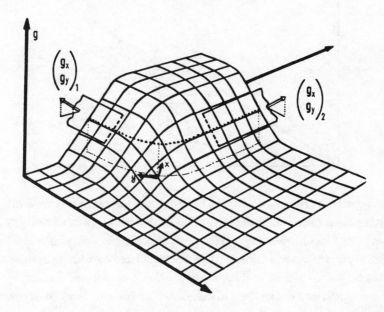

(1982) investigated various heuristic approaches to determine gray value corners. Nagel (1983) suggested a mathematical characterization in order to exploit such a gray value variation for a closed form solution to an interframe matching problem which is important for the evaluation of image sequences : a gray value corner is defined as the point of maximum planar curvature in the line of steepest gray value slope. The line of steepest gray value slope is defined as the locus of points where the gradient is maximal. If we align the x-axis with this gradient direction, the first partial derivative g_x with respect to x should be a maximum along this line, implying that the second partial derivative g_{xx} in the gradient direction crosses zero. Since the gray value distribution must be locally constant perpendicular to the gradient direction, the first partial derivative g_y vanishes, but according to the above definition of the gray value corner the second partial derivative g_{yy} with respect to y is extremal, too, at this location.

Gray value extrema provide examples for other inherently two-dimensional structural gray value variations - see Figure 9. In analogy to the gray

Figure 9 :   Gray value extremum; both first partial derivatives vanish.

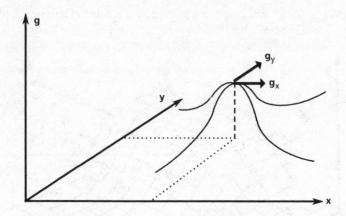

value corner, the gray value extrema can be characterized mathematically by simultaneous zero-crossings of both first partial derivatives g_x as well as g_y, combined with non-zero second partial derivatives g_{xx} as well as g_{yy}. Here again, all partial derivatives are taken with respect to a local coordinate system aligned with the directions of principal curvature for the local picture function.

Watson et al. (1985) discuss a categorization of local descriptors based on the first and second partial derivatives of the picture function.Their approach implies that the picture function can be well approximated within an acceptable environment around each pixel by a bivariate second-order Taylor series. For more complicated picture functions, these first and second partial derivatives may vary rather strongly as a function of x and y, i.e. the environment within which the Taylor approximation remains acceptable can shrink to a few pixels.

The so-called 'T-junction' - see, e.g., Waltz (1975) and Figure 10 - will be used to illustrate this. Images of straight line polyhedral edges meet in junctions. The simplest junction is the so-called 'L-junction' which can be associated with the gray value corner shown in Figure 8. The 'T-junction' is interpreted as being the image of the edge of a polyhedral surface which partially occludes the edge between two surfaces of another polyhedron. All three surfaces involved are assumed to exhibit different brightness, otherwise at least one of the edges between them would not show up in the image. A simplified picture function for this situation is show in Figure 10a. If the assumption of step transitions between

Figure 10a : Visualization of a **discrete** picture function for a T-junction. The broken lines in the image plane represent the T-junction, indicating the position of edges between the three constant gray level plateaus in the image.

Figure 10b : Visualization of a **continuous** picture function for a T-junction. The broken lines in the image plane represent the T-junction, indicating the position of transitions between the three gray levels in the image. The gray value for the 'occluding' surface has been deliberately drawn with a slope to indicate additional possibilities for variation, apart from the multiple parameters characterizing the transition regions.

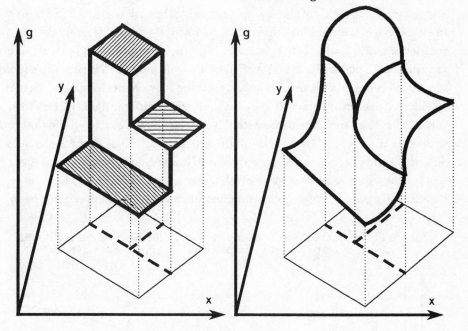

constant image intensity plateaus is dropped, the picture function becomes much more complicated: Figure 10b attempts a qualitative visualization of more or less smooth transitions between areas of reduced but nevertheless non-vanishing structural gray value variations. Whereas a straight line step transition in Figure 6a requires five parameters (the two position coordinates, the angle describing the orientation of the transition line, and the two gray values of the plateau on either side of the step transition), a multitude of parameters would be required to account in a quantitative manner for the potential variations in Figure 10b. Compared to other, multi-line junctions investigated by Waltz (1975) in his attempt to take into account the effects of non-trihedral vertices and of shadows, the T-junction appears to be simple. It has been used here just to illustrate the gap between the structural gray value variations which might occur in an image and our current (in)ability to model them precisely.

3.3   The scale problem

One might attempt to represent the 'step', 'ramp', 'roof', 'peak', and 'bar' transitions shown in Figures 5 and 6 as compound types built from elements of type 'constant' and 'linearly sloping' gray value transition as given in Figures 4a + b. Such a consideration addresses a fundamental problem, namely the question of locality: what is the proper scale for the description of a **local** structural variation of the picture function? Although the scale problem has been introduced here by reference to constant and linearly sloping components in some of the more complicated discontinuous or at least not everywhere differentiable picture function models , one can not dispense with this problem by the consideration that such picture functions are artefacts of the digitization process. Even in the continuous case, one might observe a stronger variation of limited extension superimposed on another one which extends across a much larger scale - see Figure 11 for a one-dimensional example. Analogous situations for two dimensions may occur in an

Figure 11 :   Example for a (one-dimensional) function with a small-scale variation superimposed on a variation of larger scale.

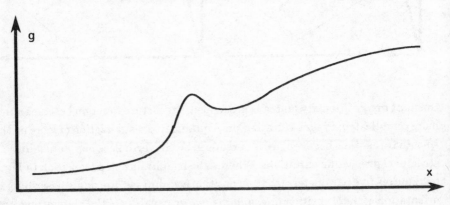

image: the gray value variations of smaller scale might represent images of real edges in the 3-D scene, whereas the variations of larger scale could be due, for example, to fading shadows.

We have to distinguish between several intertwined questions:

i) Is a single scale appropriate for the description of the gray value variation at some location in a given digitized image?

ii) Provided there is only a single appropriate scale, how can it be estimated?

iii) If gray value variations of several different scales are superimposed on each other, how can the different contributions be separated?

iv) What kind of potential relations between gray value variations of different scale have to be taken into account during the interpretation process?

Gray value variations of different scale can be separated by subjecting the image to a hierarchy of bandpass filters in the spatial frequency domain. Additional criteria are required, however, for the decision whether the variation in the result of a specific bandpass operation is significant. Although various investigations into these problems have been performed during recent years - see, e.g., Marr and Hildreth (1980), Witkin (1983), Crowley & Sanderson (1984), Koenderink (1984), Rosenfeld (1984), Korn (1985) - there are not yet any clear-cut answers.

4   DETECTION AND LOCALIZATION OF DESCRIPTORS

Once a set of admissible representations for local variations of a picture function has been defined, a process has to be designed as a next step which decomposes a given digitized image into a structure of admissible local descriptors. This decomposition process usually tends to emphasize either the representation of gray value transition areas - see Section 4.2 - or of their complement.

4.1   Region segmentation

'Segmentation' approaches as mentioned in Section 2.4 are examples for the latter case. The underlying concept for the global picture function can be characterized as a mosaic of essentially homogeneous gray value regions, i.e. the dominant representation of a local picture function corresponds to Figure 4a. For images of 3-D scenes, this model of the structural gray value variation will not be adequate in general. There are, however, special situations where a constant picture function model appears to be appropriate, for example the image of a planar polished cut through composite material made up of components with different reflectivity. Haralick (1980) admitted a linearly sloping picture function (Fig. 4b) in addition to a constant one for the description of elementary regions - see, too, Pong et al. (1984).

In analogy to clustering procedures, segmentation processes may follow an agglomerative (bottom-up, merging) approach, a divisive (top-down, splitting) approach or a combination of both approaches (split and merge). The emphasis on data structures or special algorithms for the segmentation of digitized images in many cases obscures a clear characterization of the - often only implicitly defined - model of the picture function underlying the described approach. These relations have been discussed, e.g., by Rosenfeld & Davis (1979). Numerous heuristics have been suggested to ameliorate the adverse consequences when an overly simplistic model for the picture function is employed during the segmentation process. A recent survey which compares various segmentation approaches can be found in Haralick & Shapiro (1985).

4.2 Edge detection

If the decomposition of the detailed description of the entire image into descriptors emphasizes the representation of gray value transitions, one usually employs a bottom-up or agglomerative approach: 'edge elements' are detected and joined to form contour lines.

One usually selects the desired type and scale for a significant gray value transition, thereby defining a template or a set of related templates for the associated structural gray value variation. Most early edge detection approaches used a 2x2 or 3x3 pixel template size in order to keep the required computations within manageable bounds. The orientation of an edge element was either determined by a separate template or operator mask for a small set of 4 to 8 gross orientations - for example the compass gradient masks of Kirsch (1971) or Robinson (1977) - or by estimating both components of a picture function gradient. This latter approach has the advantage to require only a total of two convolutions between the image and the gradient component templates - namely one each for the x- and the y-direction mask, respectively - compared with 4 to 8 convolutions required by the compass gradient approach. The gradient operator usually reflects a transition type represented by a constant slope - see Figure 4b. An often used template - suggested first by Prewitt (1970) - has the form given in Figure 12. This template results from fitting a linear function of the image plane coordinates to the gray value distribution. Such an approach can be extended to larger template sizes and higher order polynomials in the image plane coordinates - see, e.g., Beaudet (1978) for numerical examples. A derivation of the formulas including expressions for the

Figure 12 a: 3x3 gradient
operator according to Prewitt;
template for the x-component of
a constant slope gray value
transition as in Figure 4b

Figure 12 b: 3x3 gradient
operator according to Prewitt;
template for the y-component of
a constant slope gray value
transition as in Figure 4b

-1	0	1
-1	0	1
-1	0	1

1	1	1
0	0	0
-1	-1	-1

uncertainty of the gradient estimates due to normally distributed noise in the
measured gray values can be found in appendix 1 of Nagel (1983).

A variation of these operators has been suggested by Sobel - see Duda
and Hart (1973, page 271) and Figure 13. Experimental investigations by Abdou

Figure 13 a: 3x3 gradient
operator according to Sobel;
template for the x-component

Figure 13 b: 3x3 gradient
operator according to Sobel;
template for the y-component

-1	0	1
-2	0	2
-1	0	1

1	2	1
0	0	0
-1	-2	-1

and Pratt (1979) regarding sensitivity and fidelity to the orientation of the transition have shown that the Sobel operator appears to be slightly better than the
Prewitt operator. According to Davies (1983), this may be related to the fact that a
quadratic mask is not sufficiently isotropic with respect to orientation. By doubling
the weight in the center columns of the Sobel operator, however, the pixels closer to
the center obtain a larger influence on the operator response than the corner pixels
and thereby compensate somewhat the influence of the square mask.

A remarkably early recognition of many fundamental problems of edge detection is testified by the approach of Hueckel (1971 + 1973). He specified explicitly how the picture function is expected to vary locally, namely according to the step-type or bar-type as shown in Figure 6. He employed circular operator masks in order to reduce the orientation dependency. He investigated operator masks with different diameters which were carefully chosen to minimize approximation errors for the weight factors. In addition, he studied acceptance criteria which allow to detect the possible presence of two edge elements within the operator support. This facilitates a warning if the parameter estimates characterizing the dominant gray value transition within the operator support might become unreliable. Such an approach, however, requires considerable computations. Simplified computations suggested by Mero & Vassy (1975) have been shown by Nevatia (1977) to be more susceptible to noise than the original version of Hueckel (1971).

The selected templates have to be compared with the digitized image in order to determine the location of gray value variations with sufficient similarity to the desired transition type. Since the digitized image is more or less contaminated by noise, even an appropriate template will rarely yield a perfect match. 'Sufficient' is usually defined in terms of a threshold for the correlation between template and image. Its choice represents a formidable problem in itself. This problem is related to the fact that the majority of edge detection approaches reported so far in the literature employ a single template chosen without regard to the gray value variations actually present in the digitized image. As a consequence, the response to the chosen template is above the threshold only at some of the locations where it is expected. At other locations in the image, the response remains below the threshold although inspection of the image would justify the presence of an edge element in order to complete a desired figure. At still other locations, a response exceeding the threshold is obtained despite the fact that a transition at such a location appears incompatible with an acceptable interpretation of the resulting edge element arrangement. The commitment to a template of a fixed type and size - i.e. the latter implying a single scale for the transition - leaves the threshold as the only parameter available for the adaptation. It should not come as a surprise that fiddling around with the threshold will in general not cure the deficiencies of having chosen an inappropriate gray value transition type or scale in the first place.

In order to evade at least some aspects of this trap, Haralick (1980) studied a proper statistical test in order to decide whether two neighboring image regions can be jointly described by a single linearly sloping picture function or not. In the latter case, an edge element would have to be placed between the two test areas since they could only be approximated individually by a picture function as shown in Figure 4b.

4.3 Edge localization

Binford (1981) pointed out the distinction between the edge **detection** and the edge **localization** problem. Even if thresholding the gradient of a picture function may yield reliable results for the presence of a transition, it does not in general solve the problem where precisely in the image the edge element should be located.

The use of gradient operators corresponding to a linearly sloping picture function often produces 'broad' edge regions: a strong gray value transition may extend across many pixels. At each pixel position along such a transition, the application of, e.g., a 3x3 gradient operator corresponding to Figure 4b yields a large response. The basic inadequacy of scale between the picture function model underlying the operator and the actual gray value transition in the image would suggest to select an operator of larger scale. Instead, however, often the operator response is converted into a binary 'edge picture', followed by heuristic 'thinning' approaches. Such a combination of operations could be considered to imply a broad ramp-type picture function model (Figure 5b). The thinning procedure is expected to select the location of the center point in the transition area.

A considerable conceptual improvement consists in defining the edge to be located at the point of maximum slope. This implies a picture function model of the type 'error integral curve' (Figure 4d). The location of maximum slope corresponds to the zero-crossing of the second derivative of the picture function. Since partial differentiation corresponds to high pass filtering, the influence of noise has to be compensated for in the result of convolving the image with operators for the estimation of second partial derivatives. The edge detection approach described by Marr & Hildreth (1980) in principle convolves the image with a rotationally symmetric Gaussian smoothing filter prior to the computation of the second derivatives. Since partial differentiation and convolution can be interchanged, one may equally well convolve the image immediately with the second partial derivative of the Gaussian filter. In order to obtain a rotation invariant operator, Marr & Hildreth (1980) determined zero-crossings in the result obtained by convolution of the image with the Laplacian of a Gaussian filter. This Laplacian can be very well approximated by the difference of two Gaussian filters with a width ratio of 1:1.6, yielding the so-called 'mexican hat' operator - see Marr (1982). It has the additional advantage that the convolution of an image with a rotationally symmetric

Gaussian filter is separable into two one-dimensional convolutions which can be performed one after the other at a drastic decrease in computational costs.

The difference of Gaussians corresponds to a spatial bandpass filter. Several bandpass operations are applied to an image, each time doubling the center frequency of the preceding spatial bandpass. An edge is accepted if zero-crossings in all bandpass filtered versions of an image fall on top of each other. The undeniable advantages of this approach - see Hildreth (1983) - compared, e.g., to the thresholding of 3x3 gradient operator responses have somewhat obscured the fact that even this approach is not yet without drawbacks. One is of a more theoretical nature: the picture function model (Figure 4d) underlying this approach needs not be the correct one in all cases - see Leclerc & Zucker (1984). Another objection is basically related to the fact that Marr & Hildreth (1980) recommend fairly large operator masks in order to smooth the image sufficiently well and, moreover, to suppress approximation errors in the integer weight factors of their operators. Such an approach does not allow to detect all edges in image areas with higher frequency texture - see the debate between Haralick (1984 + 1985) and Grimson & Hildreth (1985).

It appears interesting to relate this latter problem to an observation made by Young (1983) in a different context. Young attempted to calculate certain quantitative parameters for pictorial structures extracted from images digitized at various resolutions, among them tesselations with a resolution well beyond the necessary limit of twice the highest frequency in the analog video signal. The results extracted by Young depended on the resolution of the tesselation. Young attributed this to the fact that the full information of the original video image is only recovered completely if the appropriate sinc-functions, multiplied with the corresponding digitized sample values, are integrated from minus to plus **infinity**. In practice, however, such summations are performed only with data from a finite support. When he used an apparently 'finer than necessary' resolution, the size ratio between the structure in question and the resolution cell improved. It might be sensible to investigate whether the choice of operator size required to obtain negligible approximation losses for the weight factors should be separated from the resolution required for recoverability of the original video signal from the digitized images. Sampling the bandlimited video signal at higher than twice the maximum frequency component might then allow to recover even high frequency texture contributions without adverse effects due to using an operator mask of insufficient diameter. In such cases, the continuous picture function models of Figure 4 would appear to be even more appropriate. Moreover, semi-local variations of the picture function such as the one shown in Figure 10b may be decomposed into local patches which could be well approximated by second-order Taylor expansions.

5   TRANSITION FROM PICTURE TO SCENE DOMAIN CUES

Horn (1977) has shown that some of the straight line structural gray value variations can be related to specific 3-D surface configurations provided certain assumptions about shape and surface reflectivity are satisfied. The roof-type picture function of Figure 5a corresponds to a concave edge, the peak-type picture function of Figure 5c to a convex edge, and the step-type picture function of Figure 6a to an occluding edge. In order to infer the orientation of uniformly coloured and illuminated surfaces from the observed gray value variation, Horn (1975 + 1977) has developped approaches which are based on a-priori knowledge about the reflectivity as a function of the angles between the directions of surface normal, illumination, and observation. For a static situation, this knowledge can be encoded into a 'reflectance map'. His approach is known as 'shape-from-shading'.

Recently, Bolle & Cooper (1984) as well as Cernuschi-Frias & Cooper (1984) combined a-priori knowledge about the reflectivity function and quadric surfaces in 3-D to directly infer the presence of one of these surface types from semi-local gray value variations. Babu et al. (1985) have employed two different reflectance models to infer the orientation of planar surfaces in 3-D space from the shapes of constant brightness contours. Lee & Rosenfeld (1983) adjusted image intensities in order to compensate for the effects of estimated surface orientation. The adjusted intensities can be regarded as estimates of the surface reflectivity.

If a static scene is illuminated sequentially from two or more different directions and if all images are recorded with the same camera parameters, knowledge of the reflectance map for each illumination direction facilitates the direct determination of local surface orientation - the so-called 'photometric stereo' approach investigated first by Horn et al. (1978) and Woodham (1978).

Another picture domain cue which has been studied in order to infer the local surface orientation in 3-D space is related to systematic variations of texture with image plane coordinates. This implies, of course, that the texture can be extracted reliably enough to estimate such variations. The original texture can be either projected onto the surface - in which case one talks about 'structured light' approaches - or it is assumed that observable variations of the texture can be attributed solely to changes in the relative angle between the surface normal and the line-of-sight - see, e.g., Witkin (1981) and Ikeuchi (1984).

The shape and orientation of a surface can be inferred, too, by the evaluation of surface contours - see, e.g., Stevens (1981) or Brady & Yuille (1984). A combination of shape-from-contour and shape-from-shading has been studied by Ikeuchi & Horn (1981).

6 CONCLUSION

Relating speech and image understanding requires a system-internal representation related to concepts for all aspects of a well-defined 'discourse world'. Concepts are represented internally by symbols and relations between them. It is the task of machine vision to map each pixel of a digitized image into this system-internal representation of the discourse world. This process has to map signals into symbols. It requires a clear separation between stochastic and structural contributions to the signal, i.e. the digitized image. Concepts for the structural contribution to the gray value variation have been illustrated in Section 3. The extraction of local descriptors has been discussed subsequently with the intention to show that some of the problems encountered by published approaches can be related to inadequate concepts about the structural gray value variation. Both region segmentation as well as edge detection approaches still lack a proper theoretical foundation which allows to mesh local, semi-local, and global aspects. It remains to be seen to which extent it becomes possible to characterize the global picture function as a structure of local topographic descriptors and whether such a description will be amenable to an interpretation in terms of scene domain cues.

The transition from picture to scene domain cues has been sketched only. With the exception of some structured light approaches, all the other approaches to infer shape and orientation from local gray value variations - or, in other words, from local properties of the picture function - are still in an exploratory stage. They have been mentioned here primarily to illustrate the active research into the exploitation of knowledge about the physics of the image generation process relating picture domain cues to 3-D scene domain cues, thus beginning to close the full interpretation loop outlined in Figure 2. The results should be available to study the link between understanding images and natural language text as well as speech.

ACKNOWLEDGEMENT

I thank G. Zimmermann for kindly providing the originals of Figures 1 and 3. Helpful comments on a draft version of this contribution by Th. Krämer and especially by A. Korn and G. Winkler are gratefully acknowledged.

LITERATURE

Abdou, I.E. & W.K. Pratt (1979). Quantitative design and evaluation of enhancement / thresholding edge detectors. Proc. IEEE 67, 753-763

Babu, M.D.R., C.-H. Lee & A. Rosenfeld (1985). Determining plane orientation from specular reflectance. Pattern Recognition 18, 53-62

Ballard, D.H. & C.M. Brown (1982). Computer Vision. Englewood Cliffs / NJ: Prentice-Hall, Inc.

Beaudet, P.R. (1978). Rotationally invariant image operators. Proc. Int. Joint Conf. Pattern Recognition, Kyoto / Japan, November 7-10, 1978, pp. 579-583

Binford, T.O. (1981). Inferring surfaces from images. Artificial Intelligence 17, 205-244

Bobrow, D.G. & P.J. Hayes (1985). Artificial Intelligence - where are we ? Artificial Intelligence 25, 375-415

Bolle, R.M. & D.B. Cooper (1984). Bayesian recognition of local 3-D shape by approximating image intensity functions with quadric polynomials. IEEE Trans. Pattern Analysis and Machine Intelligence PAMI-6, 418-429

Bolles, R.C. (1977). Verification vision for programmable assembly. Proc. Int. Joint Conf. Artificial Intelligence, Cambridge / MA, August 22-25, 1977, pp. 569-575

Brady, M. & A. Yuille (1984). An extremum principle for shape from contour. IEEE Trans. Pattern Analysis and Machine Intelligence PAMI-6, 288-301

Cernuschi-Frias, B. & D.B. Cooper (1984). 3-D location and orientation parameter estimation of lambertian spheres and cylinders from a single 2-D image by fitting lines and ellipses to thresholded data. IEEE Trans. Pattern Analysis and Machine Intelligence PAMI-6, 430-441

Crowley, J.L. & A.C. Sanderson (1984). Multiple resolution representation and probabilistic matching of 2-D gray scale shape. Proc. Workshop on Computer Vision: Representation and Control, April 30-May 2, 1984, Annapolis / MD, pp. 95-105

Davies, E.R. (1983). The theoretical basis and effectiveness of fast edge detection operators. British Pattern Recognition Association, Second Int. Conf. on Pattern Recognition, Oxford / UK, September 19-21, 1983, Abstracts p. 19

Duda, R.O. & P.E. Hart (1973). Pattern Classification and Scene Analysis. New York London Sydney Toronto: John Wiley & Sons

Faugeras, O. (1983) (ed.). Fundamentals in computer vision. Cambridge / UK: Cambridge University Press

Faugeras, O. (1985). Artificial intelligence techniques in computer vision (this volume)

Grimson, W.E.L. & E. Hildreth (1985). Comments on "Digital Step Edges from Zero Crossings of Second Directional Derivatives". IEEE Trans. Pattern Analysis and Machine Intelligence PAMI-7, 121-127

Hahn, W. v., W. Hoeppner, A. Jameson, & W. Wahlster (1980). The anatomy of the natural language dialogue system HAM-RPM. In Natural Language Based Computer Systems, ed. L. Bolc, pp. 119-253. München / FR Germany: Hanser / McMillan

Haralick, R.M. (1980). Edge and region analysis for digital image data. Computer Graphics and Image Processing 12, 60-73

Haralick, R.M. (1984). Digital step edges from zero crossings of second directional derivatives. IEEE Trans. Pattern Analysis and Machine Intelligence PAMI-6, 58-68

Haralick, R.M. (1985). Author's reply to Grimson and Hildreth (1985). IEEE Trans. Pattern Analysis and Machine Intelligence PAMI-7, 127-129

Haralick, R.M. & L.G. Shapiro (1985). Image segmentation techniques.

Computer Vision, Graphics, and Image Processing 29, 100-132

Hildreth, E. (1983). The detection of intensity changes by computer and biological vision systems. Computer Vision, Graphics, and Image Processing 22, 1-27

Horn, B.K.P. (1975). Obtaining shape from shading information. In The Psychology of Computer Vision, ed. P.H. Winston, pp. 115-155. New York / NY: McGraw-Hill

Horn, B.K.P. (1977). Understanding image intensities. Artificial Intelligence 8, 201-231

Horn, B.K.P., R.J. Woodham & W.M. Silver (1978). Determining shape and reflectance using multiple images. AI-Memo 490; Artificial Intelligence Laboratory, MIT, Cambridge / MA

Hueckel, M. (1971). An operator which locates edges in digitized pictures. JACM 18, 113-125

Hueckel, M. (1973). A local visual operator which recognizes edges and lines. JACM 20, 634-647; see erratum JACM 21 (1974) 350

Ikeuchi, K. (1984). Shape from regular patterns. Artificial Intelligence 22, 49-55

Ikeuchi, K. & B.K.P. Horn (1981). Numerical shape from shading and occluding boundaries. Artificial Intelligence 17, 141-184

Kanade, T. (1978). Region segmentation: signal versus semantics. Proc. Int. Joint Conf. Pattern Recognition, Kyoto / Japan, November 7-10, 1978, pp. 95-105; see also Computer Graphics and Image Processing 13 (1980) 279-297

Kirsch, R. (1971). Computer determination of the constituent structure of biological images. Computers and Biomedical Research 4, 315-328

Kitchen, L. & A. Rosenfeld (1982). Gray-level corner detection. Pattern Recognition Letters 1, 95-102

Koenderink, J.J. (1984). The structure of images. Biological Cybernetics 50, 363-370

Korn, A. (1985). Das visuelle System als Merkmalfilter. In Aspekte der Informationsverarbeitung, ed. H. Bodmann, Fachberichte Messen Steuern Regeln. Berlin Heidelberg: Springer-Verlag (in press)

Leclerc, Y. & S.W. Zucker (1984). The local structure of image discontinuities in one dimension. Proc. Int. Conf. Pattern Recognition, Montrèal / Quebec, July 30-August 2, 1984, pp. 46-48

Lee, C.-H. & A. Rosenfeld (1983). Albedo estimation for scene segmentation. Pattern Recognition Letters 1, 155-160

Marr, D. (1982). Vision - a computational investigation into the human representation and processing of visual information. San Francisco / CA: W.H. Freeman and Company

Marr, D. & E. Hildreth (1980). Theory of edge detection. Proc. Royal Society of London B 207, 187-217

Mero, L. & Z. Vassy (1975). A simplified and fast version of the Hueckel operator for finding optimal edges in pictures. Proc. Int. Joint Conf. Artificial Intelligence, September 1975, Tbilissi / Georgia, USSR, pp. 650-655

Nagel, H.-H. (1979). Über die Repräsentation von Wissen zur Auswertung von Bildern. In "Angewandte Szenenanalyse", J.P. Foith (ed.), Informatik-Fachberichte 20, pp. 3-21. Berlin Heidelberg New York: Springer-Verlag

Nagel, H.-H. (1983). Displacement vectors derived from second order intensity variations in image sequences. Computer Vision, Graphics, and Image Processing 21, 85-117

Neumann, B.(1982). Towards natural language description of real-world image sequences. In Proc. GI - 12. Jahrestagung, Informatik-Fachberichte 57, ed. J. Nehmer, pp. 349- 358; Berlin-Heidelberg-New York: Springer-Verlag

Neumann, B. (1984) Natural language description of time-varying scenes. In

Advances in Natural Language Processes vol. I, ed. D.L. Waltz, (in press)

Nevatia, R. (1977). Evaluation of a simplified Hueckel edge-line detector. Computer Graphics and Image Processing 6, 582-588

Pavlidis, T. (1977). Structural Pattern Recognition. Berlin Heidelberg New York: Springer-Verlag

Pong, T.-C., L.G. Shapiro, L.T. Watson & R.M. Haralick (1984). Experiments in segmentation using a facet model region grower. Computer Vision, Graphics, and Image Processing 25, 1-23

Prewitt, J.M.S. (1970). Object enhancement and extraction. In Picture Processing and Psychopictorics, eds. B.S. Lipkin & A. Rosenfeld, pp. 75-149. New York / NY: Academic Press

Robinson, G.S. (1977). Edge detection by compass gradient masks. Computer Graphics and Image Processing 6, 492-501

Rosenfeld, A. (ed.) (1984). Multiresolution Image Processing and Analysis. Berlin Heidelberg New York Tokyo: Springer-Verlag

Rosenfeld, A. & L.S. Davis (1979). Image segmentation and image models. Proc. IEEE 67, 764-772

Rosenfeld, A. & A.C. Kak (1982). Digital Picture Processing, second edition. New York / NY: Academic Press

Stevens, K.A. (1981). The visual interpretation of surface contours. Artificial Intelligence 17, 47-73

Waltz, D.L. (1975). Understanding line drawings of scenes with shadows. In P.H. Winston (ed.) The Psychology of Computer Vision, pp. 19-91. New York / NY: McGraw-Hill

Waltz, D.L. (1979). Relating images, concepts, and words. Proc. NSF Workshop on the Representation of Three-Dimensional Objects; R. Bajcsy (ed.). Philadelphia / PA, May 1-2, 1979

Waltz, D.L. (1981). Towards a detailed model of processing for language describing the physical world. Proc. Int. Joint Conf. Artificial Intelligence, Vancouver / BC, August 24-28, 1981, pp. 1-6

Watson, L.T., T.J. Laffey, & R.M. Haralick (1985). Topographic classification of digital image intensity surfaces using generalized splines and the discrete cosine transformation. Computer Vision, Graphics, and Image Processing 29, 143-167

Witkin, A.P. (1981). Recovering surface shape and orientation from texture. Artificial Intelligence 17, 17-45

Witkin, A.P. (1983). Scale-space filtering. Proc. Int. Joint Conf. Artificial Intelligence, Karlsruhe / FR Germany, August 8-12, 1983, pp. 1019-1022

Woodham, R.J. (1978). Photometric stereo. AI-Memo 479; Artificial Intelligence Laboratory, MIT, Cambridge / MA

Young, I.T. (1983). Measurement accuracy in digital image analysis. British Pattern Recognition Association, Second Int. Conf. on Pattern Recognition, Oxford / UK, September 19-21, 1983, Abstracts p. 17

SOME ARTIFICIAL INTELLIGENCE TECHNIQUES IN COMPUTER VISION

O.D. Faugeras
INRIA, Domaine de Voluceau, Rocquencourt, BP 105,
78153 Le Chesnay, France

INTRODUCTION :

Computer Vision is dedicated to the task of finding interpretations in images. There are several related disciplines which it might be interesting to mention to point out similarities and differences.

First there is Computer Graphics which deals with models of objects, both physical in terms of their reflectance and transparency and geometrical in terms of their volume or surface. Models of illumination, diffusion of light, textures are also becoming increasingly important in order to obtain more and more realistic pictures. All this is definitely relevant to Computer Vision where object modelling is used intensively but in a somewhat different context since the problem is to use models to understand the content of images not to create images.

Second, there is Computer Aided Design/Manufacturing which deals with models of trajectories and object surfaces to program machine tools to perform useful industrial tasks. Again, this is relevant to Computer Vision but with the obvious difference that the kind of very high accuracy that is needed in CAD-CAM is usually not needed for Computer Vision where less accurate descriptions but somewhat broader in scope are necessary.

Third, there is Image Processing where, starting from an image, the goal is to produce another image which may be more pleasant to look at, easier to analyse, or need less bits to be represented and is therefore easier to store or to transmit. Image Processing deals with images as signals, not fundamentally different from any other signals and uses sophisticated models both for images and for acquisition and degradation systems. These models come from the Signal Processing and Automatic Control galaxy and are extremely relevant to Computer Vision, mostly at the preprocessing stage as we shall see in a moment.

Fourth, there is Pattern Recognition where the goal is to recognize objects from measurements. Again, this is a relevant discipline which has been extensively applied to images. One of the main differences is that Pattern Recognition, when it deals with images, deals only with 2D scenes and more importantly uses mostly purely numerical representations and processes directly the image without building another representation.

In contrast, Computer Vision builds rich symbolic descriptions from images and manipulates these descriptions, as opposed to the images themselves, in order to come up with interpretations.

Figure 1 is a schematic description of Computer Vision where the process of building interpretations has been split in four stages which are very much interrelated but that it is interesting to separate conceptually. Each of those four stages is articulated to a module containing models. These models can be either world models or perception models.

The preprocessing stage is the one that has been studied the more within the Image Processing community. It is concerned with Image acquisition to digitize video signals for example; enhancement and restauration to get rid of or reduce degradations caused by poor illumination, out of focus or motion blur; coding to exploit the spatial and temporal redundancy of images to reduce the bandwidth necessary to transmit them over channels of limited capacity. All these techniques are essentially numerical and share among themselves the fact that, in order to compute the new value of a pixel, some processing is applied to a usually small neighborhood around that pixel, and that this processing is the same for each pixel neighborhood. A simple example of this is the operation of convolution. Therefore, tremendous possibilities for parallelization exist that are currently being investigated in many places. To summarize, the only data structure used at this stage is the image grid, and the processing is basically numerical with large possibilities for parallelism.

At the feature extraction level we find an interesting situation that differs from what is encountered in Speech Understanding, for example, where good models of Signal formation are available and one knows, more or less, how to define and compute elementary symbols, the phonemes, from where to start building interpretations.

From that standpoint, Computer Vision is not so easy and it is just recently that people in the field have agreed on the need to compute, depending on the application to be solved, four types of features.

EDGES : edges happen in a picture at places where the intensity or a function of some of its derivatives varies rapidly and significantly. They allow to determine in part the boundaries of objects present in the scene. Most of the time, they are not sufficient to completely identify those objects because of things such as shadows, strong variations in the illumination, texture variations, etc....

TEXTURES : textures are local variations of intensity within the areas delimited by edges. These variations allow to distinguish between a corn and a wheat field in an aerial photograph or to characterize various geological formations.

DISTANCES : distances are generally lost in the acquisition process. For many applications this information is essential because from it, it is possible to compute the actual shape of objects in 3D space and as a consequence to reason about and act on them. We may say that recovering distances from images has been a very active research area in Computer Vision in the last few years.

MOTION : dynamic interactions between objects and the observer are also clearly relevant for many applications. Computing motion is usually very closely tied to computing distances and again, motion analysis is at the heart of the current research activities in Computer Vision.

Basically, the role of the feature extraction stage is to compute at every pixel of the image grid a description tying the intensity variations around that pixel to intrinsic properties of objects, i.e. properties depending only upon its physical and geometric structure and not upon the position of the sensors, the kind of lightning, etc.....

The symbolic description phase is concerned with building a rich symbolic description of the scene that can be efficiently exploited by the semantic description module. Many such dexcriptions are of course possible, but it seems that here again some sort of consensus has appeared recently within the Computer Vision community about the need to explicitely store in that description the information that is needed to solve the application at hand.

Such a description which is interesting both because it is fairly general and because it has been inspired by a deep analysis of Human Vision is called the 2 1/2 D sketch and has been proposed by David Marr [Marr 1982]. The basic idea is to build from the feature measurements some sort of three-dimensional map of the scene in which are represented pieces of surfaces characterized by the constancy or slow variation of some of those attributes. For example, the silhouette of an object is characterized by its continuity and the slow variation of its curvature, the surface of that object is characterized by the homogeneity of its texture, its motion field, the slow variation of its Gaussian curvature, etc...

The description is not completely three-dimensional because that information is not computable in general at every pixel. Therefore it is incomplete, a situation most often encountered in Artificial Intelligence.

At the semantic description stage, the problem is to match the models which are present in the data base with the previous symbolic description. The goal is to produce an interpretation of the content of the scene in order, for example, to act on that scene with manipulators, if we are interested in Robotics applications, or to update the current data base of models, if we are more interested in learning. Here again, just as at the symbolic description stage, we have to solve some difficult knowledge representation problems.

For applications such as the recognition and positioning of objects, the data structures that seem the most suitable are relational structures such as graphs, hypergraphs, labeled or not. These structures are very convenient to represent objects, their geometric structures, their functions, their spatial relationships. In AI language, such structures are called semantic networks. For applications such as geometric learning where not only representations of instances of objects, but also representations of classes of objects are needed, semantic networks are not as useful and people prefer to use things such as "frames" proposed a long time ago by psychologists and more recently by Minsky [Minsky 1975]. Of course, just as in many other disciplines of AI, there is no good consensus as to which are the best data structures for a given application.

In this Chapter, we would like to illustrate the above analysis of Computer Vision by three systems which are intended to solve problems at the symbolic and semantic description levels and are representative of the AI approach to Computer Vision.

RULE BASED SYSTEM FOR 2D IMAGE SEGMENTATION :

This work has been reported in a recent paper by Nazif and Levine [Nazif and Levine 1984] who have attempted to solve the image segmentation problem, one of the crucial steps in obtaining a useful symbolic description of images, by a system that uses rules and is declarative rather than procedural.

In the past, there has been two approaches to the problem of segmenting a picture into significant areas. The first approach is edge-based : find the borders of the regions by looking for discontinuities in the intensity. This works in special cases where contrast is high between the objects of interest and the background. The second approach is region-based : find the regions in the image where some feature, for example the intensity, is constant or more generally satisfies some uniformity predicate. Again this is limited to the case where the uniformity predicate is indeed true within objects which is again only true in very special cases.

Both techniques appear to be complementary and in fact should be applied to the same picture and their results combined. Moreover, both work incrementally, starting from very inaccurate and noisy descriptions, and improving them through heuristics such as edge linking, region growing or splitting. Decisions as to whether an edge exists in an area of the image should be influenced by the fact that two adjacent regions have been found in that same area. Also, decisions as to whether to split a region in several should be influenced by the existence of lines of high contrast within that region. "Interesting" areas should be processed first, because they may provide clues as to how to segment other neighboring regions by providing "islands of truth" allowing the use of context. This implies that the order in which the picture areas are to be processed is very data dependent and that therefore the segmentation strategy should vary from picture to picture.

All these ideas are exploited in the Levine and Nazif system represented in Figure 2. It is composed of a modular set of processes that can access the information stored in a long time memory (LTM) and read and modify data stored in a short term memory (STM). The STM contains the input image, the segmentation data and the output. The LTM contains the knowledge about low-level segmentation and control strategies.

The INITIALIZER module generates the initial region and line maps by standard techniques. The REGION, LINE and AREA ANALYSER modules match rules stored in the LTM to data stored in STM. The FOCUS OF ATTENTION module directs the attention of the system and the SUPERVISOR module matches the strategy rules to select the appropriate control strategy.

The system uses production rules at several levels. We discuss here knowledge and control rules. Knowledge rules act on regions, lines and areas and take the form of the conjunction of a set of conditions which, if satified, starts a set of actions. Actions on regions can be to merge two into one or to split one into several; actions on lines can be to extend a line, merge two lines or delete one.

These rules attempt to model Gestalt principles for perceptual grouping such as similarity, proximity, uniform destiny, good continuity and closure. An example of a rule dealing with regions is :

> if :   (1) The region size is very low
>
> (2) The adjacency with another region is high
>
> (3) The difference in region features is not high
>
> then : merge the two regions

An exemple of a rule dealing with lines is :

> if : (1) The line end point is open
>
> (2) The line gradient is not very low
>
> (3) The distance between to the line in front is not very high
>
> (4) The two lines have the same region to the left
>
> then : join the two lines

Control rules are of two kinds : focus of attention rules and metarules. The focus of attention rules perform two levels of data selection. At the first level, they decide which area in the image needs to be processed next, and at the second level they decide which region and line should be processed in the current area. This is a very flexible control system that allows many different strategies to be tried and even to drive the strategy from the data.

The metarules coordinate the activities of all processing modules by deciding which process to activate next given the previous history of the segmentation task.

This technique has been tried on a number of images and compared to more standard ones such as split-and-merge [Tanimoto and Pavlidis 1975] and histogram segmentation [Ohlander 1975]. The Levine and Nazif technique is consistently slower than the other two due to the more flexible data structure, and it produces outputs which conform more closely to the human expectations of low level segmentation.

As a conclusion, the rule-based system achieves several major accomplishments. First, it introduces the rule-based approach to the image segmentation problem whereas previous vision systems limited the use of explicit knowledge to the semantic interpretation level. Second, regions and lines are combined and simultaneously used in the analysis while the introduction of focus of attention areas provides spatial boundaries across which the processing strategy is adjusted. Therefore, the system can execute the best strategy based on the properties of each area.

INTERPRETING 2D IMAGES WITH 3D MODELS : ACRONYM

The Acronym system [Brooks, 1981] deals with a higher level than that of the segmentation, namely with the interpretation of an image with the help of three-dimensional models. His approach is first to predict image features from 3D models, then to match predicted to observed features and to reject incorrect matches by consistency checking. The key points of this work are the way objects are modelled, the way predictions are made from those models and the way interpretation of image descriptions are built in terms of models.

Let us look at the models first. In Acronym, the world description is in terms of volume elements, the so-called generalized cones and their spatial relationships. These volume elements are used to represent classes of objects and their subclass relationships through the manipulation of algebraic constraints.The idea of a generalized cone is indicated in Figure 3.

In practice, the spine is straight or circular and the section is polygonal or circular. The representation is frame-like and objects are nodes of the object graph with two classes of directional arcs : subpart and affixment.

In the frame-like representation, numeric slots are filled with algebraic expressions with constants and variables; classes of objects are then specified with algebraic inequalities. Here is an example of a generalized cone model of a generic electric motor body :

Node : ELECTRIC_MOTOR_CONE

```
CLASS :              SIMPLE_CONE
SPINE :              Z0014
SWEEPING_RULE :      CONSTANT_SWEEPING_RULE
CROSS_SECTION :      Z0013
```

Node : Z0014

CLASS :   SPINE
TYPE :   STRAIGHT
LENGTH : MOTOR_LENGTH

Node : CONSTANT_SWEEPING_RULE

CLASS :   SWEEPING_RULE
TYPE :   CONSTANT

Node : Z0013

CLASS :   CROSS_SECTION
TYPE :   CIRCLE
RADIUS : MOTOR_RADIUS

An example of the associated object graph is in figure 4.

Let us now look at the constraint manipulation system. One of the key features of Acronym is the ability to manipulate constraints. The general requirements for such a system are the following. Given a set of constraints S on n quantifiers and the corresponding satisfying set C_S, a subset of $\mathbf{R}^n$, there are three kinds of questions that the system should be able to answer :

1. Given S, decide whether or not C_S is empty

2. Given a satisfiable set S and an expression E, compute the minimum and maximum of E in C_S

3. Given constraints sets S and R, calculate $T = S^\frown R$

If the constraints are linear, the problem can in principle be solved by the simplex method. For general constraints, it is a very difficult problem and in order to come up with a feasible system, the requirements have to be relaxed :

A1. Given S, partially decide whether C_S is empty or not :

if the constraint manipulation system (CMS) can prove that S is unsatisfiable, it should indicate so, otherwise indicate that it may be satisfiable

A2. Given a satisfiable S and an expression E, compute l and u such that :
$$l \le \inf E \le \sup E \le u$$

A3. Given constraint sets S and R, calculate T such that
$$C_S \cdot C_R < C_T < C_S \ C_R$$

Acronym's CMS is built around an algebraic simplifier and a number of bounding algorithms. It has been initially implemented as a production rule system but, being highly recursive, it was too slow and rewritten in MACLISP. We give here an example taken from [Brooks 1981] : there are a number of variables expressing errors in the position and location of a box, a manipulator hand, and the orientation of a screw on the end of a screwdriver. It is desired to find upper and lower bounds on an expression Δy in terms of a single quantifier DRIVER_LENGTH where Δy is given by a one page long expression in ten variables which we do not reproduce here. Given numerical constraints on the variables, the CMS is able to deduce that :

$$-0.164-0.0044209*\text{DRIVER\_LENGTH} \le \Delta y \le$$
$$0.164+0.00442042*\text{DRIVER\_LENGTH}$$

Let us now look at the geometric reasoning in Acronym. There are two requirements for the geometric reasoning system. The first is to identify image features that an object will generate and find characterizations of them which are invariant over the modeled range of variations (quasi-invariant features). The second is to discover further constraints which can be used to split the range of variations into cases in which further quasi-invariant observables can be predicted.

Let us take an example taken again from [Brooks 1981] where we have two views with different camera geometries of an electric screwdriver sitting in his holder. The problem is that in order to compute the orientation and position of the screwdriver in the camera coordinates, large products of rigid displacements have to be simplified. Here again, an algebraic simplifier has to used, the goals being to decide whether objects are in the field of view and what objects might be expected to occlude others. Indeed, simplified expressions are in a form which allows for prediction of invariant and quasi-invariant features. In particular, they can be used to predict the projected 2D image shape of objects.

One possible approach for this simplification is to turn everything into products of 4*4 matrices, multiply them out and use an algebraic simplifier. This is a bad idea because we have to search for trigonometric simplifications which are obscure in expanded form and better use can be made of expressions describing spatial relations as combinations of simple geometric transforms than could be made of a single complex rotation and translation expression.

Acronym uses eleven simple rules and uses them for prediction which operates in five phases. First, all the contours on a generalized cone which could give rise to image shapes are identified. This is object centered. Second, the orientation of the generalized cone relative to the camera is examined to decide which contours will be visible and how their image shapes will be distorted over the range of variations in the model parameters that appear in the orientation expressions. Third, relations between contours of a single generalized cone are predicted. Fourth, actual shapes that the contours will generate are predicted and expected values for shape parameters in the image are estimated as closed intervals. Fifth, back constraints used in the interpretation are instantiated.

ANALYSIS OF 3D IMAGES FROM 3D MODELS : HYPER3D

Industrial Vision is a good example of an application domain where rich geometric models of objects are available. The system HYPER3D developed at INRIA [Faugeras and Hebert 1983] demonstrates the use of such models for the recognition and location objects when active sensing with a laser range finder is available.

In order to avoid the difficult problems posed by the 'shape from' processes including shape from stereo [Grimson, Baker and Binford], shape from shading [Ikeuchi and Horn], and shape from contour [Witkin, Brady and Yuille], we have decided to use structured light. We have developed a laser range finder which has been described in several publications [Faugeras and Hebert 1983, Boissonnat and Germain] and is based on active stereoscopy. Several versions of this device exist, including one commercially available. The slowest version can measure the (x, y, z) coordinates of a point on the surface of an object in 2 milliseconds with an accuracy of .5 mm.

The primitives used in the object representation are planar patches approximating its surface. This description has several advantages which are :

1. It is local, meaning that occlusion or distorsion of one part of the object does not change the description of the other parts.

2. It is compact, meaning that most objects can be accurately represented by a small number of planar patches.

3. It is general, meaning that it can be applied to any 3D shape.

4. It is sensitive to variations in the position and orientation of the objects and allows to recover those parameters accurately.

5. It is simple, meaning that the techniques used to go from the range data to the description are straightforward and fast.

Model data, as explained in [Faugeras and Hebert 1983, Faugeras et al. 1984], are obtained by combining laser scanning and object rotation so as to cover the whole surface of the object. A simple processing [Faugeras et al. 1984] yields a triangulation of the surface (Figure 5). Scene data is obtained by raster scanning the scene with the laser, yielding a range 'image'. Points in that image and triangles in the above triangulation are then grouped by a simple region growing technique into larger planar patches. A typical result is shown in Figure 6.

The problem is then to identify and locate in a scene one or several models while allowing partial occlusions (always present in 3D). The problem of finding the location of a model implies the computation of the 'best' rigid motion (product of a translation and a rotation) that brings a recognized model onto the scene. The basic matching technique used is that of Hypothesis Generation and Evaluation.

To generate an hypothesis is to predict the position of the model in the scene. This prediction can only be attempted when we have found two pairs of corresponding non-parallel planar patches, which allow to determine the rotation, or three such pairs in order to obtain also the translation.

Once the rotation and translation have been computed using three pairs of non-parallel planar patches in the model and scene descriptions (MD and SD), the hypothesis is evaluated by identifying other patches in the MD and the SD. Each new identification is used to update the estimation of the position of the model by minimizing an error criterion [Faugeras and Hebert 1985]. This minimization can be efficiently performed by using the quaternion representation of the 3D rotations [Faugeras and Hebert 1985].

We present an example of the analysis of a complex scene. Figure 7 shows the segmentation of a scene which contains three objects; the contours are the contours of the detected regions. The reference model is presented in Figure 6. Figure 8 shows the result of the identification of each part of the scene. Each identification is visualized by showing the initial set of primitives, the orientation of the identified part, and the superposition of the recognized model primitives (in dotted lines) with the corresponding scene regions in order to show the quality of the estimation of the transformation.

CONCLUSIONS :

It appears that powerful techniques borrowed from IA can be successfully applied to a number of Vision problems. We think that this trend will become stronger in the next few years. But more importantly, we believe that Vision is probably the best paradigm around for a large number of fundamental problems in AI such as learning, geometric and temporal reasoning, generalization, and will appear more and more so to the researchers in the field.

REFERENCES

H. Baker and T. Binford, "Depth from edge and intensity based stereo," Proc. Int. Jt. Conf. Artif. Intell., Vancouver, 1981.

J.D. Boissonnat and F. Germain, "A new approach to the problem of acquiring randomly oriented workpieces out of a bin," Proc. Int. Jt. Conf. Artif. Intell., Vancouver, 1981.

M. Brady and A. Yuille, " An extremum principle from shape from contour," MIT AI Lab., MIT-AIM 711, 1983.

R.A. Brooks, "Symbolic reasoning among 3D objects and 2D models," Artificial Intelligence, 285-348, 1981.

O.D. Faugeras and M. Hebert, "A 3D recognition and positioning algorithm using geometrical matching between primitive surfaces, Proc. Int. Jt. Conf. Artif. Intell., Karlsruhe, 996-1002, 1983.

O.D. Faugeras et al., "Object representation, identification and positioning from range data," in Robotics Research, M. Brady and R. Paul eds, MIT press, 1984.

O.D. Faugeras and M. Hebert, "The representation, recognition and localization of 3D objects from range data", to appear in the International Journal of Robotics Research, 1985.

W.E. Grimson, "From images to surfaces : a computational study of the early vision system," MIT Press, Cambridge, 1981.

K. Ikeuchi and B.K.P. Horn, "Numerical shape from shading and occluding boundaries," Artificial Intelligence, 17, 141-185, 1981.

D. Marr, Vision, Freeman, San Francisco, 1982.

M. Minsky, "A framework for representing knowledge," The Psychology of Computer Vision, P.H. Winston ed., New-York : McGraw-Hill, 406-450, 1975.

A.M. Nazif and M.D. Levine, "Low level image segmentation : an expert system", IEEE Trans. on PAMI, Vol. PAMI-6, 555-577, September 1984.

R. Ohlander, "Analysis of natural scenes," Ph.D. dissertation, Carnegie-Mellon Univ., Pittsburgh, PA, April 1975.

S. Tanimoto and T. Pavlidis, "A hierarchical data structure for picture processing," Computer Graphics and Image Processing, VOL-4, 104-199, 1975.

A.P. Witkin, "Recovering surface shape and orientation from texture," Artificial Intelligence, 17, 17-47, 1981.

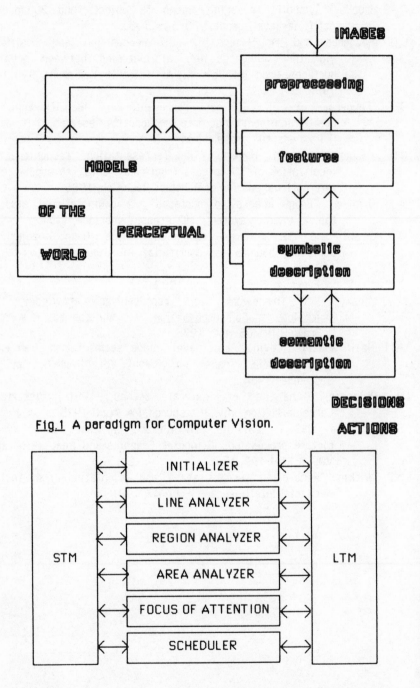

Fig.1 A paradigm for Computer Vision.

Fig.2. The Nazif and Levine System for image segmentation.

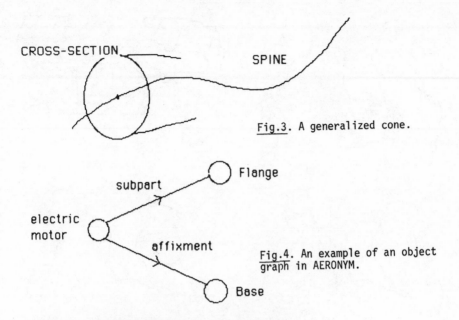

Fig.3. A generalized cone.

Fig.4. An example of an object graph in AERONYM.

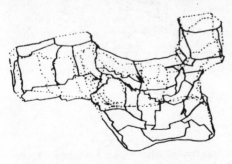

Fig.5. Triangulation of a 3-D object.

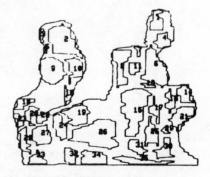

Fig.6. Model used for recognition and localization (60 planar faces).

Fig.7. Segmentation into planar faces of a scene containing three partially overlapping objects like the one in Figure 6.

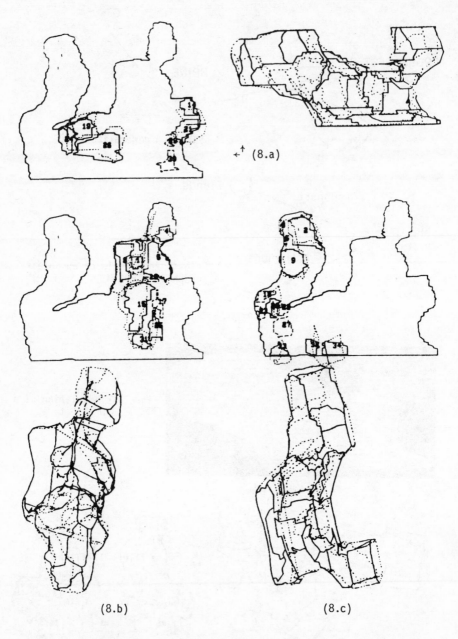

(8.a)

(8.b)   (8.c)

Fig.8. : a) Recognition and localization of the first instance of the
            model.
         b) Recognition and localization of the second instance of the
            model.
         c) Recognition and localization of the third instance of the
            model.

RULE-BASED DETECTION OF SPEECH FEATURES
FOR AUTOMATIC SPEECH RECOGNITION

Renato De Mori, Lily Lam and David Probst

Department of Computer Science, Concordia University
Montreal, Quebec H3G 1M8 Canada.

1. INTRODUCTION

At present, a number of scientists and engineers seem to be quite interested in doing research in the area of speech recognition by computer. Different workers in the field have different approaches, and might even describe their motivations for doing speech recognition research somewhat differently. A very common position, for example, is that the main goal of speech recognition research is to develop techniques and systems for speech input to machines. Indeed, if both speech recognition and general machine intelligence make sufficient progress in our lifetimes, we could conceivably encounter computers that not only listen but also reply sensibly. Even so, this ambitious desire to make spoken input part of the human-computer interface, while undoubtedly deeply rooted in genuine practical concerns, is only one of several possible motivations; we now argue that speech recognition is not only useful but also interesting.

To begin with, some workers in speech recognition are excited by a research program which suggests that, in the long run, very high performance computer recognition of unconstrained, large-vocabulary, speaker-independent, continuous speech will be most effectively obtained through the use of *knowledge-based* computer speech recognition systems; the knowledge in question is first and foremost knowledge of *speech*, the kind of knowledge that would be contained in deep linguistic theories and deep models of speech. The use of speech knowledge in computer speech recognition points to one additional motivation for doing speech recognition research. Just as we go to cognitive psychology to get ideas for computer perception, so we use computer models of perception to test and refine our theories of human perception. In this connection, it is instructive to read what Church [CHURCH 83] has written about probabilistic methods, and in particular his discussion of whether allophonic constraints can be explained in terms of more basic linguistic fundamentals. From motivations we move on to a very simple scheme of the process of spoken language generation and understanding.

Fig. 1 shows the essential transformations of information involved in speech communication.

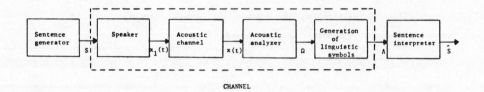

CHANNEL

Fig. 1   Transformations of information in speech communication. S — Sentence
representation; $x_1(t)$ — generated signal; $x(t)$ — received signal; Ω —
acoustic pattern; Λ = lattice of hypotheses composed of linguistic symbols;
$\hat{S}$ = interpretation.

Initially, a sentence generator produces an abstract representation S of the sentence
to be transmitted. This abstract representation S is then converted by the speaker
into a sequence of sets of discrete articulatory commands which drive the vocal tract
actuators, producing a continuously time-varying pressure signal $x_1(t)$. The signal
$x_1(t)$ is transmitted through a noisy acoustic channel, resulting in a different signal
$x(t)$ which is perceived by the listener. The listener transforms the signal $x(t)$ into
an acoustic pattern Ω. The purpose of this transformation is to have a
representation of the spoken message which better exhibits the linguistic features than
does the signal itself. The acoustic pattern is then interpreted by a
recognition/understanding system which first transforms the acoustic information in Ω
into an abstract, linguistic representation Λ. Unfortunately Λ is not S. Rather, it
may be a continuous string or a lattice of characters or of word hypotheses which
has to be interpreted in order to produce $\hat{S}$, the recognition system's final
interpretation of $x(t)$. In a satisfactory recognition system, the self-correcting
mechanisms of perception function well enough to produce an $\hat{S}$ which is S most of
the time.

Some speech recognition workers have chosen to apply the discipline of
information theory to the construction of recognizers. That theory as originally
conceived is a mathematical theory designed to measure the amount of information
necessary to reduce the receiver's doubt concerning given alternatives. The
contrasting approach taken here is to model both the source and the sentence

interpreter as rule-based systems, where the rules encode the a priori knowledge we have about human speech generation and understanding.

Knowledge-based speech recognition systems require mechanisms to pay attention to distinctive acoustic information, detailed phonetic features, and the like. These mechanisms can perhaps be justified by considering alternate recognizers which use little or no speech knowledge. For example, many workers use a recognition model based on feature extraction and classification. With such an approach, the same set of features are extracted at fixed time intervals (typically every 10 msecs.) and classification is based on distances between feature patterns and prototypes [LEVINSON 81] or likelihoods computed from a Markov model of a source of symbols generated by matching centisecond speech patterns and prototypes [BAHL 83].

These methods are usually speaker dependent and are made speaker independent by clustering prototypes obtained from many speakers. The classifier is not capable of making reliable decisions about phonemes or phonetic features; rather, it generates scored competing hypotheses that are combined together to form scored word and sentence candidates. If the protocol exhibits enough redundancy it is likely that the cumulative score of the right candidate is significantly higher than the scores of competing candidates. If, however, there is little redundancy in the protocols, as in the case of connected letters or digits or in the case of a large lexicon, then it is important that ambiguities at the phonetic level are resolved before hypotheses are generated. Examples of these difficulties have been reported in the recent literature [BAHL 84, RABINER 84].

We have referred to the fact that most of the systems proposed so far take advantage of the *redundancy* of the protocols they use. The most difficult and unsolved problems arise when tasks have little redundancy or when speaker independence is required for complex tasks. Examples of such complex tasks are the recognition of letters and digits (isolated or connected) and the recognition of large vocabularies. For such problems, it seems reasonable to extract a large variety of acoustic properties.

Drawing on important computer science and machine intelligence motivations, a system has been implemented in which both the extraction of acoustic properties and the generation of syllabic hypotheses result from the collaboration of several distinct processes. This cooperation of computational activities has been conceived using the paradigm of an *Expert System Society* [MINSKY 75, ERMAN

80]. Each expert is associated with a *Long Term Memory* (LTM) containing the specific expert's knowledge and a *Short Term Memory* (STM) where data interpretations are written. Experts are computing agents which execute reasoning programs using structural and procedural knowledge. The knowledge of each expert is expressed by a set of *plans*, some of which can be executed in parallel. Communication between cooperating tasks is performed by message passing.

The novelty of the knowledge-based approach under discussion is that descriptions of acoustic properties are extracted and related to phonetic feature interpretations using plans which have been learned. More specifically, these plans result from a long (human) learning effort in which a large number of patterns have been analyzed in order to extract invariant properties; this extraction process makes essential use of knowledge about speech analysis, production and perception. For example, it is known that the burst spectrum of an alveolar plosive constant must be compact, but rules for detecting burst spectra and for characterizing compactness have to be inferred and statistics about their performance have to be collected.

The system under discussion is based on rules which capture many speaker-independent relations between phonetic features and acoustic cues. These rules are a kernel which can be enriched when new knowledge is acquired regarding new pronunciations and new languages.

2. MODELS FOR COMPUTER PERCEPTION OF SPEECH

It is well known that various simplifications to the general speech understanding problem exist; depending on the task complexity, two different types of models can be used for speech decoding : a passive model and an active model.

In the *passive* model, human reception of speech is viewed as consisting of sensation followed by perception, followed by cognition. This model has been used for designing systems for the recognition of isolated words and consists of acoustic preprocessing, feature extraction, and pattern matching. It is clear that human listeners use expectation for understanding what is being said. Human perception is thus likely to be an *active* process in which cognition may even guide the lower levels of decoding. None of the components using different types of knowledge can currently be made to perform reliably. A strategy must be found to combine information from all the components in order to profit from redundancy and resolve the ambiguities.

An *active* model for speech understanding involves the representation of knowledge at various levels (Knowledge Sources : KS) : procedural knowledge containing rules on how to use the KSs effectively in order to solve the problem of interpreting a signal, and a set of data structures where the interpretation hypotheses may be written. An essential feature of the active model is that cognition and expectation may drive decoding.

Perhaps the most important idea in the active, knowledge-based model is that of knowledge-based focusing of attention. We now describe a perceptual model which has important similarities to our computer speech recognition system. We find a certain plausibility in the idea that the brain contains anticipatory schemata that condition the perceiver to pick up certain kinds of information from the signal rather than others, and thus control the activity of perceiving. Perception is a constructive process in which anticipations of certain kinds of information are first constructed, and then allow the receipt of that information as it becomes available; the anticipatory schemata are plans for perceptual action as well as expectations in the classical sense. Directed explorations of the signal occur which, to some extent, modify the original schema, and lead to further exploration. In the case of speech, the listener continuously develops anticipations of what will come next, based on what he has already heard. These anticipations control what he will pick up next, and in turn are modified by it. The preceding account of perceptual activity has been borrowed from Neisser [NEISSER 76].

We now provide an outline of an expert system for interpreting speech patterns. The achievement of complex tasks such as speech understanding and speech recognition can be conceived in the framework of *quasi-distributed problem solving*. Another term would be *collaborative problem solving*. The simplest description would be to say that the system consists of a collection of specialized experts. Each expert has both a private short term memory and a private long term memory, and communicates with other experts through a message exchange network according to message passing semantics.

We now describe the structure of the Expert System Society. Interpretations of the speech waveform are generated by an Expert System Society implemented on a VAX 11/780. Its structure is shown in Fig. 2.

EXP$_1$ is the Acoustic Expert (AE). It has the task of sampling and quantizing the signal, performing various types of signal transformations, and extracting and describing acoustic cues. The term *acoustic cues* will be used for indicating spectral or signal properties describing aspects that are relevant for hypothesizing phonetic features. Examples of acoustic cues are formant loci, characteristics of burst spectra like compactness, and peaks and valleys of signal energy. EXP$_1$ can perform, for example, an analysis based on Linear Prediction Coefficients (LPC) for segments labelled with vocalic hypotheses in order to find formant loci capable of describing the place and manner of articulation. EXP$_1$ can also perform a broad-band spectral analysis based on the Fast Fourier Transformation (FFT) when hypotheses of nonsonorant continuant sounds have been made. Like other experts, EXP$_1$ may carry out both spontaneous *data-driven* activities and *expectation-driven* activities arising out of requests issued by other experts.

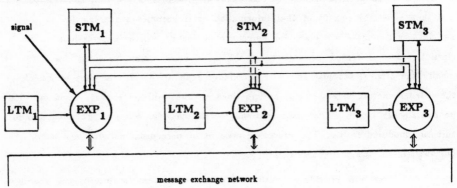

Fig. 2   Structure of the Expert System Society

Requests and control messages are exchanged among experts through the message exchange network shown in Fig. 2. Data, cues, descriptions and hypotheses are written by an expert into its own Short Term Memory (STM). Only the expert which owns the STM can write into it, but any expert can read any STM.

EXP$_2$ is the Phonetic and Syllabic Expert (PSE). It translates descriptions of acoustic cues into *phonetic feature hypotheses*. These features describe the *manner* and the *place* of articulation of each segment of the spoken utterance. This translation may involve the extraction of new acoustic cues by asking EXP$_1$ to execute sensory procedures. There are some acoustic cues, like peaks and valleys of time evolutions of energies in fixed bands of the signal, that can be extracted by context-independent algorithms. These acoustic cues will be called

Primary Acoustic Cues (PAC) and the phonetic features related to them will be called *Primary Phonetic Features* (PPF). A definition of the primary cues and features used in the system described here is given in Tables I, II and III. These algorithms for extracting PACs generate descriptions of a time interval of the signal without being constrained by contextual information extracted from adjacent segments.

Examples of various types of PACs are shown in Fig. 3. The two curves in Fig. 3a represent the time evolution of the signal energy (—) and the zero-crossing counts (---) in successive 10 msec intervals of the first derivative of the signal. The phrase is the sequence of letters and digits K3VPCB. Fig. 3b shows the corresponding PAC description. The time unit is 0.01 sec. LONG and SHORT refer to the dip duration. DEEP, MEDIUM and HIGH refer to the height of the minimum energy in the dip with respect to the background noise energy.

Other functions of EXP_2 include those of segmenting the speech signal into Pseudo Syllabic Segments (PSS) and of checking or evaluating phonetic hypotheses. In EXP_2, the activity of generating PPFs is *data-driven*, while the activities of extracting other phonetic features are *expectation-driven*. Expectations may arise from a strategy inside EXP_2 or they can be requests transmitted by EXP_3.

EXP_3 is the Lexical Expert (LE) that generates lexical hypotheses based on prosodic features, phonetic hypotheses, and syntactic and semantic constraints.

3. ACOUSTIC PROPERTIES, PHONETIC FEATURES, AND PLANS

This section describes how relations of phonetic features to acoustic properties are embedded in *plans* which are executed by the expert system. With this approach a phoneme PH_i is expressed by a set of phonetic features, i.e.

$$PH_i = (pf_{i1}, pf_{i2}, ..., pf_{ij}, ..., pf_{iJ})$$

Each phonetic feature pf_x is represented by a relation R_x to a set of acoustic properties ap_x, i.e.

$$pf_x = R_x (ap_{x1}, ap_{x2}, ..., ap_{xk}, ..., ap_{xK})$$

For example, the phoneme /p/ is represented as follows:

/p/ = (nonsonorant-interrupted-consonant,tense,labial) = (nit,labial).

The phonetic feature 'labial' in the context of 'nit' features is represented by the following relation R_k :

Table I

Primary Acoustic Cues

Symbol	Attributes	Description
LPK	tb,te,ml,zx,	long peak of total energy (TE)
SPK	"	short peak of TE
MPK	"	peak of TE of medium duration
LOWP	"	low energy peak of TE
LNS	tb,te,zx	long nonsonorant tract
MNS	"	medium nonsonorant tract
LVI	tb,te,ml,zx	long vocalic tract adjacent to a LNS or a MNS in a TE peak
MVI	tb,te,ml,zx	medium vocalic tract adjacent to a LNS or a MNS in a TE peak
LDD	emin,tb,te,zx	long deep dip of total energy
SDD	"	short deep dip of total energy
LMD	"	long dip of total energy with medium depth
SMD	"	short dip of total energy with medium depth
LHD	"	long non-deep dip of total energy
SHD	"	short non-deep dip of total energy

Table II

Attribute description

Attribute	Description
tb	time of beginning
te	time of end
ml	maximum signal energy in the peak
emin	minimum total energy in a dip
zx	maximum zero-crossing density of the signal derivative in the tract

Table III

Primary Phonetic Features

Symbol	Primary Phonetic Feature
VF	Front vowel
VC	Central vowel
VB	Back vowel
VFC	Front or central vowel
VCB	Central or back vowel
VW	Uncertain vowel
NI	Nonsonorant interrupted consonant
NA	Nonsonorant affricate consonant
NC	Nonsonorant continuant consonant
SON	Sonorant consonant
SONV	A sonorant or the /v/ consonant
PP	Possible pause

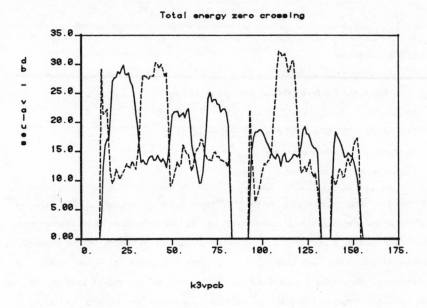

PAC	tb	te
LDD	1	10
LPK	10	47
LPK	47	65
SMD	65	67
LPK	67	83
LDD	83	92
LPK	92	110
SHD	110	111
LPK	111	132
LDD	132	137
LPK	137	155

Fig. 3   (a)   Total energy (---) and zero-crossing counts (---) divided by 6 of the pronunciation of the sequence K3VPCB (time references are in tenths of milliseconds).   (b)   Examples of PAC description for the sequence K3VPCB.

(*relation* R$_k$

(*left-side*

(*feature* (labial))

    (*feature context* (nit))

    (*temporal context* (*followed-by* front vowel)))

(*right-side*

(suprasegmental and time-domain properties)

(formant-transition properties)

(burst—spectra properties)))

The rule for 'labial' takes into account different types of *contextual dependencies*.
One contextual dependency is represented by the other features that appear with
'labial' in a plosive phoneme. The other contextual dependences are represented by
the class of phonemes that can follow or precede the plosive phoneme under
consideration. Relations are used by *plans* executed by the expert system. In many
cases, acoustic property extraction is context dependent; for example, we may be
forced to impose precedence relations on the extraction processes. For more on the
latter, we refer the reader to [DEMICHELIS 83] and [KOPEC 84].

A *plan* is a sequence of items. Each item may contain a *precondition
expression* for applying rules of the type R$_k$, *operators* containing sensory procedures,
for extracting the properties used by R$_k$, and an *algorithm* for evaluating the
evidence of the hypothesis generated by R$_k$.

The operators of plans are signal processing and property extraction
algorithms. Property extraction can be organized as a hierarchy of actions.
Important material on hierachical planning and networks of action hierachies may be
found in [STEFIK 80] and [SACERDOTI 75]. Actions can be associated with
constraints that have to be verified in order for an action to be executable. For
example, an action may consist in the extraction of buzz descriptors for characterizing
the manner of articulation of plosive sounds. Buzz descriptors can be extracted only
in time intervals where the speech loudness curve has deep dips. Once a network of
actions has been conceived, constraints of actions are propagated backward and
upward and used for setting *preconditions*. Action hierarchies are executed through
elaboration-decision cycles. During the *elaboration phase* a set of executable actions
is performed. Actions may result in the generation of *objects* or in the updating of
existing objects. Objects are data structures containing structured descriptions of

segments of signal to be interpreted. During the *decision phase* all the actions that can be executed in the next elaboration phase are considered. The preconditions for the new actions are evaluated and those actions for which some precondition is not met are ruled out. The choice among competing action candidates is also performed in the decision phase. A simple *fuzzy algebra* is used for ordering competing action candidates. It is based on voting criteria that combine different supports from different sources that match partially or totally descriptions contained in the preconditions.

Planning starts by considering *abstract objects* and *operators*. An example of an abstract object is "description of properties of a plosive sound" and an abstract operator is the one that extracts such description. The abstract operator is then decomposed into abstract actions derived from the knowledge human experts in acoustic phonetic have about the phonetic event that has to be described. The abstract actions are deliberately *redundant* in order to allow discrimination of ambiguities that may arise from signal variability. For the sake of economy only a limited number of abstract actions are implemented with real actions. The purpose is that of ensuring discriminability among descriptions of signal segments belonging to different classes while using algorithms that have been proved reliable and fast. The action hierarchy is modified when discrimination becomes poor as new data from new speakers are analyzed. The new real actions are decided and implemented by a human expert who bases his decision on his knowledge, the type of patterns that require better discriminant descriptions and the statistics of the ambiguous descriptions of these patterns as obtained by the available system. Discriminant descriptions are generalized by a learning system and acceptance of generalizations is decided by a Truth Maintenance System.

Three major abstract actions are considered at the top of the hierarchy. Classical vector-quantization is performed by an action named "distance-based centisecond labelling". Another action called "knowledge-based centisecond labelling" attempts to label each speech spectrum using knowledge based on spectral morphologies, relations with morphologies preceding and following spectral and suprasegmental features. A third action corresponds to a plan called "Asynchronous Description of Speech Segments" (ADSS). We will show how the third plan alone has been built as a network of action hierarchies and used for a multi-speaker recognition of connected letters.

ADSS, as the other plans, is based on actions implemented by using real signal processing and property extraction operators. From now on we will use the term *operator* for indicating real operators. The plan ADSS is built incrementally with the help of a program that performs inductive learning. The general goal of the plan is that of producing descriptions of speech segments suitable for discriminating among phoneme classes. As the goal is a complex one, it is achieved through incremental subgoaling. The application of the above mentioned planning paradigm for designing pattern descriptors and recognizers is a significant novelty. Other relevant aspects are the use of learning and recognition performances for plan refinement and subgoaling.

DEVELOPMENT OF PERCEPTUAL PLANS

The example we will use in this section refers to the speaker-independent recognition of connected letters belonging to the E1 set defined as follows

$$E1 = \{ P, T, K, B, D, V, E, G, C, 3 \}$$

It has been shown that acoustic segments obtained automatically correspond to letters with few errors that are very well detected by the fact that the number of detected acoustic segments does not corrrespond to the number of pronounced letters. During learning, labelling of acoustic segments is done automatically and it is modified manually when a segmentation error is detected. Each segment is described by a sequence of PACs. At the beginning an initial set of sequences of letters is analyzed. Each phoneme generates a different sequence of PACs. The plan ADSS is initially set in order to be used in the following elaboration-decision cycle:

elaboration-phase(1)

build an object containing the PACs of the segment to be described; associate to each PAC its time references (the beginning time: t_b and the ending time: t_e) and other attributes.

decision-phase(1)

apply rule-set(1) and generate letter hypothesis.

"rule-set(1)" contains rules of the form:

antecedent → consequent

where "antecedent" is a sequence of PACs and "consequent" is an action. The object built in the "elaboration-phase(1)" is part of a network of data descriptions called the Data Description Network (DDN). The "antecedents" of rule-set(1) are matched against the DDN. The antecedent expressions are built by a program that performs Inductive Learning (IL). This program is capable of generalizing antecedent expressions and produces in any case disjoint expressions. If a perfect match between a rule antecedent and DDN is not possible, then a Similarity Measure (SM) normalized in the (0,1) interval is computed based on a voting procedure as described by [LAIRD 84].

Rule actions, at the beginning, generate letter hypotheses. The letter hypothesis that receives the highest SM is taken as the description label of the segment whose time interval is described in DDN. An example of rule in rule-set(1) is:

$$(MNS) \ (MVI) \ (LPK) \ \rightarrow \ generate \ "3".$$

This rule means that if a tract of medium duration having the characteristic of frication noise (MNS) is followed by a sonorant tract of medium duration (MVI) which is followed by a vocalic peak of the signal energy (LPK), then the label is "3". Description labels may vary depending on the purpose of coding. As rule-set(1) does not have a rich enough discrimination power because it is built only on PACs, planning is used for producing plans capable of extracting properties with discrimination power. The planning system compares the rule antecedents with prototypes of the classes of descriptions corresponding to the labels that can be hypothesized by the action part. Prototypes are based on human expert knowledge in acoustic-phonetics.

Based on a distance computation between a rule-antecedent and prototypes, the planning system uses its meta-knowledge and tries to predict possible confusions represented by *confusion sets*. A *meta-reasoning phase* takes place at this point trying to find out a *set of physical operators* that can be applied, when preconditions represented by the antecedent expression are verified, in order to resolve the confusion described by the confusion set. An example of *meta-knowledge* used for predicting a confusion set is the following:

$$(LDD) \ (LPK) \ \rightarrow \ (plosives, \ vowels \ or \ sonorant \ sounds \ after \ a \ pause)$$

LDD means a long deep dip in the signal energy. An example of *meta-knowledge* used for proposing physical operators is the following:

$$(LDD) \ (LPK) \ and \ confusion \ set \ [e, \ b] \ \rightarrow \ operators \ for \ buzz-bar \ detection$$

Each physical operator can be applied under some constraints. A plan, consisting of a sequence of operator applications, is generated by the planning system in such a way that the constraints are satisfied. These plans will be executed for extracting new objects to be placed in DDN. These objects are not used immediately. New examples involving new speakers are proposed to the system for recognition. The recognition errors identify some rules that have caused them. These rules are tagged. For all the examples that are classified correctly or wrongly by tagged rules, the corresponding DDNs are kept. When enough DDNs have been collected, learning is performed.

Learning has, first, the purpose of reducing the level of generalization of the tagged rules so that new rules can be introduced in order to reduce the confusion rate. The second purpose of learning is that of taking the rules whose level of generalization cannot be further reduced and using each of them as precondition for the execution of the plan that was already conceived for it. Each plan introduced into the system has already generated objects collected through DDNs. Discriminant descriptions are learned for the classes and objects produced by plans that have just been included into the system. The plan ADSS is now expanded because some of the rules in "rule-set(1)" invoke the execution of another plan involving an elaboration-phase(2), followed by a decision-phase(2) that uses a new rule-set(2). Plans in elaboration-phase(2) are built by the planning system. Rules of rule-set(2) are learned by the learning system.

The strategy algorithm of the planning system can be summarized as follows:

strategy algorithm
learn rule-set(1);
i:=1;
repeat
    compute possible confusion-sets for rule-set(i);
    for every rule r(i) in rule-set(i)
        define plan for resolving possible confusion set of r(i);
        run experiments and tag rules that generate real confusions;
        adjust through learning antecedents of tagged rules in rule-set(i);
    for every tagged rule where two or more classes may have high similarities
    do
    begin
        insert the execution of resolving plan as action;
        learn new rules for rule-set(i+1) based on objects produced by resolving
        plans during experiments;
    end
    i:=i+1;
until confusion rate is sufficiently low;

For the sake of simplicity all the rules that are used after the execution of each plan are considered to belong to rule-set(i).

The plans generated in this way belong to a hierarchy of actions that are executed according to the following algorithm:

action hierarchy execution algorithm

  next-plan := spontaneous activities;

  j := 1;

  repeat

    elaboration-phase (next-plan)

    decision-phase (rule (j), result)

    if (result = execution of plan) *then begin*

      specify next plan;

      isolate rule (j) as a subset of rule set (j)

    end

  until the most detailed descriptions have been generated

The following example refers to the calculation of the evidence of hypotheses about the place of articulation of the consonant /p/ of the utterance shown in Fig. 3. We have obtained some experimental results about the recognition of letters ending with the vowel /i/. For this particular vocabulary it was found [DEMICHELIS 83] that burst information is not reliable enough, so only formant pseudo-loci were considered. Pseudo-loci are extracted with a spectral analysis performed every 2 msec in an 80 msec interval starting 10 msec before the beginning of the vocalic segment.

Three formant estimations are used in the relations R_{lp}. These estimations are shown in the example of Fig. 4.

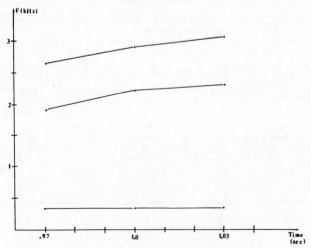

Fig. 4 Example of formant transition analysis.

Formant slopes are then computed from the samples of formant transitions. Formant slopes are then compared with fuzzy sets defining "ascendent" for labial, "moderately ascendent" for alveolar and "moderately descendent" for palatal. Evidences may range from 0 to 1. The following values have been found for the example of Fig. 4.

for-labial-evidence = 1.0;

for-alveolar-evidence = 0.5;

for-palatal-evidence = 0.

Fuzzy sets were obtained from histograms of formant slopes.

4. A SYSTEM OF PLANS FOR THE RECOGNITION OF CONNECTED LETTERS

The speech signal is first analyzed on the basis of loudness, zero-crossing rates and broad-band energies using an expert system described in [DE MORI 82]. The result of this analysis is a string of symbols and attributes. Symbols belong to an alphabet of Primary Acoustic Cues (PAC) whose definition is recalled in Table I. A Semantic-Syntax-Directed-Translation scheme operates on PAC descriptions and, through the use of sensory procedures, identifies the vocalic and the consonantal segments of syllable nuclei; for the vocalic segments, the scheme hypothesizes the place of articulation of the vowel. Plans are then applied for interpreting the consonantal segment of every syllable. An overview of the plan PE1 for the recognition of the E1 set is shown in Fig. 5.

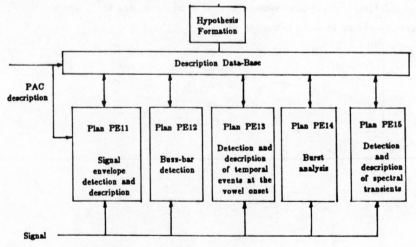

Fig. 5   Overview of the plan PE1.

The purpose of PE1 is that of discriminating among the elements of the E1 set.

The plan is subdivided into sub-plans (PE11,PE12,PE13,PE14,PE15).

PE11   produces an envelope description by analyzing the signal amplitude before
and after preemphasis. Envelope samples are obtained every msec by taking the
absolute value of the difference between the absolute maximum and the absolute
minimum of the signal in a 3 msec interval. The envelope description is made
by the following alphabet (⁻ represents negation) :

EDA = {SHORT—STEP(ST),

LONG—STEP(LST),

NO—STEP(NST),

STEP WITH HIGH LOW FREQUENCY ENERGY(BZ),

BURST—PEAK(BUR),

POSSIBLE—BURST(PBU),

NBZ=⁻BZ,

NBU =⁻BUR,

NPB=⁻PBU.}

PE12   detects a buzz-bar by analyzing the shape of FFT spectra before the voice
onset. The alphabet of the descriptions it produces is :

BZA = {NOB,BU1,BU2,BU}

NOB means no buzz and the other three symbols describe degrees of buzz-bar
evidence (BU1 : little evidence, BU : strong evidence)

PE13   analyzes temporal events at the voice onset. These events are related to
voice onset time. They are :

D   :   the delay between the onset of low and high frequency energies,

ZQ   :   the duration of the largest zero-crossing interval of the signal at the
onset,

ZR   :   the number of zero-crossing counts in the largest sequence of sucessive
zero-crossing intervals with duration less than 0.5 msecs.

PE14 and PE15 perform respectively burst and formant transition analysis as
described in [DEMICHELIS 83].

Preconditions for plan execution may be learned with a general-purpose
algorithm whose details are given in [DEMORI 84]. The highlights of this algorithm
are summarized in the next section.

Expressions made of symbols extracted by subplans PE11 and PE12 and
representing positive and negative evidence have been inferred for each PAC
description and for each phoneme using this learning algorithm. Examples of such

rules are given in the following :

E := NOB NBZ NST NBU NPB

B := BU BZ NST NBU PBU

There are 96 such rules in the system. A PAC description is used for indexing a set of rules that is matched against the input description produced by the plan. As rules and descriptions contain the same number of symbols, a similarity index between a rule and a description is computed in closed form.

A similarity index is computed by using the *max* operator for disjunctions and by summing the contributions of each clause and then dividing the sum by the number of clauses. Parameters extracted by subplans are used in fuzzy relations. Examples of such fuzzy relations are given in the following :

E :=   short   D   short   ZQ low   ZR

K :=   long   D   short   ZQ high   ZR

where "short, long, high, low"are fuzzy sets. There are 43 such relations. A priori probabilities of the two similarity indices are inferred from experiments for every phoneme. These probabilities can be supplied to the language model for further preprocessing. A simple recognition strategy based on similarity indices has been used for the experiment described in this section. Its details are omitted for the sake of brevity.

Fig. 6 shows the similarities S1 and S2 computed for the phrase of Fig. 3. Notice that similarities are computed only for those phonemes whose relations are selected by preconditions.

Similarity Values

Pronounced Symbol	Preconditions	Similarities		
K	LDD LPK			
		S1(K)—1.000	S2(K)—0.800	S12(K)—0.900
		S1(T)—1.000	S2(T)—0.648	S12(T)—0.824
		S1(D)—0.833	S2(D)—0.500	S12(D)—0.667
		S1(G)—0.875	S2(G)—0.373	S12(G)—0.624
		S1(E)—0.833	S2(E)—0.407	S12(E)—0.620
		S1(P)—0.667	S2(P)—0.333	S12(P)—0.500
		S1(B)—0.571	S2(B)—0.200	S12(B)—0.386
3	LPK LPK	Identified as 3	based on preconditions	
V	SMD LPK	Identified as V	based on preconditions	

Fig. 6   Similarity indices S1 and S2 and their average S12 for the phrase of Fig. 3.

The proposed approach has been tested on a protocol of 1000 connected pronounciations of symbols of the El set in strings of five symbols each. The strings were pronounced by five male speakers, and five female speakers the voice of which was not used for deriving the rules. As the recognition algorithm is syllable based, it is not constrained by the number of syllables. Percentage errors are shown in Table IV.

PRONOUNCED

		P	T	K	B	D	6	C	V	E	3
R	P	93		1	2					2	
E	T		92	4		2	2			1	1
C	K		2	94						1	
O	B	5			93	4			3	1	
G	D		2		2	90			2		
N	6		3		1	2	97		1		1
I	C						1	100			
Z	V				2	2			92		1
E	E	2		1					1	95	
D	3		1						1		97

TABLE IV   INSERTION ERROR RATE: 0.5%
                  DELETION ERROR RATE : 0

No results have been reported so far on the multi-speaker recognition of connectedly spoken letters. The idea of using a number of phonetically significant properties in a recognition system based on the planning paradigm appears very promising. The analysis of the behavior of each plan and of the errors generated by their application suggests the actions that have to be taken in order to improve recognition accuracy.

5.   LEARNING METHODOLOGY

Learning rules from examples can be seen as the process of generalizing descriptions of positive and negative examples and previously learned rules to form new candidate rules. When applied incrementally this methodology can produce results which depend on the order in which examples are supplied and on the occurrence of examples which are exceptions to the relevant rules. Incremental learning of rules has to come out with a set of rules that is the most consistent with the examples encountered so far.

In order to allow dynamic preservation of consistency among the set of rules, an algorithm has been conceived which uses the *Truth Maintenance System* formalism [DOYLE 79] and which is reminiscent of previous work by Whitehill [WHITEHILL 80]. Both the choice of a *description language* for examples and rules and the choice of the *generalizing algorithms* are critical in a learning system in the sense that they may or may not allow the learning of relevant rules. A description language and rule generalization heuristics have been defined based on knowledge about rule-based continuous speech recognition (CSR). A relevant aspect of the learning system developed for CSR is that generalization rules are not constrained by the Maximally Common Generalization property introduced in [WHITEHILL 80]. Positive and negative evidence used for learning operator preconditions are described by their relevant concept and a conjunction of predicate expressions. Each predicate expression or selector [MICHALSKI 83] asserts that an acoustic property has been detected or that an acoustic parameter has been extracted with some specified value. A generalization rule derives, from two conjunctions C1 and C2, a conjunction C3 that is more general than both C1 and C2, i.e., C1 $\Rightarrow$ C3 and C2 $\Rightarrow$ C3.

The generalized rules themselves are the nodes of a TMS [DOYLE 79]. Each node represents a rule with left-hand-side (LHS) CONJ and right-hand-side (RHS) CONC, having a support list SL whose IN and OUT parts are respectively the list of nodes with RHS CONC and LHS less general than CONJ, and the list of nodes with RHS different from CONC and LHS less general than CONC. With each node are kept the lists of consistent examples (PE for positive evidence) and inconsistent examples (NE for negative evidence). Lastly each node has a STATUS property which is IN when the corresponding rule is accepted (regarded as holding) and OUT otherwise. A node is IN, i.e., its STATUS is IN, if and only if all of the nodes in the IN part and all of the nodes in the OUT part of its SL are respectively IN and OUT, and the numbers of examples in PE and NE satisfy a given predicate P (for example NE $\geq$ 2 PE). As the numbers PE and NE keep changing during learning, a generalization can be accepted at a certain moment but be rejected later. This justifies the use of TMS.

The proposal, which was implicit in previous sections, to take seriously the value of a *knowledge base* in both human and machine learning suggests possible improvements to the learning methodology of the current system implementation. We would like to think of very high quality learning, whether human or machine, not as a matter of filling in detail within a pre-determined structure nor as a matter of inducing concepts which are learned item by item, but rather as a highly selective and directed process which, above all, is *knowledge intensive* : it is a large amount of *old* knowledge which makes possible the learning of *new* knowledge. Perhaps some day we can use truth maintenance (or reason maintenance) systems as engines within more general computer systems for improving knowledge; we might even call the latter Partially-Inadequate-Knowledge Improvement Systems (PIKIS).

Just as learning methodology needs to be improved, so does the methodology for constructing rule-based expert systems. A recent contribution along these lines, [MCCARTHY 83], suggests incorporating our common sense background knowledge into some free-standing expert systems. In knowledge-based computer recognition of continuous speech, where the expert systems are embedded rather than free standing, both the expert systems involved in computer speech perception and the ones involved in machine acquisition of new speech knowledge require, we suggest, a knowledge base which is common in a somewhat different sense : we suggest that this knowledge base should be an approximation to the speech knowledge and recognition ability which are encoded in the brains of normally constituted very young, young and mature human speech recognizers. The irony of all this is that it is far from easy to get this knowledge and this ability, which are neurally encoded in our brains, out onto paper as deep models and theories so that we may put them back into our programs.

6. CONCLUSION

In the preceding sections we have discussed aspects of both a research program and a current system implementation for knowledge-based computer recognition of continuous speech. We hope we have made it clear that the research program is not intended as a mere description of the implementation, but rather as a long-range plan which can be used to extend, modify and improve the existing implementation; indeed, in some contexts, most notably with respect to machine learning, the research program is clearly in advance of the current system. The most important aspects of the continuous speech recognition system are that it is active, quasi-distributed, feature-based and knowledge-based. The system uses a set of algorithms for extracting acoustic cues and phonetic features; these algorithms have been embedded in a system of plans implemented using the frame paradigm.

Experimental results show that these features can be useful both for segmenting continuous speech into syllabic segments and for the bottom-up generation of hypotheses.

We will now attempt to summarize a number of important lessons which have emerged from work on this continuous speech recognition system.

1) A knowledge-based speech recognition system with a distributed knowledge base makes it possible to find a detailed explanation for any error which occurs; this system has been designed in such a way that a careful *diagnosis* can be made for each error, in order to understand which feature was misrecognized and what acoustic property was wrongly detected. Human learning, whether about speech or the visual world or whatever, takes place only gradually starting roughly from birth. Human perceptual activity, for example, listening to speech, depends critically on error-correcting mechanisms; communication is a process of repair. All of this is modelled in our speech recognition system not only by explicitly programming the error-correcting mechanism and allowing system restructuring through machine learning, but also by intentionally providing aids through knowledge distribution for the successive human redesign of the recognition system.

2) The use of PPFs simplifies the problem of dealing with speaker dependencies. Remember that a PPF is represented by a relation with acoustic properties. In this way, the speaker-dependent knowledge can be cleanly separated from the speaker-independent knowledge. Similarly, one and the same coarticulation instance may be represented by a large variety of qualitatively different patterns; to deal with this complexity we need to go behind the variability to discover some essential features of the coarticulation. Both of these separations or abstractions are instances of a more general principle : at the level of surface appearance, a speech signal is not cleanly structured; only by using a deep model of the underlying speech reality can a human or computer recognizer succeed in dealing adequately with unconstrained continuous speech.

3) Morphological features are useful ingredients for plan preconditions. Segmentation and recognition of place of articulation do not appear to be speaker dependent. Good segmentation techniques allow one to significantly

lower the difficulty of continuous speech recognition. Moreover, in this system, segmentation errors are easily explained, which allows improvement of the segmentation techniques.

4) As we have said, phonetic features are characterized by acoustic properties. Redundancies in this representation improve the recognition accuracy; specifically, redundant acoustic properties are extracted for each PPF in order to achieve low error rates. Human grasp of ordinary language profits from high redundancies. We can afford to miss or mishear individual sounds or even words without losing the meaning. Here again, computer perception may profitably be modelled on human perception.

This consideration of redundancies leads to a parenthetical remark that we should like to make in the guise of a conclusion. It is fairly clear that, in the presence of noise, a recognizer of a language which makes use of redundancy will be more successful the better he (or it) knows both the language and the context. Like some other speech recognition workers, we have been attracted to the problem, which we now recognize as deep, of characterizing or modelling the intrinsic difficulty of speech recognition tasks. In building this model we would like to learn from computer experience but see the possibility of a logical problem in discovering an intrinsic model using experiments performed by a particular recognizer. The solution to this difficulty, we suggest, is not only to construct an independently checkable, deep model of speech for hierarchically modelling the intrinsic complexity of speech recognition tasks, but also to build this model into the recognizer for doing computer experiments.

Modelling the complexity of speech recognition tasks, designing computer systems for continuous speech recognition, learning more about speech ourselves, designing computer systems for machine learning about speech — all these, we suggest, require large amounts of prior deep knowledge about speech. And yet, how should this knowledge be organized? We suspect that a remark by Moses [MOSES 82] concerning the relatively low overall complexity of an organizational structure designed as a pyramid or tower of linguistic abstractions has not yet been fully assimilated by the designers of knowledge-based computer systems for continuous speech recognition or, indeed, for other computer tasks.

ACKNOWLEDGEMENTS

This research was partially supported by the Natural Sciences and Engineering Research Council of Canada with grant no. A2439. The force of the distinction between shallow, single-level, rule-based systems and deep, hierarchical, knowledge-based systems was suggested to us by J. Moses (MIT). We suspect that the current system is at least partially consistent with the latter's suggestion that very large knowledge-based systems should be designed as layered towers or pyramids.

REFERENCES

[BAHL 83] Bahl L. R., Jelinek F., Mercer R. L., A Maximum Likelihood Approach to Continuous Speech Recognition, IEEE Trans. on Pattern Analysis and Machine Intelligence, Vol. PAMI-5, No. 2, pp. 179 - 190, March 1983.

[BAHL 84] Bahl L. R., Das S. K., de Souza P. V., Jelinek F., Katz S., Mercer R. L., Picheny M. A., Some Experiments with Large-Vocabulary Isolated Word Sentence Recognition, Proc. of the IEEE Conference on Acoustics, Speech, and Signal Processing, San Diego, CA., pp. 2651 - 2653, March 1984.

[CHURCH 83] Church K. W., Phrase-Structure Parsing : A Method for Taking Advantage of Allophonic Constraints, MIT/LCS/TR-296, Cambridge, MA, January 13, 1983. (MIT Ph.D. thesis)

[DEMICHELIS 83] Demichelis P., De Mori R., Laface P. and O'Kane M., Computer Recognition of Plosive Sounds Using Contextual Information, IEEE Trans. on Acoustics, Speech, and Signal Processing, Vol. ASSP-31, No. 2, pp. 359 - 377, April 1983.

[DE MORI 82] De Mori R., Giordana A., Laface P., Saitta L., An Expert System for Interpreting Speech Patterns, Proc. of the AAAI-82, pp. 107 - 110, 1982.

[DE MORI 83] De Mori R., Computer Models of Speech Using Fuzzy Algorithms, Plenum Press, New York, NY, 1983.

[DE MORI 84] De Mori R. and Gilloux M., Inductive Learning of Phonetic Rules for Automatic Speech Recognition, Proc. of the CSCSI-84, London, Ontario, pp. 103 - 106, May 1984.

[DOYLE 79] Doyle J., A Truth Maintenance System, Artificial Intelligence, Vol. 12, No. 3, pp. 231 - 272, 1979.

[ERMAN 80] Erman L. D., Hayes-Roth F., Lesser V. R., Reddy D. R., The HEARSAY-II Speech-Understanding System : Integrating Knoweldge to Resolve Uncertainty, Computing Surveys, Vol. 12, No. 2, pp. 213 - 253, June 1980.

[KOPEC 84] Kopec G. E., Voiceless Stop Consonant Identification Using LPC Spectra, Proc. of the IEEE Conference on Acoustics, Speech, and Signal Processing, San Diego, CA., pp. 4211 - 4214, March 1984.

[LAIRD 84] Laird, J. E. : Universal Subgoaling; Carnegie-Mellon University, Department of Computer Science, Pittsburgh, Pennsylvania, Report No. CMU-CS-84-129, May 1984.

[LEVINSON 81] Levinson S., Rabiner L. R., Isolated and Connected Word Recognition : Theory and Selected Applications, IEEE Trans. on Communications, Vol. COM-29, No. 5, pp. 621 - 659, May 1981.

[MCCARTHY 83] McCarthy J., Some Expert Systems Need Common Sense, in The Computer Culture, H. Pagels, ed., Annals of the New York Academy of Sciences, Vol. 426, pp.129-137 (1984).

[MICHALSKI 83] Michalski R. S., A Theory and Methodology of Inductive Learning, in Machine Learning : An Artificial Intelligence Approach, Tioga Publishing Company, Palo Alto, CA, pp. 83 - 134, 1983.

[MINSKY 75] Minsky M., A Framework for Representing Knowledge, in The Psychology of Computer Vision, P. Winston, ed., McGraw-Hill, New York, NY, 1975.

[MOSES 82] Moses J., Computer Science as the Science of Discrete Man-Made Systems, Knowledge : Creation, Diffusion, Utilization, Vol. 4, No. 2, pp. 219 - 226, December 1982, reprinted in The Study of Information : Interdisciplinary Messages, F. Machlup and U. Mansfield, eds., John Wiley and Sons, New York, NY, 1983.

[NEISSER 76] Neisser U., Cognition and Reality : Principles and Implications of Cognitive Psychology, W. H. Freeman and Co., San Francisco, CA, 1976.

[RABINER 84] Rabiner L. R., Wilpon J. G., Terrace S. G., A Directory Listing Retrieval System Based on Connected Letter Recognition, Proc. of the IEEE Conference on Acoustics, Speech, and Signal Processing, San Diego, CA, pp. 3541 - 3544, March 1984.

[SACERDOTI 75] Sacerdoti, E. D. : The nonlinear nature of plans, IJCAI-4, International Joint Confrence on Artificial Intelligence; Tbilisi, Georgia, USSR, September 1975, pp. 115-135.

[STEFIK 80] TStefik, M. J. : Planning with Constraints; Stanford Heuristic Programming Project, Memo HPP-80-2; Computer Science Department, Report No. STAN-CS-80-784, January 1980.

[WHITEHILL 80] Whitehill S. B., Self Correcting Generalization, Proc. of the AAAI-80, pp. 240 - 242, 1980.

READING SPECTROGRAMS :

THE VIEW FROM THE EXPERT

F. LONCHAMP
Institut de Phonétique, Université de Nancy II, B.P. 33-97
54015 NANCY Cedex, FRANCE.

1- INTRODUCTION

The purpose of this chapter is to survey selected problems in
the automatic segmentation and labeling of utterances made of several words
spoken in a natural, connected manner. The author will report on insights
gained in the course of a spectrogram reading experiment that is part of
the SYSTEXP project of the Pattern Recognition - Artificial Intelligence
group headed by Professors HATON and PIERREL at C.R.I.N.-Nancy. This chapter has been written with two different publics in mind - those who wonder
why spectrograms are read, and those who wonder how they are read - and therefore runs the risk of pleasing neither. But we must first make it clear
that the word 'expert' in the title was preferred to the more accurate
'experienced reader' because of its brevity, and also its reference to the
'expert system' approach. A second caveat is necessary. Although spectrogram
reading involves labeling at the phone (phoneme) level, we will not argue
that segmenting and labeling in phone-sized units is the only, or the best
way to process acoustic data for all speech recognition or speech understanding systems. The dozens of isolated word recognizers using pattern -
matching techniques that do not involve phone-sized segmentation which already exist either commercially or as laboratory prototypes, are ample proof
that alternative approaches are fruitful.

But we believe that phonetic labeling has some advantages for multi-speaker connected speech understanding systems with a large vocabulary of
a few thousand words, a 'comfortable' range of syntactic rules and requiring
only a modest amount of speaker-specific training. On the credit side, one
can point to:
- the small size of the inventory, even if allophones are taken into account,
  contrasting with the much larger number of diphones or syllabic units;
- straightforword addition and/or modification of phonological rules provided

by linguists;
- simple inputting of lexical pronunciation data from available sources;
- the possibility to use existing data on the acoustic specification of
speech sounds.

Drawbacks do exist, however. One very serious one is that boundaries between phones can often only be placed arbitrarily, and a heavy reliance is put on the segmentation process (see Klatt 1979 and Shoup 1980
for further comments on other types of units such as diphones or syllables).

Below, we will examine the reasons why spectrogram reading was
felt to be a worthy topic of research. Then we will outline what makes speech
labeling difficult. In a third part, we will report on some results and implications of our spectrogram experiment. Finally, some of the problems involved in the writing of rules in an expert-system framework will be discussed. Space prevents giving background information on the acoustics and phonetics of speech. Pickett(1980)provides an excellent treatment. The spectrogram
in fig. 1 illustrates some of the acoustic events we will be referring to.
The important topic of phonological rules will not be covered, as it is too
highly language-specific.

2- IMPROVING THE ACCURACY OF SEGMENTATION AND LABELING

It is now widely, but not universally agreed that continous
speech understanding requires accurate labeling and segmentation   (Lea &
Shoup 1980). Two of the ARPA contracting teams (BBN and SDC) strongly emphasized the need for good acoustic-phonetic recognition in their review of
their own work (Lea 1980). "... the fact that our performance decreased
only slightly with (an) increased vocabulary ... (seems to us) due to an
acoustic-phonetic recognizer that is generally very good... but making occa-
sional serious mistakes... There is a long list of acoustic phonetic phenomena to be studied and incorporated into (our system)..."(Wolf & al. 1980 on
BBN "HWIM"). "...Were the SDC project to continue, it would concentrate on
several crucial elements... Various changes would be made in the acoustic-
phonetic processor to improve its accuracy... Much more effort must be ex-
pended in identifying and classifying fricatives, plosives and nasalized
sounds... The more reliance the rest of the system can put on the output
of the acoustic phonetic processor, the more efficient the total system will
be... There is more leverage to be gained at the bottom end than almost any-
where else in the total system..."(Barnett & al. 1980 on their SDC system).
During the ARPA project, the SDC team produced a series of valuable reports

Fig. 1 - Spectrogram of (French) sentence "C'est de l'eau"
[sedəlo] (It's water). Range of analysis: 0-8 KHz.

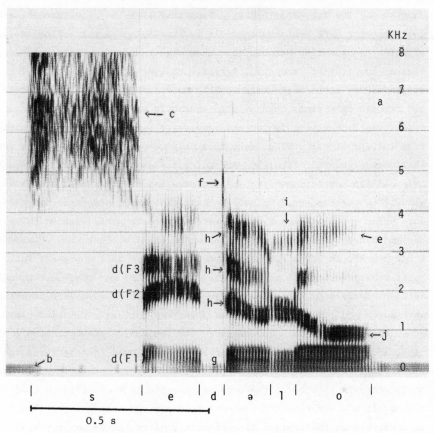

a: Calibration lines at integer multiples of 1 KHz.
b: 'Baseline' produced by spectrograph when signal enegy is low.
c: Patch of friction noise (fricative) for phone [s̄] .
d: Formants; note frequency and intensity variations in time
e: Note energy modulation at the fundamental frequency.
f: plosive burst.
g: voice bar.
h: Formant transitions.
i: Low-energy 4th formant of [l] glide.
j: Frequency level at which second formant of [o] is measured.

on the identification of nasals (Gillman 1974), vowels and sonorants
(Kameny 1975, 1976), fricatives and plosives (Molho 1976).

The fact that HARPY, and HEARSAY II to a lesser extent, successfully met the ARPA performance goals is attributed to the following factors:
efficient cooperation between many knowledge sources in HEARSAY II, and efficient 'merging' of acoustic, lexical and syntactic informations into a
single 15000 state network for HARPY. More specifically, both systems imposed strong constraints on available syntactic patterns, used a language
with a small branching factor and required a significant amount of training
from individual users. They were thus able to overcome the problems resulting
from coarse phonetic labeling. According to Lea (1980), HARPY, for instance,
only had the correct phonetic label as the top choice in 42% of the segments,
and within the top three 65% of the time. The input utterance was segmented
into brief quasi-stationary segments that were compared with 98 talker-speci-
fic templates, yielding a set of distances based on Itakura's LPC residual
error metric. In BBN's HWIM system, on the other hand, a segment lattice was
built from a variety of measurements includind LPC spectra, formant frequency
data, zero-crossing rates and energy-in-bands values. Specific procedures
were developed to deal with complex phenomena such as unreleased plosive pairs
or syllabic nasals. As a consequence, the top choice was correct 52% of the
time, and an impressive accuracy of 80% was achieved for the three top candidates, although Wolf & al. carefully point out that this value is not totally adequate in view of the way the phonetic lattice is later used in their
system. It may surprise the newcomer to the field that no comprehensive data
is available on the contextual variability of speech sounds for even a single
language. After all, the sound spectrogram has been commercially available
since the mid-fifties, and computers for nearly as long. The sheer amount of
work should not, however, be underestimated. Assuming a phoneme inventory
size of only 35, about 20000 tokens would have to be analyzed in order to gather data on all possible pairs of phonemes with a rough estimate of individual variability based on 15 speakers. Part of the answer may also be that
this type of data-gathering is not academically rewarding. Recently however,
advances in acoustic-phonetic labeling for several classes of consonants have
been reported (De Mori & al. 1979; Demichelis & al. 1983; Kopec 1984). For
French, a nation-wide project has been started (Carre & al. 1984).

An alternative to painstaking data-gathering suggested itself in
1979 when it was reported that Dr. V. Zue from MIT had taught himself to read
spectrograms to a very high degree of accuracy, after about 2000h of training.

Previous attempts, a review of which can be found in Cole & al.(1980) or
Greene & al.(1984), had concluded that there was not enough information on
a spectrographic display to allow accurate labeling. Clearly, this type of
expertise could be tapped in the expert-system framework that had been developed in the artificial intelligence field. But before covering this last
development, we will outline the reasons why speech sounds are difficult
to identify on any acoustic display.

3- THE ACOUSTIC VARIABILITY OF SPEECH SOUNDS
Speech is mainly difficult to segment and label because of the
large contextual variability in the acoustic structure of phonetic segments.
Because detailed statements are scattered throughout the specialised literature, we will attempt to characterize the major processes involved.

Unvoicing of voiced glides
Glide consonants (i.e. w, r, R, 1, ...) normally exhibit laryn-
geal periodic voicing unless they occur next to a voiceless stop (i.e. p, t,
k...) or fricative (f, s, ∫ ,t ...). Voicing being inhibited in this case, the
vocal tract is excited by a turbulent noise source at the larynx and/or at the
most constricted part of the tract. A large difference in spectrum between
voiced and voiceless glides occurs because the voiced harmonic spectrum has
a -12dB/octave slope above 0.3KHz, while the noise spectrum has a shallower
slope with a low-pass characteristics below 0.5 to 3KHz, depending on the
size and location of the constriction and also on flow-volume velocity. Also,
when the noise source is not at the larynx, the part of the vocal tract behind the source introduces zeros in the spectral transfer function that damp
or cancel some of the characteristic poles (formants). Comparing [dRe] - with
voiced R glide - with [tRe] - unvoiced R - in figs. 2 and 3, note the lack of
energy below 1 KHz and around 3 KHz, exemplifying attenuation of the lower
part of the spectrum and cancellation of some higher poles. Glide devoicing is
frequent. From Rossi's (1968) statistics on French consonants clusters in
conversational speech, it can be gathered that 70% of all consonants occur
in clusters, and that 42% of all clusters involve a glide and a voiceless
consonant. 5 out of 6 of the most frequent clusters, totalling 23% of all
clusters, are concerned:[tR, sj, pR, Rt, pl] . When template matching is
used, it is clear that at least two templates should be available for glides.

Fig. 8: Spectrogram
   of [te]

Note higher burst than
for [tRe] in fig. 3 (+)

Fig. 3: Spectrogram
   of [tRe]

Note unvoiced [R](*)

Fig. 2: Spectrogram
   of [dRe]

Note voiced [R] (*)

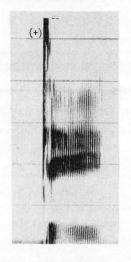
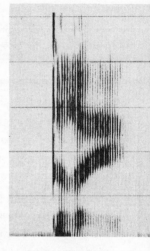

(+)

t   e   t   R(*)   e   d   R(*)   e

Fig. 4: Spectrogram
   of   [ʃi]

Fig. 5: Spectrogram
   of [sy]

Note lower frequency cut-off (*) at approximately the
same level for [ʃi]   and [sy] .

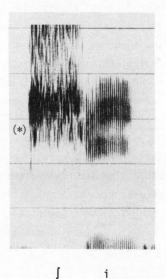
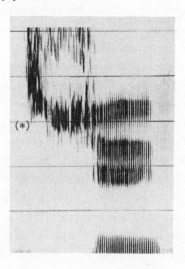

(*)   (*)

ʃ   i   s   y

Labial coarticulation

Lip-rounding is mandatory for back vowels(i.e. ɔ,o, u,ʊ ...) in
most languages, and for front rounded vowels (y, ø, ʉ ...) and some consonants
(w, ʃ ,ʒ ...). It increases the vocal tract length, thereby shifting the
higher poles to lower frequencies. Of major concern is the fact that lip
rounding often extends on neighbouring sounds that are not intrinsically
rounded (i.e. t, s) with large acoustic effects. On figs. 4 and 5, it can
be seen that the major identification cue for [s] - its lower frequency cut-
off - is brought to the level it has in[ʃ] , when followed by labial [u] .

Tongue coarticulation

Possibly in order to minimize the articulatory distance to be
travelled, the tongue often fails to reach its 'normal' target position in
certain contexts. Fig. 6 shows the tongue position for a [u] in both dental
and neutral (labial) contexts. A fronter tongue position is obvious in the
dental context, leading to a shorter displacement between the vowel and the
dental articulations. The acoustic consequence is shown in fig. 7: we note
a much higher F2 frequency in the dental context. Another example (figs. 3
and 8) is the lower burst frequency for[t] when followed by glide consonant
[R] .

Nasal coarticulation

Even in languages without phonemic nasal vowels, such as English,
vowels are often nasalized when in contact with a nasal consonant (n, m ...),
as the velum opening and closing gestures extend into neighbouring sounds.

Vocal tract length difference

Vocal tract length for females (and children) is shorter than
for males. Consequently, vowel formants for instance can be shifted up to 25%
from their nominal male malues. This effect can be seen from a comparison of
the same sentence spoken by female talker (fig. 9) and a male speaker (fig. 1).
No satisfactory solution exists for this so-called 'normalization' problem,
which is a major problem in designing a successful multi-speaker system.
Use of a short training sentence set seems the most practical solution at
the moment.

Vocal source spectral slope variability

The spectral slope of the vocal source exhibits large variations

Fig. 6: Composite X-ray tracing of tongue position for
    ------ u in a dental context (d - t)
    ——— u in a labial (neutral) context
    —.—.   tongue tip position for dental consonant
Note fronter position of tongue in dental context as a
result of coarticulation.

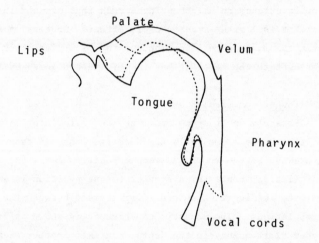

Fig. 7 - A: Spectrogram of vowel [u] in context-free position

      B: Spectrogram of vowel [u] in a dental context. Note
         higher F2 resulting from a fronter articulation (*).

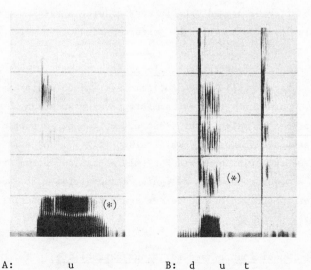

A: u   B: ḍ u t

from its nominal -12dB/octave value, even for a single speaker, depending
on the vocal intensity. For a 'soft' voice, the slope may be closer to -18dB
per octave, which implies significant reduction of the high-frequency spectral amplitude. A soft voice is typically used for the last syllable(s) of
long utterances. Perceptually, the frequency position of spectral maxima matters much more than their absolute level. Computing spectral mismatch between tokens and templates is often too dependent on these amplitude differences.

In many cases, allowance must be made for contextual influences
before a labeling decision can be reached. There is no guarantee that a 'coarticulated' spectrum will be closer to its corresponding 'neutral' template than to the template of another phone. Intimate knowledge of coarticulation rules is the major reason why spectrograms can be labeled with a high
degree of accuracy.

In view of the spectral variability of speech sounds, the question of the amount of phonetic information that is really conveyed by acoustic patterns has been raised. Obviously, semantic and syntactic information
is used by human listeners in understanding speech. It is therefore difficult to assess how much phonetic information there actually is. We do know
that there are clear intelligibility differences between carefully articulated
and conversational speech. Picheny & al. (1985), using hard-of-hearing listeners, found that that the average increase in intelligibility attributable
to clear speech is about 17%. All classes of phonemes are involved. Talkers
vary in their overall intelligibility and their ability to speak more clearly.
Acoustically, the following factors have been shown to contribute:
- longer sounds;
- vowel formant frequencies achieving target values, with tighter within-
  phoneme clustering and greater acoustic distances between classes (Chen
  & al. 1983, Lindblom & Lindgren 1985);
- more distinctive location of spectral maxima for consonants;
- stronger plosive bursts;
- greater intensity of consonants relative to neighbouring vowels.
Winitz & al. (1972) demonstrated a correlation between both frequency and
duration of plosive bursts isolated from conversational speech and correct
identification level.

Similar findings are available for speech in masking noise for
normal hearing listeners, although the increase due to careful articulation

Fig. 9 - Spectrogram of unknow utterance from our spectrogram
reading experiment.

Segments are visually defined and may correspond to
more than one phone. The expert's labels are rank-
ordered. Crossed segment indicates rejected hypothesis
after labeling the following segment. Dubious segment
within brackets.

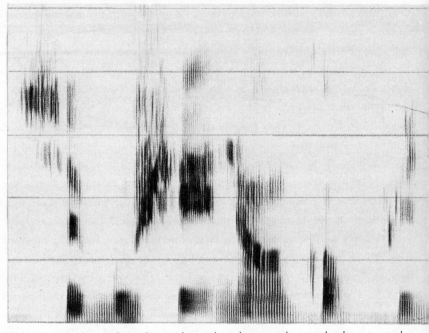

Segments	1	2	3	4	5	6	7	8	9	10	11	
Expert's labels	s / ʃ̸	ə / v / m	b	u	ʃ	e	ɲ / n	ã̲ / ɛ / ã	k	o	(R)	
Aural transcription	s	ə	b	u	ʃ	e	n	a	ã	k	ɔ	R

(ce boucher n'a encore (plus...))

seems smaller (10%). Informal listening to computer-gated phones in routine
phonetic analysis indicates wide variation in identifiability. Doddington
(1980) confesses to categorizing speakers as 'sheep' or 'goats'. Despite
being a minority (10-20%), 'goats' are responsible for most of the recognition errors in a system. Measuring intrinsic aural identication levels for
isolated and consonant-embedded vowels is beset with methodological pitfalls
(see Assmann & al. 1982 for a review and discussion). An often quoted, but
unpublished, experiment by Shockey & Reddy suggests that trained phoneticians
are unable to transcribe more than 60 to 70% of the phonemes in a foreign
language, that is without the benefit of lexical and syntactic information.
Moreover, they agree amongst themselves only about 50% of the time.

We can now turn to an examination of spectrogram reading.

4- READING SPECTROGRAMS: AN EXAMPLE AND SOME RESULTS

Before summarizing results from a spectrogram reading experiment
involving 50 sentences from 5 different speakers, we will describe the way
in which phonetic labels can be derived from the spectrographic representation of a sentence. This sentence, only the first part of which will be analyzed, has been picked at random from the set used in the experiment (see
fig. 10 for details). Zue (1982) provides a longer example of the decoding
of a difficult English sentence.

1- This high-frequency noise with a lower cut-off frequency at about 3 KHz
is either a 'low' $[s]$ (i.e. followed by a labial vowel or consonant) or a
'high'$[\int]$ (i.e. followed by a high front vowel or a dental consonant). The
$[s]$ noise is usually above 4 KHz, while$[\int]$ extends down to 2 KHz. The weaker
noise patch below is not taken into account, as it is recognized as being a
not completely cancelled pole/zero pair, a typical speaker-specific feature.

2- Visually, the following sound is a typical vowel. Its low F3 signals a
labial vowel. Going back to the previous sound, we may now label it as $[s]$
without hesitation. The values of F1 and F2 point to $[\phi]$ or$[\ni]$ (a mere notational variant in French). The gap between $[s]$ and$[\ni]$ is too short to cue
the presence of a stop consonant.

3- The following segment shows merely a low-frequency, low-level 'formant'.
This feature cues either a voiced plosive, or fricative $[v]$ if we assume
that the frication noise is below the threshold of visibility, or a nasal consonant with the upper formant(s) also below threshold. The downward-sloping
formant transitions of the preceding vowel indicate a labial consonant, therefore ruling out dental and velar consonants (d, g, n ...). Although the

formant intensity varies somewhat in time, its duration is too short to suggest two contiguous phones. A very weak burst may be present at the end, but it is too weak to rule out [v] or [m] as labels. The rank ordering of labels is [b, v] and [m].

4- The next sound has a single vowel-like formant. Its intensity is equal to that of the first formant of the vowel [ə], which prompts us to reject consonantal labels. Although vowels usually have several visible formants, we hypothesize that it is a very softly articulated vowel. From the value of F1 alone, it could be an [i, y] or [u]. But only [u] may show complete loss of high-frequency energy.

5- The following consonant is a definite [ʃ]. Its rising low-frequency edge confirms that the preceding vowel is a rounded one, which is compatible with our choice. But it also means that the next sound is not labial.

6- The formant pattern of this vowel points to an [e], although its third formant is rather low. This is most likely due to a carry-over of the lip-rounding gesture of the preceding consonant. We note that this vowel is longer than the previous ones, but not enough to suggest two identical vowels side by side. In retrospect, this lengthening is due to the vowel being in 'group final' position in the utterance. The short noise-filled gap between [ʃ] and [e], which bears a remote resemblance to a devoiced [l] pattern, is not taken into account because of the lack of formant transitions associated with laterals.

7- The next pattern is immediately visually identified as a nasal consonant. Characteristic features are: a low-frequency, low-level first formant; a single upper formant; clear offset and onset. The high upper formant rules out [m]. The large falling F2 transition on the next vowel suggests palatal [ɲ] or dental [n]. Note that the true label is not our first choice.

8- This long vowel is mainly characterized by a diffuse first formant and a low F2. Several possibilities come to mind: either a long nasal vowel (ã), with length ascribed to group-final position, or an oral vowel nasalized by the previous nasal consonant, followed by a true nasal vowel. Insufficient compensation for the effect of formant transition led us to suggest [εã] instead of [aã]. We failed to consider the case of two true nasal vowels side by side.

9- We find next a typical velar stop (k), with a 'compact' low-frequency burst made of two distinct spikes followed by a clear gap of low-level noise. But this labeling crucially depends on our identification of the following vowel as a back vowel.

10- The formant pattern of this vowel points to a [o] , as Fl is rather high
and F2 quite low. The true label is, however,[ɔ], with the velar tongue coarticulation responsible for the downward shift in F2 that we failed to take
into account.

11- The long gap is not easy to interpret. We identify a stop burst at the
end. A first possibility is a pause followed by a voiceless stop consonant.
But the previous vowel does not seem to have undergone group-final pre-pausal
lengthening. So we also have to consider a voiceless [R] in front of a voiceless stop, as we know that devoiced R's often have spectral maxima below
the treshold of visibility. A third possibility that we failed to consider is
a sequence of stops, either identical, to account for the lack of burst within
the gap, or different, assuming the first to have been unreleased (i.e. without burst).

In fig. 11, we illustre interspeaker variability by pointing out
discrepancies between this utterance and the same one spoken by the author.

We will defer a discussion of the implications of the expert's
labeling strategy until the final part of this chapter. But the following aspects are worth noting right now:
- immediate recognition of some patterns vs analytical matching of partial cues
  for others;
-'normalizing' patterns before labeling and use of some cues as confirmatory
  evidence.

We will now present some results from a spectrogram reading experiment. 5 male speakers produced a different set of 10 phonetically balanced
sentences in a small noise-free recording room. The speakers, who are all computer scientists at CRIN, have slight but recognizable dialectal features from
several areas. To avoid wide variations in rate and reading style, a practiced
female speaker read aloud each sentence at a fairly brisk pace with the speaker immediately repeating it from memory. 0-5KHz spectrograms were produced
and processed by the expert over a period of 4 weeks. Then, using the spectrograms and the recording, the expert provided an aural transcript.

A- Consonant recognition results
The overall recognition score for consonants is 80%. This is definitely less than the 89% agreement achieved by expert VZ in a similar experiment (Cole & al. 1980), as we do not include voicing 'errors'. Voicing is not

Fig. 11 - Spectrogram of same sentence as in fig. 9 spoken by
the author, illustrating a number of inter-speaker differences.
Speech rate is slightly slower. Note greater amount of high-frequency energy.

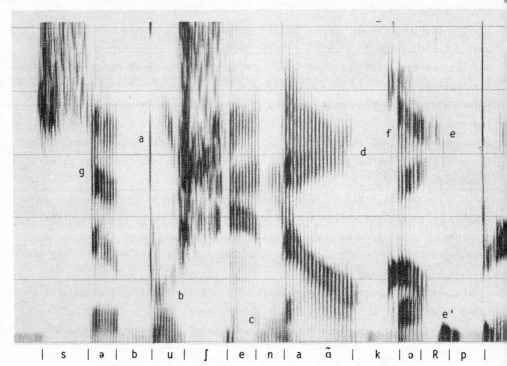

| s | ə | b | u | ʃ | e | n | a | ɑ̃ | k | ɔ | R | p |

a- Clear diffuse plosive burst pointing to [b].
b- 2nd formant of [u] is clearly visible.
c- 1st formant of [e] is unexpectedly reduced
d- Higher formants of [ɑ̃]are at a much higher frequency.
e- Weak patch of noise pointing to [R] .
e'-Low patch of noise ruling out a plosive as the first element
    in the silent gap. Convergence of F1 and F2 of previous vowel
    signals [R] .
f- Higher formants (F3 and F4) of [ɔ]are readily visible.
g- absence of noise patch below 3 KHz.

Table I: Spectrogram reader's performance on consonants

Nb. occur. in transcript.	correct 1st rank	correct 2nd rank	correct 3rd rank	total correct	%(°)	omission no answ.	nb. errors
p	44	17	18	3	38	86	2	4
b	13	5	1	-	6	(46)	-	7
t	62	54	5	-	59	95	-	3
d	37	17	1	-	18	49	1	18
k	41	34	2	2	38	93	-	3
g	6	6	-	-	6	(100)	-	-
f	13	5	2	-	7	(54)	-	6
v	29	20	2	-	22	76	3	4
s	68	59	2	-	61	90	-	7
z	11	7	-	-	7	(64)	-	4
ʃ	13	11	1	-	12	(92)	-	1
3	22	16	4	-	20	91	-	2
l	76	53	5	1	59	78	4	13
R	86	55	8	2	65	76	13	8
j	22	14	2	-	16	73	-	6
w	19	12	-	-	12	(63)	5	2
ɥ	5	2	-	-	2	(40)	1	2
m	41	30	6	2	38	93	1	2
n	38	22	10	1	33	87	1	4
ɲ	4	1	-	1	2	(50)	1	1
	650	440	69	12	521	80.2	32	97

(°): % based on less than 20 tokens are within brackets.

Table 2: Index of expert's confidence in labeling. The ratio of the number of alternative labels to the number of tokens in the corpus gives a rough measure of the expert's degree of confidence. The greater the ratio, the greater the uncertainty. Values based on less than 20 tokens are starred. For glottal stops [ʔ], the number of wrong hypotheses is reported.

consonant	nb of alternative labels (A)	nb of tokens in corpus (B)	ratio A/B
p	54	44	1.23
f	12	13	0.92 *
d	31	37	0.84
b	10	13	0.77
3	17	22	0.77
z	7	11	0.64 *
ɥ	3	5	0.60 *
v	17	29	0.59
m	24	41	0.59
n	22	38	0.58
l	40	76	0.53
t	30	62	0.48
k	17	41	0.41
R	34	86	0.40
ʃ	4	13	0.31 *
s	21	68	0.31
w	5	19	0.29 *
ɲ	1	4	0.25
j	4	22	0.18
g	0	6	0.00 *
ʔ	13	-	-

always clearly marked on spectrograms, and a speech understanding system
will have to incorporate a pitch detector that will provide this type of
information. Perhaps a more meaningful figure is the percentage of correct
first choice labels: 68%. VZ achieved 70%, but under more stringent scoring
rules. Apart from voicing, we often labeled a token as [b-v] or [m-n], and
tallied the answer as 'correct first rank' if either consonant appeared in
the transcript. The mean number of symbols (or pairs such as [b-v]) is
1.51, about equal to VZ's average for consonant and vowel symbols. Detailed
results are given in table 1 (Carbonell & al. 1984). Among the more frequent
consonants, 3 glides (1, R, j), fricative [v] and stop [d] (only 49% correct)
are below average. Sensitivity to context and devoicing readily explains the
poor results on glides. [d] (and [b])have much less distinct bursts than
their voiceless counterparts (t, p). On the other hand, the typical formant
transition pattern for [g] followed by a front vowel - F2 and F3 diverging
from a common area - and the compact low frequency burst when followed by a
back vowel, are never missed. [v] is difficult to distinguish from [b] when
softly articulated, but easily confused with [1] at higher vocal effort when
(pseudo)formants often appear. That some sounds are harder to identify is
readily seen on table 2, where the number of incorrect alternatives are lis-
ted with the ratio of these labels to the number of tokens. It can be seen,
for instance, that 54 incorrect labels were specified for the 44[p] sounds,
in addition to the 38 correct ones, as seen on table 1. This amounts to
1.23 extra labels per token. We therefore recognize that the high recognition score for [p]was achieved at the expense of increasing the range of labels to more than 2 on average. This underlines the fact that there is often
no well-defined cue to positively identify this sound. Conversely, all 6 [g]
were correctly identified without hesitation, as no alternative symbols were
reported. Table 2 therefore gives a rough measure of the degree of confidence
each identification label is granted. Table 3 provides a detailed breakdown
of the alternative labels in the form of a confusion matrix. This gives an
indication on how confusable two particular sounds are. It can be seen, for
example, that [m] is easily confused with [1] . A comparison with a similar
matrix from a machine speech-labeling task could help identify strong and
weak points in the identification routines.

B- Vowel recognition results
We have used a rather lax criterion for assessing labeling

Table 3 - Distribution of (incorrect) alternative labels.

labels from aural transcript.	\	alternative labels																				
	p	t	k	b	b~v	d	g	f	v	s	z	ʃ	ʒ	l	R	j	w	m	n	m~n	?	Voy.
p		20	20			1		1													13	
t	12		17							2					1						1	1
k	6	8					2			5											1	
b	2	1	2		11	1		1	6					3		1						
d				11			4	1														3
g					6				2													
f	2	1							1	2	7						1					
v				1					2	5	9	1			2			4	2			
s			1	3			2		5		19	3	2					2	5			
z				1	2	1	1	1	4	8		4	2	12			6					
ʒ	1			3		1						2	1	3	1	2	4	3	7	3		
ʃ										1				4	2	4	3					
l										1				2			1	1				
R						1			1													
j							5	1									6					
w																	2					
ɥ	1	1	1	1		1	8	4	1		2	1	2	1	1				1			
m												1		1					14	1		
n								6				14	2		1	1			14	1		
ɲ	5	2	3	1				1		2		2										
?																						

Table IV: Spectrogram reader's performance on vowels.

nb occur. in transcript.		nb correct	%(°)	missed	Main feature errors			
					High/low	Round	Nasal	Front/Back
i	55	47	85	5	2	–	–	1
e	70	66	94	–	–	4	–	–
ɛ	42	32	76	–	6	4	–	(2)
a	99	75	76	4	20	(12)	(1)	–
ɔ	20	10	50	1	6	–	3	(2)
o	21	16	76	–	4	–	–	1
u	32	21	66	1	(4)	(5)	(3)	10
y	22	14	64	–	(1)	8	–	–
ø	4	3	(75)	–	1	(1)	–	(1)
oe	7	1	(14)	–	5	1	–	–
ə	67	43	64	–	10	8	2	4
ã	35	23	66	1	3	–	8	–
õ	29	23	79	–	–	–	1	5
ɛ̃	15	5	(33)	–	–	–	6	–
œ̃	4	0	(0)	–	(4)	–	2	–
	522	379	73					

(°) % based on less than 20 tokens are within brackets.

Fig. 10 – Spectrogram by a female speaker of same sentence as in fig. 1. Note approximate 15% upward shift of all frequency cues, especially formants (but not F2 of last vowel !).

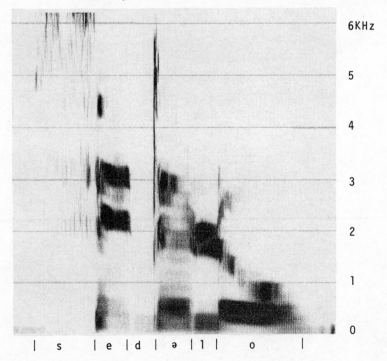

6KHz

5

4

3

2

1

0

| s | e | d | ə | l | o |

accuracy for vowels. The expert almost invariably gave two unordered labels.
Formant frequencies were estimated by eye using the spectrographic calibration lines 1 KHz apart. An answer is deemed correct when the high/low feature is wrong by at most one step (i.e. [e] reported instead of [i]), except
for nasal vowels. Failure to detect either labiality, nasality or the front/
back feature was scored as an error. Detailed results appear on table 4. We
have attempted to list the major feature error for each vowel, with less
frequent errors in brackets. Note that multiple errors are possible on a
single segment. No meaningful comparison with VZ's performance can be made.
French has a rich inventory of oral and nasal vowels, none of which is diph-
tongized or distinguished by length. Vowels are very much affected by coarticulation and speaker-specific differences such as vocal tract length. Most
errors occur for heavily coarticulated patterns.

C- Segmentation results

32 consonants were missed (4.9%), and only 12 vowels (2.3%). 75
extra consonant segments were wrongly hypothesized, but 39 were explicitely
marked as very dubious. [l] and [R] make up 63% of these extra consonants.
The pattern for the 32 omitted consonants is straightforward. We find 12 [R],
all either in sentence final position or next to a consonant, 5 [w] next to
a voiceless consonants, 4 [l] next to consonants, 3[v] next to glide consonants. Of the 12 vowels that were missed, 5 are devoiced [i] and 5 occur
next to another vowel. Extra vowels were reported in 19 cases, 7 being very
dubious.

Counting only omitted segments, segmentation accuracy is slightly above 96%. How crucial segmentation is, can be inferred from a simulation
experiment described in Sakai (1980). Using randomly-occuring substitutions,
omissions and insertions patterned on their experimentally determined distribution, recognition rates for 100 Japanese city names dropped 4% when
phonetic labeling accuracy alone was reduced by 10% for vowels and unvoiced
consonants (90 to 80 % accuracy) and by 20% for voiced consonants (60 to
40%). The recognition rate remained constant for insertion rates up to 20%,
but omitting 10% of the segment caused a 20% drop in performance. While the
insensitivity to labeling accuracy may be due to the limited size of the vocabulary in this isolated word recognition task, there is no reason to believe that the effect of omissions would be less in continous-speech recognition.

Mean identification results for the 5 speakers were 85.3, 83.0, 79.8, 77.3 and 76.6%, revealing a 8.5% difference between the most and least 'intelligible' speakers. Great caution should therefore be exercized in comparing machine recognition scores for different speakers. The poorest results seem to be due to speakers showing a large reduction in vocal effort on final syllable(s), with a corresponding loss of spectral details for the softly-articulated consonants. But, as will be seen from our discussion above, part of the difference may also be due to global differences in articulatory precision and 'clearness' of elocution.

5- IMPLICATIONS FOR SPEECH UNDERSTANDING

In this final section, we consider a range of issues that have to be dealt with in the development of the acoustic-phonetic front-end of a speech understanding system. Present limitations in the phonetic labeling of acoustic patterns are recognized as forming a major bottleneck: accuracy remains in the 60-70% range for one to three labels per segment, even though elaborate pattern-recognition techniques are employed. Spectrogram reading by human expert has shown that labeling performance could be improved, up to 80 or 90%, provided the essence of this human expertise can be incorporated within the system. This level is deemed by many experts (Klatt 1977, Haton 1985) to be high enough to allow the higher levels - syntactic, semantic and pragmatic analysers - to come up with the correct sentence interpretation in almost all cases.

Developing an expert-system for speech segmentation and labeling has been considered a worthwhile investment by several research groups (Memmi & al. 1984, Gillet & al. 1984, Mizoguchi & Kakusho 1984, Carbonell & al. 1984) in their effort to acquire relevant decoding rules, with a view to testing them for comprehensiveness and coherence.

There are basically two ways in which a sound can be identified. Firstly, labeling decisions can be based on the immediate visual identification of a specific pattern. This pattern may be visually complex and not very salient. The [l] in fig. 1 provides a good example. A most characteristic feature is the very fast transition linking the F2-F3 formant complex near 1.7 KHz to the 3rd formant of [o] , and also the sharp downward transition seen on the 4th formant of preceding [ə]. Another elusive but unambiguous cue is the merging of F2 and F3, which, apart for transition continuity, is mostly seen as a broadening of the second spectral maximum. Secondly,

identification can be secured through analytical matching of all available
acoustic cues. This strategy is used by the expert when an unambiguous cue
is not available, often as a result of strong coarticulation. Again, taking
the same [1] as an example, the low F1 is compatible with a large range of
sounds, including some vowels (i, u, y ...), nasal consonants (m, n ...)
and glides (j, 1, w...). Even if the merging of F2 and F3 goes undetected,
the value of this 'second' formant points to vowel [∅] or glide [1] . Combining our hypotheses already leaves only [1] as a suitable label. Very importantly, the remaining cues can be used in a top-down strategy to confirm -
or reject - this hypothesis. The third maximum at 3.5 KHz cannot be the third
formant of [1] , as it is too high. Therefore F3 may have merged with F2,
a fact which may be revealed by a detailed acoustic analysis of the second
spectral peak. Also, the third formant of [∅] should show up at about 2.2 KHz.
Failure to find it allows this vowel to be rejected with a high degree of
certainty.

Clearly, the (cognitive) visual ability of the human expert is of
paramount importance. Identification is based on visually extracting significant patterns, such as formants, plosive gaps and bursts, fricative noise,
transitions, etc... He is also able to compensate for changes in absolute intensity level for some cues while still taking into account small intensity
variations. It has been suggested that automatic speech labeling should be
dealt with by several cooperative experts, one of them being a 'visual' expert (Johanssen & al. 1983). Apart from its inherent complexity, this proposal subordinates speech recognition to progress in another domain of artificial intelligence. There are two ways out of this problem. First, the human spectrogram reading expertise seems to transfer to less visually exacting
representations, such as temporal plots of formant frequencies (Mizoguchi &
al. 1984), frequency/intensity LPC static spectral plots or even tables of
numerical measurements for burst spectral shapes (Bush & al. 1983). A second
possibility is to break up the labeling problem into two parts: identifying
speech classes using standard pattern-recognition techniques and then looking
for specific, possibly complex acoustic events to confirm - or refute -
a limited number of hypotheses. The human expert is asked to provide lists
of possible 'events' that may be present, as well as rules that will take
care of the influence of coarticulation. Immediate 'visual' identification
is therefore by-passed to a certain extent. Analytical matching, as described above, can also be employed. Production rules as used in expert-systems

seem best suited to deal with coarticulation variability. A simple but efficient way of building up a phonetic lattice from incomplete information allowing subsequent pruning of hypotheses invalidated by incoming contextual
data, has been developed at CRIN (Carbonell & al. 1985). It incorporates
the typical backward-chaining capacity of expert-systems.

Suppose the following 'facts' have been extracted from 5 segments
(S1 to S5) by a preliminary, non-contextual, treatment:

S1: vowel (i.e. syllabic peak); F1=800, F2=1200, F3=2500 Hz.

S2: silent gap + burst = plosive; spectral maximum at 3 KHz.

S3: vowel; F1=300, F2=1950, F3=2500 Hz.

S4: fricative; mean lower cut-off=3KHz; rising to 3.5 KHz toward S

S5: vowel; F1=550, F2=1750, F3=2450 Hz.

S1 is unambiguously labeled as [a], S5 as [ɛ], whereas S3 is either [i] or
[y] (i.e. high front non-labial or labial vowel). Also, the following production. rules are available:

R1: <u>if</u> plosive <u>true</u>

<u>and</u> burst maximum between 3 and 4.5 KHz

<u>and</u> right context = labial (i.e. u, o, y, w.....)

<u>then</u> [t]

R2: <u>if</u> plosive <u>true</u>

<u>and</u> burst maximum between 2.5 and 3.5 KHz

<u>and</u> right context= unrounded front vowel (i.e. i, e ...)

<u>then</u> [k]

R3: <u>if</u> fricative <u>true</u>

<u>and</u> lower cut-off between 3 and 4 KHz

<u>and</u> context = labial

<u>then</u> [s]

R4: <u>if</u> fricative <u>true</u>

<u>and</u> lower cut-off between 2 and 3 KHz

<u>and</u> context = non-labial

<u>then</u> [ʃ]

R5: <u>if</u> fricative <u>true</u>

<u>and</u> lower cut-off rising

<u>then</u> left context=labial; right context=non-labial

Both R1 and R2 apply to S2, given that S3 is either labial or unrounded. A
two-branch tree is generated:

$$a \Big<^{t \text{ --- } y}_{k \text{ --- } i}$$

Note that the following sequences are not hypothesized: [ti] and [ku].
Both R3 and R4 also apply to S4, due to the incomplete specification of S3.
But R3 applies only to the upper branch of the tree, and R4 to the lower
branch, yielding

$$a \Big\langle \begin{array}{l} t \text{---} y \text{---} s \\ k \text{---} i \text{---} \int \end{array}$$

R5 is relevant, as it allows pruning the lower branch: the left context is
labial, therefore excluding [i] , which is non-labial. The second conclusion of
R5 provides a welcome check as it suggests that the right context is non-labia
in agreement with our labeling of S5 as [ε]. The lattice reduces to

$$a - t - y - s - ε \quad .$$

Tactics and strategies used in spectrogram reading have been
expertly covered in Cole & al. (1980), Zue (1982) or Memmi & al. (1984).
We concur with most of their description. Several aspects must be emphasized.

Segmental accuracy is very high. But it is clearly achieved partly as a result of accurate labeling. There is no way in which the 'pure'
segmentation ability of the expert can be measured. A mere glance at the
spectrogram allows the expert to recognize many spectral patterns leading to
identification, at least at the level of broad classes: vowels, plosives,
fricatives... The expert can then compute a fairly accurate estimation of expected vowel and consonant durations, which is very helpful in breaking up
clusters of similar sounds (Carbonell & al. 1984). A possible bias, due to
the typical (French) pre-pausal lengthening can be avoided by concentrating
on the non-final part of the utterance, and also by looking for the shorter
units. Note that general comments by the expert on using spectral and intensity breaks do not tell the whole story, as immediate identification is also
involved. We believe that segmentation at the phone(me) level is not possible without attempting recognition at the same time. Fortunately, syllabic
segmentation, or more precisely syllabic peak picking, is possible using
gross intensity variations (Mermelstein 1975, Fohr & al. 1985). The rate of
speech can be deduced from the mean vocalic length, and even an estimate of
articulatory precision and clearness of speech can be gained by spotting details such as the extent of high-frequency noise in plosive bursts.

Building the labeling string from islands of phonetic reliability has been reported. This may be a psychologically rewarding strategy for
the human reader, but we find it possible to label from left to right, provided we are given access to a significant amount of context on both sides

of the pattern we are examining. The previous and following syllables seem
necessary, but longer streches do not carry much useful information as coarticulation influence does not extend on several syllables.

Finally, the expert often recognizes the phonetic class a phone
belongs to, even if he fails to report the correct label. Also, multiple
labels can be taken as pointing to a class of sounds rather than to a specific phoneme. Huttenlocher & Zue (1984) describe a model of lexical access
based on partial phonetic information. A coarse classification of segments
into broad classes such as plosive, fricative, vowel, or nasal consonant provides a very large reduction in the number of lexical candidates, even for
very large vocabularies in their isolated word recognition task. But it must
not be assumed that labeling at the phonetic class level is much easier than
at the phone level. Although the number of errors will be reduced, their
seriousness will increase as the redundancy is also reduced. It may be a
better idea to combine detailed labeling where possible with coarser parsing when it is recognized that little information is available at the acoustic level.

To conclude this brief assessment of the implications of spectrogram reading, we must emphasize that, although an expert-system framework
is a convenient way of testing the rules a human expert has developed in the
course of his training, the actual structure of a practical acoustic-phonetic front-end processor will be different (Haton 1985).

o o o

ASSMAN P.F., NEAREY T.M. & HOGAN J.T. (1982),"Vowel identification; ortho-
        graphic, perceptual and acoustic aspects", JASA, 71(4), 975-989.

BARNETT J., BERNSTEIN M.I., GILLMAN R. & KAMENY I. (1980),"The SDC speech
        understanding system", in LEA (1980), 272-293.

BUSH M.A., KOPEC G.E. & ZUE V.W. (1983),"Selecting acoustic features for
        stop consonants identification", ICASSP-1983, 742-744.

CARBONELL N., FOHR D., HATON J.P., LONCHAMP F. & PIERREL J.M. (1984),"An
        expert-system for the automatic reading of French spectrograms",
        IEEE-ICASSP 1984, paper 42-8.

CARBONELL N., DAMESTOY J.P., FOHR D., HATON J.P., LONCHAMP F. & PIERREL J.M.
(1984),"Techniques d'intelligence artificielle en décodage acoustico-phonétique", Actes 14ème JEP/GALF, Paris, 299-303.

CARRE R., DESCOUT R., MARIANI J., ESKENAZI M. & ROSSI M. (1984),"The French
language database", IEEE-ICASSP 1984, Paper 42-10.

CHEN F.R., ZUE V.W., PICHENY M.A., DURLACH M.T. & BRAIDA L.D. (1983),"Speaking clearly: acoustic characteristics and intelligibility of
stop consonants", MIT Speech Com. Group Working Papers, II, 1-8.

COLE R.A., RUDNICKY A.I., ZUE V.W. & REDDY D.R. (1980),"Speech as patterns on
paper", in COLE R.A. (ed.), Perception and production of fluent
speech, L.E.A., 3-50.

DEMICHELIS P., DE MORI R., LAFACE P. & O'KANE M. (1983),"Computer recognition
of plosive sounds using contextual information", IEEE-ASSP, 31(2),
359-377.

DE MORI R., GUBRYNOWICZ R. & LAFACE P. (1979),"Inference of a knowledge source for the recognition of nasals in continous speech", IEEE-ASSP,
27(5), 538-549.

DODDINGTON G.(1980),"Whither speech recognition?", in LEA (1980), 556-561.

FOHR D., HATON J.P., LONCHAMP F. & SAUTER L. (1985),"Méthodes de segmentation syllabique en reconnaissance de la parole", Actes 14ème
JEP/GALF, Paris, 164-167.

GILLET D., MERCIER G. & al., (1984),"SERAC: un système expert en reconnaissance acoustico-phonétique", 4ème Congrès Reconn. des Formes
et Intellig. Artif., AFCET-INRIA, 1984.

GILLMANN R.,(1974),"Automatic recognition of nasal phonemes", Proc. IEEE
symp. on Speech Recognition, 74-79.

GREENE B.G., PISONI D.B. & CARRELL T.D. (1984),"Recognition of speech spectrograms", JASA, 76(1), 32-43.

HATON J.P. (1985),"Compréhension de la parole et intelligence artificielle:
état des recherches", T.S.I. , in press.

HUTTENLOCHER D.P. & ZUE V.W. (1984),"A model of lexical access based on partial phonetic information", IEEE-ICASSP 1984, paper 26-4.

JOHANSSEN J., Mac ALLISTER J., MICHALEK T. & ROSS S. (1983),"A speech spectrogram expert", IEEE-ICASSP 1983, 746-749.

KAMENY I.(1975),"Comparison of foramnt spaces of retroflexed and nonretro-
flexed vowels", IEEE-ASSP, 23(1), 38-49.

KAMENY I. (1976),"Automatic acoustic-phonetic analysis of vowels and sonorants, IEEE-ICASSP 1976, 166-169.

KOPEC G.E. (1984), "Voiceless stop identification using LPC spectra", IEEE-
ICASSP 1984, paper 42-1.

LEA W.A. (1980), Trends in speech recognition, Prentice-Hall.

LEA W.A. & SHOUP J.E. (1980),"Specific contribution of the ARPA-SUR project", in LEA (1980), 382-421.

KLATT D.H. (1977),"Review of the ARPA speech understanding project", JASA, 62, 1345-1366.

KLATT D.H. (1979),"Speech perception: a model of acoustic-phonetic analysis and lexical access", J. of Phonetics, 7(3), 279-312.

LINDBLOM B. & LINDGREN R. (1985),"Speaker-listener interaction and phonetic variation", French-Swedish Seminar on Speech, Grenoble, April 1985

MEMMI D., ESKENAZI M., MARIANI J. & STERN P.E. (1984),"SONEX: système-expert en lecture de spectrogrammes", Rapport Final ATP-IA 1982, LIMSI.

MERMELSTEIN P. (1975),"Automatic segmentation of speech into syllable units", JASA, 58, 880-883.

MIZOGUCHI R. & KAKUSHO O. (1984),"Continuous speech recognition based on knowledge engineering techniques", Proc. Int. Conf. Pattern Recognition, Montreal 1984, 678-680.

MOLHO L.M. (1974),"Automatic recognition of fricatives and plosives in continuous speech", Proc. IEEE Symp. on Speech Recognition, 68-73.

PICHENY M.A., DURLACH N.I. & BRAIDA L.D. (1985),"Speaking clearly for the hard-of-hearing I: Intelligibility differences between clear and conversational speech", JSHR, 28(1), 96-103.

PICKETT J.M. (1980) The sounds of speech communication, University Park Press.

ROSSI M. (1968)," Au sujet des groupes consonantiques du français", Revue d'Acoustique, 3-4, 306-313.

SAKAI T. (1980),"Automatic mapping of acoustic features into phonemic labels", in SIMON J.C. (ed.), Spoken Language Generation and Understanding, Reidel, 147-190.

WINITZ H., SCHEIB M.E. & REEDS J.A. (1972),"Identification of stops and vowels from the burst portion of /p, t, k/ isolated from conversational speech", JASA, 51, 1309-1317.

WOLF J.J. & WOODS W.A. (1980),"The HWIM speech understanding system", in LEA (1980), 316-339.

ZUE V.W. (1982),"Acoustic-phonetic knowledge representation: implications from spectrogram reading experiments", in HATON J.P. (ed.), Automatic speech analysis and recognition, Reidel, 101-120.

o o o

STATISTICAL METHODS FOR SPEAKER INDEPENDENCE

Stephen E. Levinson

Speech Research Department
AT&T Bell Laboratories
Murray Hill, NJ 07974

ABSTRACT

Contemporary efforts toward speaker independence in automatic speech recognition usually take one of three approaches. Either one seeks to extract speaker-invariant information directly from the signal or one tries to devise a transformation which may be applied to the signal to normalize speaker differences or one may simply characterize speaker variability statistically.

It is generally agreed that the extraction of speaker-invariant features is the most elegant solution and most probably the way humans understand speech. Unfortunately, we presently do not know enough about the process to simulate it on a computer. Speaker normalization is attractive but still presents some difficulties. The merits and liabilities of this method are discussed by Wakita (1977).

As a practical matter, the present state of the art weighs heavily in favor of statistical methods. Admittedly these are techniques based on the doctrine of "ignorabimus". We can never know exactly what speaker-invariance is but we can make probabilistic models of it. In fact, here, as elsewhere in science, statistical methods have been remarkably successful.

There are two ways to characterize speaker variability statistically. One may take the non-parametric approach by simply collecting and storing large numbers of prototypes of speech patterns and then use nearest-neighbor rules for classification. A refinement of this technique uses clustering as a method of data reduction to lessen the computational cost of storing the prototypes. Clustering also increases robustness.

Alternatively one may use techniques such as hidden Markov modelling to make parametric models of speech patterns and then use maximum likelihood classification rules.

Both methods have been quite effective in a variety of speech recognition experiments, on both isolated words and continuous speech and on vocabularies ranging from tens to hundreds of words. In addition to being practical, these methods, in conjunction with multidimensional scaling techniques, may lead to a better understanding of speaker-invariant features.

INTRODUCTION

The utility of speech recognition devices would be substantially increased if their performance could be made robust to variability in the characteristics of the speaker. Efforts to achieve robustness independent of speaker usually involve one or more of three strategies: (i) extraction of and subsequent classification based upon features of the speech signal which are invariant across speakers, (ii) derivation and application of a transformation to the speech signal so that idiosyncracies of the speaker are suppressed, or (iii) statistical characterization of variability in the signal across large populations.

There is reason to believe that we humans use invariant features and cues in our ordinary spoken communication. It would be a most elegant solution to our problem if we could simulate that ability in our devices. Unfortunately, we cannot presently name, let alone extract, a complete — in the sense of spanning the space of speech signals — set of invariants. Obviously more research is needed on this topic.

The strategy of speaker normalization has been examined by Wakita (1977) and needs no further examination here. It is fair to say, however, that this very attractive concept is incompletely understood.

As a practical matter, then, we have little choice but to use statistical techniques in present, state-of-the-art devices. Indeed, experiments in both the laboratory and realistic environments have provided reason to be optimistic. Unfortunately, probabilistic laws of nature are doctrines of "ignorabimus" in which we admit that we can never know the "truth" about the phenomenon under study and so content ourselves with a statistical description. As such, these methods are often referred to in pejoratives suggesting that they are, at best, conveniences which do not increase our understanding. Perhaps the best known example of the deep distrust that science harbors for probability is Einstein's denial of quantum mechanics framed in his dictum "God doesn't play dice... ." Einstein (1942). Yet, quantum mechanics has proven to be an enormously successful theory even causing many areas of science to discover their own "uncertainty principles" e.g. Copeland (1981). Clearly, then, this argument can only be conducted on a dangerous philosophical battleground mined with such contradictions as randomness versus process and free will versus determinism. I do not intend to venture onto that treacherous terrain. I simply call it to your attention as evidence of two honorable traditions in science, successful probabilistic theories and stubborn objections to them. In this paper I shall describe statistical approaches to speaker independence for speech recognition devices. I shall conclude by suggesting that these methods can even be used as tools in the search for underlying (deterministic) invariants.

STATISTICAL TECHNIQUES

In this paper I shall discuss four fundamental techniques which have been applied to speaker independent speech recognition. The first and simplest of the methods I shall call the unedited sampling approach. The idea is that in a large enough population there will be found enough different acoustic patterns to subsume any individual variant. The technique then simply consists of collecting data from a substantial population. Once a similarity criterion is formed, an unknown utterance can be compared to all of the labelled patterns and classified as an instance of the category to which the sample it best matches belongs. This technique was used in the VOCAL system, Levinson (1975), and performed moderately well. In fact, it was never even contemplated that the system be trained to an individual speaker.

At approximately the same time, a study was in progress, Itakura (1975), on the now well known minimum prediction residual principle which was incorporated into an isolated word recognizer. This technique achieved high accuracy on moderately sized vocabularies for designated speakers. Therefore, it seemed natural to try to extend the method to the speaker independent case. It was suggested, Rabiner (1978), that this might be accomplished by averaging several Itakura templates together to produce a new template which would be representative of a large spaker population. Subsequently, it was found that the desired speaker independent templates could best be produced by clustering techniques, interactive ones at first, Levinson et al. (1979), and later fully automatic ones of both the hierarchical and, borrowing from studies of vector quantization, agglomerative varieties, Rabiner and Wilpon (1979).

While these studies were going on, several others, most notably Baker (1975), Jelinek (1976), Bahl and Jelinek (1975), Bahl et al. (1978), Bahl et al. (1984) and Lowerre (1976) were conducted to explore techniques for stochastic modelling. This research was not explicitly aimed at achieving speaker independence but there is at least anecdotal evidence that the prototypical systems were, to some extent, speaker independent. Recently, my colleagues and I, Levinson et al. (1983), Rabiner et al. (1983) and Rabiner et al. (1984) conducted some isolated word recognition experiments based on stochastic models which were designed to be speaker independent.

Finally, there is an approach to speaker independence which I call the method of pseudo-invariants. The recent work of Vysotsky (1984) is a good example of this approach. I shall not say a great deal about this technique except to describe it and show how it follows the general paradigm of the other techniques.

PRINCIPLES OF THE STATISTICAL METHODS

At first, it might appear that these four statistical techniques are quite different. In fact, they are all different, sometimes very cleverly disguised, methods for producing class-conditional probability density functions and can thus be easily and usefully cast in a Bayesian framework in the sense of Patrick (1972).

In all cases we begin by representing acoustic patterns (e.g. isolated words) as points in an abstract metric space as is depicted in Figure 1. We expect that, usually, points corresponding to two utterances of the same word will be closer to each other than either of them is to an utterance of a different word. If this assumption is most often satisfied, then one can reliably classify an unknown utterance as an instance of the same word as its nearest neighbor amongst a set of labelled samples. From the Loftsgaarden and Quesenberry (1965) result, we know that this minimum distance decision rule is equivalent to identifying an unknown word as the one whose probability conditioned on the measurements (i.e. the point z) is largest.

NON-PARAMETRIC METHODS

The most obvious way to use this principle for speaker independent speech recognition is to make the bold assumption that, given enough labelled samples from sufficiently many different speakers, a nearest neighbor classifier will give robust performance across a large speaker population. The extent to which the assumption is justified may be judged from an early experiment which I conducted based on a 42 word vocabulary, Levinson (1975). The training set comprised 882 utterances obtained from one rendition of the entire vocabulary by each of 21 speakers. A recognition system using a 5NN rule based on the Euclidean distance in a 10-dimensional space of FFT-filterbank outputs was tested on a set of 384 words collected from 11 speakers 4 of whom were not subjects for the training data. A correct recognition rate of 55% (210 words) was observed. Given the stark simplicity of the signal processing used and the difficulty of the task, this is a remarkable result.

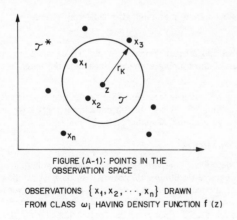

FIGURE (A-1): POINTS IN THE
OBSERVATION SPACE

OBSERVATIONS $\{x_1, x_2, \cdots, x_n\}$ DRAWN
FROM CLASS ω_i HAVING DENSITY FUNCTION $f(z)$

Fig. 1   Acoustic patterns as points in an abstract feature space.

The basic idea underlying the naive system described above can provide much more impressive results when implemented with more sophisticated techniques. In particular, substantial improvement results from replacing the FFT "front end" with the Itakura method and from refining the probability estimators by clustering algorithms.

The motivation for using clustering techniques is that just as the samples of the pooled training set display clusters corresponding to different words, these clusters in turn can be resolved into smaller clusters corresponding to different pronunciations of the same word. Furthermore, this fine structure can be more efficiently and more robustly represented by using a single derived prototype for each cluster and eliminating outliers. When we do this we are effectively locating the centers of those regions of the space where the probability of a given vocabulary word is high.

In our early clustering experiments we used the interactive strategy depicted in Figure 2. In this scheme four separate clustering algorithms were applied by a human operator to a matrix of pairwise distances between the samples of each single word. The intuition gained with the interactive system led to the design of the autonomous system shown in Figure 3. The details of this algorithm are given in Rabiner and Wilpon (1979). The important concept for purposes of this discussion is that the

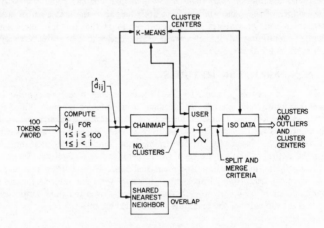

Fig. 2   Block diagram of an interactive clustering system.

inner loop is an alternating "label and estimate" procedure that seeks to isolate one mode of the underlying probability distribution of the training samples. Each time the outer loop is executed, a new mode is found and labelled.

The results of using this method in a speaker-independent digit recognition experiment, Rabiner et al. (1979), are given in the second column of Table I. In this experiment there were only 15 errors in 1000 trials using test samples from 50 men and 50 women.

PARAMETRIC METHODS

An alternative to the above described non-parametric probability estimation method is the complementary method based on parametric families of stochastic models. According to this method one estimates the parameters of a stochastic model for each word in the vocabulary. If the parameters are estimated from training data collected from a diverse speaker population, then the models themselves should possess reasonable speaker-independence. Associated with each model is a likelihood function which provides a measure of the probability that an unknown point in the abstract space represents an instance of the corresponding word. Thus, finding the model whose likelihood function has the largest value when evaluated at a given point is equivalent to finding the label on the nearest neighbor to that point.

One type of model which has proven effective for speech recognition is the hidden Markov model as depicted in Figure 4. In such models the parameters are the probabilities of state transitions and the probabilities of spectral prototypes conditioned on the state. These parameters can be estimated from training data by the method of Baum (1972) or other techniques outlined in Levinson et al. (1983). Once the parameter values have been determined, the likelihood function can be evaluated at any point in the feature space.

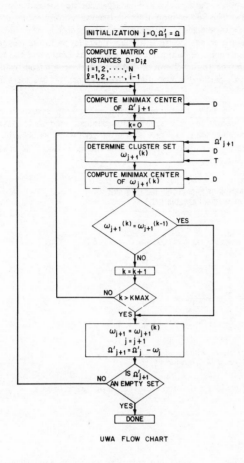

UWA FLOW CHART

Fig. 3   Flow chart of the automatic clustering algorithm.

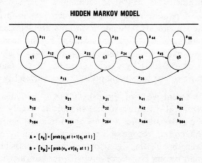

Fig. 4   Structure of hidden Markov models for isolated words.

The theoretical equivalence between parametric and non-parametric methods is borne out by experiment, Rabiner et al. (1983). The first column of Table I shows the results of a digit recognition experiment based on hidden Markov models. The experimental conditions were identical to those under which we tested the Itakura method. There is a slight degradation in the performance of our HMM method which is due to our choice of quantized LPC spectra as symbols of the HMM. This is verified by the numbers shown in the third column of Table I which result from using the Itakura method with quantized LPCs. Comparing the first and third columns, the two methods are seen to perform nearly identically.

It is also worthy of note that the IBM continuous speech recognition system based on HMM techniques was also capable of operation in a speaker independent mode. The system was not explicitly designed to be speaker independent and thus no formal results for its behavior in that mode have been reported. I have, however, seen it so operated on the Raleigh Task, Bahl et al. (1978), and in that demonstration it performed flawlessly.

TABLE I—COMPARISON OF RESULTS ON HMM/VQ AND
LPC/DTW WORD RECOGNIZERS

DIGIT	RECOGNIZER		
	HMM/VQ	LPC/DTW	LPC/DTW/VQ
0	98	99	99
1	98	98	99
2	96	100	96
3	99	99	97
4	93	97	96
5	97	96	93
6	96	100	94
7	99	100	94
8	92	98	96
9	95	98	96
AVERAGE	96.3	98.5	96.5

RESULTS (AVERAGE WORD ACCURACY (%))
100 TALKERS, 10 DIGITS PER TALKER

Table I   Results for isolated digit recognition experiments.

PSEUDO-INVARIANTS

I use the term pseudo-invariant not in a derogatory sense but simply to emphasize that we do not know which invariant features humans use for speech recognition. As a result, the features that one may propose as invariants are not truly invariant and are only useful as statistical features. As such, they are simply a priori labels for the axes of the abstract feature space of Figure 1 and are amenable to both the parametric and non-parametric classification techniques described above. The principle difference, from the point of view of pattern recognition, between pseudo-invariants and ordinary statistical features lies in the extraction process. Pseudo-invariants are selected on the basis of the experimenter's intuition about or understanding of the physical and psycho-acoustic characteristics of speech whereas statistical features are extracted by convenient mathematical algorithms using purely statistical criteria. The hope is, of course, that by careful selection of the features, they will have lower variances and hence will be more robust to, among other things, variability across speakers.

A paradigm of this approach is the recent work of Vysotsky (1984). His idea was to choose some easily measurable spectral and temporal features which should be highly information bearing, characterize them by first and second order statistics and use them in a sequential decision algorithm. Using this scheme he achieved a 96% correct recognition rate on digits and a 95% rate on a 20-word vocabulary including the digits. Even though the signal processing and classification algorithms are computationally simple, the performance compares favorably with the parametric and non-parametric methods described above.

COMPARISON OF THE METHODS

The recognition experiments cited in this paper were, except in one case, all performed at different times with different data. It is thus difficult to make any direct comparison of the relative performance of these methods as measured by recognition accuracy. In this respect, the robustness of the several methods rests on how well they estimate the tails of the distributions of whatever features they use. It is my experience that whenever small sample statistics are involved (as is always the case in speech research) there is a small but consistent advantage to the non-parametric methods.

A much more interesting basis on which to compare the methods is computational complexity. This comparison is shown schematically in Figure 5. Here we see that the possibility of obtaining a slight advantage in accuracy with the non-parametric methods must be weighed against the significant

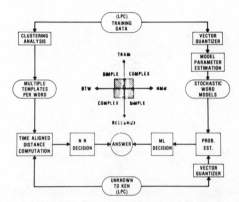

Fig. 5 Comparison of computational complexity of parametric and non-parametric statistical methods.

advantage in computational complexity which accrues to the parametric methods. The figure illustrates that the parametric methods relegate the complex processing to the training phase which need be done but once thus allowing the recognition process, which is performed continually, to be simple. The non-parametric methods distribute the computational burden in exactly the reverse order. As a result, the parametric methods are less costly in terms of both arithmetic and memory. In fact, the recognition phase of both the parametric and pseudo-invariant methods is simple enough to be accomplished on a single custom VLSI device. Of course, the penalty paid for this simplicity is that the training must be done off-line on a substantial computer. In the non-parametric case, training consists merely of data collection and is thus easily added to a self-contained recognition system.

Thus we see that while conceptually all of the methods are identical, their respective implementations have practical implications which may indicate an advantage for one system or another depending on the nature of the task.

STATISTICAL METHODS AND THE SEARCH FOR INVARIANT FEATURES

If there are truly such things in speech as invariant features, they are almost certainly very intricately encoded in the acoustic signal. To discover them, we need powerful tools such as are provided by statistical methods.

An example of the power of the statistical approach for understanding the structure of the speech signal emerged from our early experiments on clustering. We use a technique for data analysis called multidimensional scaling which is complementary to clustering, Kruskal (1977). This procedure seeks a configuration of points in an n-dimensional space such that given similarity measures (distances) are preserved. Thus if both clustering and scaling algorithms are run on the same data, the results should agree in the sense that the clusters should appear in the scaled data. Figure 6 shows the first two dimensions of a six-dimensional space with the location of points as determined by a scaling procedure and their assignment to clusters as separately determined by a clustering procedure. The scaled configuration has been rotated to principle components so that the nth axis is the direction in which the nth largest variation occurs in the data. It is very often possible to ascribe meaning to these axes. For example, the major axis in Figure 6 is a "male/female" axis. Unfortunately, at the time this experiment was done, we could not analyze enough data to find interpretations for the other axes. However, I have no doubt that useful interpretations are possible and perhaps it is a propitious time to undertake a more ambitious scaling experiment.

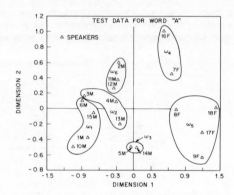

Fig. 6   Multidimensional scaling and cluster configurations of speech data.

Another source of information about invariants can be obtained by synthesizing speech from the models or templates that are derived from the original statistical analyses. In this way, we are able to use our human perceptual mechanisms to determine what kinds of information are preserved by various methods of analysis. For example, by synthesizing speech from our computed HMMs, we discovered that they contain almost no prosodic information. This in turn, suggests that improvements in performance can be achieved by introducing some physical correlates of prosody, e.g. energy, Rabiner et al. (1984), into the model.

A final example of the use of statistical techniques to discover structure in the speech signal is that of segmentation. It has been shown, Höhne et al. (1982), that what dynamic programming template matching is sensitive to is syllabic structure. Thus the image under the alignment function of a

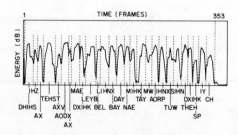

Fig. 7   Syllabification of continuous speech by dynamic programming techniques.

known syllable boundary in a reference utterance is the corresponding boundary in the unknown test utterance. The syllable boundaries shown in Figure 7 were computed in this way and agree with those determined by expert phoneticians to within a few milliseconds.

CONCLUSION

Statistical techniques in speech recognition are capable of providing a reasonable degree of speaker independence. The various methods are simply different ways of estimating class-conditional probabilities and are successful to the extent that they are able to capture the information bearing structure of the speech signal. As such, they are not only of practical utility but also potentially of value in providing insight into the invariant features of speech by means of which it may be possible to achieve truly robust mechanical speech recognition.

REFERENCES

Bahl, L. R. and Jelinek, F. (1975), "Decoding for Channels with Insertions, Deletions and Substitutions with Applications to Speech Recognition," IEEE Trans. Inform. Theory, vol. IT-21, July, pp. 404-11.

Bahl, L. R., Jelinek, F. and Mercer, R. L. (1984), "A Maximum Likelihood Approach to Continuous Speech Recognition," IEEE Trans. Pattern Analysis and Machine Intelligence, vol. PAMI-5, March, pp. 179-90.

Bahl, L. R., Baker, J. K., Cohen, P. S., Cole, A. G., Jelinek, F., Lewis, B. L. and Mercer, R. L. (1978), "Automatic Recognition of Continuously Spoken Sentences from a Finite State Grammar," Proc. IEEE Int. Conf. on Acoust. Speech and Signal Processing, Tulsa, OK, April, pp. 418-21.

Baker, J. K. (1975), "The DRAGON system — An Overview," IEEE Trans. Acoust. Speech and Signal Processing, vol. ASSP-23, Feb., pp. 24-9.

Baum, L. E. (1972), "An Inequality and Associated Maximization Technique in Statistical Estimation of Probabilistic Functions of Markov Processes," Inequalities, vol. 3, pp. 1-8.

Copeland, J. A. ed. (1981), "Special Issue on Fundamental Limits in Electrical Engineering," Proc. IEEE, vol. 69, no. 2, Feb., pp. 147-278.

Einstein, A. (1942) unpublished letter to C. Lanczos from Princeton dated 21 March. loc. primo cit. Dukas H. and Hoffmann B. (1979), Albert Einstein — The Human Side, Princeton Univ. Press, Princeton, NJ, p. 68.

Höhne, H. P., Coker, C., Levinson, S. E. and Rabiner, L. R. (1983), "On Temporal Alignment of Sentences of Natural and Synthetic Speech," IEEE Trans. Acoust. Speech and Signal Processing, vol. ASSP-31, August, pp. 807-13.

Itakura, F. (1975), "Minimum Prediction Residual Principle Applied to Speech Recognition," IEEE Trans. Acoust. Speech and Signal Processing, vol. ASSP-23, Feb., pp. 67-72.

Jelinek, F. (1976), "Continuous Speech Recognition by Statistical Methods," Proc. IEEE, vol. 64, Apr., pp. 532-56.

Kruskal, J. B. (1977), "The Relationship Between Multidimensional Scaling and Clustering," in Classification and Clustering, J. Van Ryzin, ed., New York, Academic Press.

Levinson, S. E. (1975), "The VOCAL Speech Understanding System," Proc. 4th Int. Conf. on Artificial Intelligence, Tbilisi, USSR, Sept., pp. 499-505.

Levinson, S. E., Rabiner, L. R., Rosenberg, A. E. and Wilpon, J. G. (1979), "Interactive Clustering Techniques for Selecting Speaker Independent Reference Templates for Isolated Word Recognition," IEEE Trans. Acoust. Speech and Signal Processing, vol. ASSP-27, April, pp. 134-41.

Levinson, S. E., Rabiner, L. R. and Sondhi, M. M. (1983), "An Introduction to the Theory of Probabilistic Functions of a Markov Process in Automatic Speech Recognition," Bell Sys. Tech. J., vol. 62, April, pp. 1035-74.

Loftsgaarden, D. O. and Quesenberry, C. P. (1965), "A Nonparametric Estimate of a Multivariate Density Function," Ann. Math. Stat., vol. 36, pp. 1049-51.

Lowerre, B. T. (1976), "The HARPY Speech Recognition System," unpublished Ph.D. dissertation, Department of Comp. Sci., Carnegie-Mellon Univ., Pittsburgh, PA.

Patrick, E. A. (1978), Fundamentals of Pattern Recognition, Prentice-Hall, Englewood Cliffs, NJ.

Rabiner, L. R. (1978), "On Creating Reference Templates for Speaker Independent Recognition of Isolated Words," IEEE Trans. Acoust. Speech and Signal Processing, vol. ASSP-26, Feb., pp. 34-42.

Rabiner, L. R. and Wilpon, J. G. (1979), "Considerations in Applying Clustering Techniques to Speaker Independent Word Recognition," J. Acoust. Soc. Am., vol. 66, Sept., pp. 663-73.

Rabiner, L. R., Levinson, S. E. and Sondhi, M. M. (1983), "On the Application of Vector Quantization and Hidden Markov Models to Speaker Independent Isolated Word Recognition," Bell Sys. Tech. J., vol. 62, April, pp. 1075-1106.

Rabiner, L. R., Levinson, S. E., Rosenberg, A. E. and Wilpon, J. G. (1979), "Speaker Independent Recognition of Isolated Words Using Clustering Techniques," IEEE Trans. Acoust. Speech and Signal Processing, vol. ASSP-27, Aug., pp. 336-49.

Rabiner, L. R., Sondhi, M. M. and Levinson, S. E. (1984), "A Vector Quantizer Combining Energy and LPC Parameters and Its Application to Isolated Word Recognition," AT&T Bell Lab. Tech. J., vol. 63, May-June, pp. 721-36.

Rabiner, L. R., Levinson, S. E. and Sondhi, M. M. (1984), "On Recognition of Isolated Words From a Medium-Size Vocabulary," AT&T Bell Lab. Tech. J., vol. 63, April, pp. 627-42.

Vysotsky, G. J. (1984), "A Speaker Independent Discrete Utterance Recognition System Combining Deterministic and Probabilistic Strategies," IEEE Trans. Acoust. Speech and Signal Processing, vol. ASSP-32, June, pp. 489-98.

Wakita, H. (1977), "Normalization of Vowels by Vocal-Tract Length and Its Application to Vowel Identification," IEEE Trans. Acoust. Speech and Signal Processing, vol. ASSP-25, April, pp. 183-92.

ON THE ROLE AND STRUCTURE OF THE LEXICON IN LANGUAGE UNDERSTANDING

G. PERENNOU
Laboratoire C.E.R.F.I.A., UA CNRS # 824
Université Paul Sabatier
118 Route de Narbonne
31062-TOULOUSE CEDEX

1 INTRODUCTION

Whenever the dialog between human and machine is approached through Artificial Intelligence (AI), drastic changes are brought to bear on the linguistic questions this type of dialog raises. Indeed, what is at stake ceases to be the study of languages for their own sake to become the challenge of achieving entirely new systems. These are founded, to some extent of course, in linguistic knowledge-bases, but even more so in a set of otherwise extraneous mechanisms --e.g., reasoning strategies, knowledge retrieval, etc. In other words, it often becomes impossible to discern the substantial linguistic contributions invoked from the very systems that bring them to play within specific applications.

In AI, awareness of the above progressed over the last decade, as it became obvious that, for certain achievements to come through, some well-defined sub-problems relating to machine capabilities had to be dealt with on their own. Therefore, between human and machine, dialoging in natural language often turned exclusively to question-answer systems that were confined to some limited universe. However, as Weizenbaum comments upon both his own system, ELIZA, and a few others, these tend to provide more room for illusion than for anything else; being extremely limited, they end up dodging most of the fundamental problems that lie at the center of contemporary linguistic debate.

A similar remark could be made concerning the voice entries now being released: whatever advantage such systems can offer, their performance is still pegged at the level of simple commands through a limited set of words or word-groups. Yet a definite evolution is occurring in these matters; indeed, the various systems now being worked on in a number of laboratories, as well as the heralded fifth-generation computers both foreshadow the advent, within the coming decade, of genuine dialog systems embodying a non-trivial linguistic dimension.

The present exposé fits within the perspective of such

progress, for in reality specifically lexical problems otherwise threaten to remain ancillary. At least, so long as the level of linguistic communication and the extent of a speech universe are too narrowly confined, and do not justify what is referred to below as the **lexical component** of grammar.

When considering that AI man-machine dialog systems contain at best a few hundred words, it is no wonder if publications in the matter display but a practically empty index, when it comes to the notion of lexicon. Although things are different in the case of automated translation, in which each well-delimited domain requires a vocabulary of no more than a few thousand words -- for example, some six thousand for mathematical articles, according to a U.S.S.R. Academy of Science estimate.

At the same time, it should be borne in mind that, within the field of speech recognition, particular importance has been ascribed to the "lexical question;" namely in matters of word access through their acoustic and phonetic forms. Admittedly, words have up to now been limited in number within a given system, but laboratories do handle systems that contain more substantial numbers of them (thousands).

Questions of Terminology. Since the term **lexicon** is likely to convey several different things, the following meaning will be uniquely understood here:

> A lexicon is a set of terms; a set we shall call a vocabulary and understand as being endowed with various access and transformation mechanisms that are necessary to its use within the framework of a given grammar.

In this sense, **vocabulary** comes to mean **store** or **repertory** endowed with an appropriate **structure**. As for **dictionary**, it can then be used to mean a work that is released in public life, with the purpose of informing its users about the lexicon of one or of several languages. Of course, the meaning of **terms** of the vocabulary should be specified. Inasmuch, however, as utter precision is not needed on this point, the usual meaning of **term** as **dictionary entry** can temporarily be retained.

2 A FEW HISTORICAL LANDMARKS

Paradoxically, it is within contemporary linguistics that lexicology has been severely relegated to a place of less importance. For example, while initialling the advent of generativism, N. Chomsky's **Syntactic Structures** (1957) does not even once address the question.

But, whenever an in-depth and thorough study of language is undertaken, lexical problems cannot that easily be dismissed. These days, they are at the very center of major controversies within the generativist movement. Following works by Katz and Fodor (1963) and Katz and Postal (1964), the very notion of **lexical entry** gained some status in the ("standard") 1965 version of the generativist theory; viz. **Aspects of the Theory of Syntax.** The relationship this notion entertains to phonology became the subject of important contributions, particularly: Chomsky and Halle, Schane, Kiparsky (all published 1968), etc.

The question as to how to deal with morphology ignited a controversy between lexicalists and non-lexicalists, the former --Chomsky among them-- holding it that derivational morphology should be made a part rather of the lexicon than of grammar. Finally what is called "lexical decomposition" constitutes a major source of disagreement between, on the one hand, those favoring "semantically founded theories" (Chomsky's terminology) which include generative semantics and various forms of case grammar and, on the other hand, those behind an interpretative theory of semantics. This latter controversy can be considered to be summed up, as it happens, in the title of a 1970 article by Fodor: "Three Reasons for not Deriving 'Kill' from Cause to Die."

Unlike theoretical linguistics, which relegated lexicology to some purgatory, ethnology, psycho- and socio-linguistics, etc., have been experiencing a growing interest in this discipline.

Historically, a very long lexicological tradition is available to us. The earliest lexicons no doubt came into existence at the same time as writing became an important means of communication; maybe, asserts S. N. Kramer, in the earliest Sumerian schools, whose numerous tablets definitely point to a preoccupation both with grammar and with the drafting of lengthy wordlists. At some later point (3rd mil. BC) Sumerian masters undertook the compilation of what constitutes the oldest bilingual (Sumerian-Accadian) dictionary. As of the 1st century AD, Chinese lexicons containing some 8,000 signs, and later over 50,000 signs, are known to have been compiled.

The advent of printing, coupled with an urgent need for dictionaries in almost-modern European languages, conferred to lexicographic work yet another dimension.

Throughout the period extending from French Classicism to the 19th century scientific revolution --including therefore the Encyclopedic movement-- lexicological problems will remain ever present in grammarians' and philosophers' thinking. By the same token, there occurs a profuse diversification of the ways these problems are approached: philology, history, sociology, phonetics, psycho-linguistics, information theory, etc., shed so many different lights upon the word and the lexicon.

Lexical questions are also due to acquire growing importance in man-machine dialog systems designed for fifth-generation processing. Already existing achievements of this kind, in the area of automated speech recognition, deserve to be mentioned: Cohen and Mercer (1974) have integrated the phonology of American English to a lexical component, to be used within a speech-recognition system that is geared to entering texts in the computer (Jelinek IBM Project). Later achievements, such as BDLEX-0; first version of a lexical data-base to integrate the phonological and morphological aspects (Developed within the CNRS Speech Communication GRECO). And the various, more ambitious versions of this which are being readied.

Within these studies, the originality of the AI approach seems to reside, first of all, in the goal assigned to any man-machine dialog system; namely therefore, in its functionality with respect to a given application --an exigency which, in turn, requires that the problem be recognized in all of its dimensions (Cohen & Mercer, 1974; Haton, 1981; Perennou, 1980; Pierrel, 1981; De Mori, 1983). As is mentioned below, there already exist computerized lexicons involving vocabularies larger than AI ones (over 50,000 words for graphic or phonetico-graphic lexicons) but their entries do not really allow for the coverage of mechanisms that are necessary to the generating and understanding of natural language.

3 THE LEXICON AND THE MAIN COMPONENTS OF A GRAMMAR

What status is to be given to the lexical component of a grammar that may satisfy the needs of man-machine communication in natural languages?

The next sections attempt to supply some elements of an answer, ones that are inspired by contributions from modern linguistics.

Linguists consider that a grammar must entail at least three essential elements: syntax, phonology and semantics. Unlike phenomena pertaining to syntax and phonology, phenomena relating to semantics have only more recently been drafted into theories. This relatively new practice requires a level of "logical" representation whose very themes happen to be shared by A.I. --while, at the same time also, A.I. ascribes a lot of importance to a pragmatic component that is supposed, given a certain context, to attribute a meaning to a message.

To many linguists, and particularly to the generativists among them, the purpose of any grammar of a language is mainly to make explicit those mechanisms that underlie message production and comprehension. Clarification of such mechanisms, by means of "a set of rules which, in the case of this language, will express the correspondance between sound and meaning,"(Chomsky) meets the real purpose of grammar. Work leading to the emergence of "generative semantics" --especially, McCawley's (1967)-- has done a lot to render such a view prevalent.

Be it as it may, two remarks are in line here:

1) The lopsided weight given to speaking over writing and, consequently, the prime importance ascribed to phonology proceed from a view that is bound to be well received by many; especially, by automated speech-processing specialists. However, such favor should not go to hide the fact that many fundamental problems pertaining to natural language are independent of a choice between the oral and the written modes of communication. In this context, Lakoff's preference of "rules that connect logical forms and surface forms together" is noteworthy. In A.I., the written form is the one used in the case of many applications of the question-answer type. The relationship of the written mode to the oral one constitutes a specific problem of great interest, that lies at the very base of future applications in the area of oral text-entering into the computer.

2) The absence of any reference to "meaning" or "signification," or to any term of the kind, reveals that pragmatics --as well as any instrument of expressiveness, style, etc.-- is assigned a very low priority of concern. And yet, the difficulty encountered by theoreticians, whenever they try to draw a clear demarcation-line between syntax, logic and pragmatics, is notorious. To take one example, among many available, Fauconnier can be observed to conclude a study on polarized-element[1] distribution by a remark on how his study "proceeds from semantic and pragmatic principles that are much more general... [than those of a "hypothetical level of logic"]." This observation coincides somewhat with A.I. practices of considering pragmatics as essential.

It remains that the best way of co-articulating the various grammatical components is still a matter open to controversies. Some --e.g., Chomsky and Gross-- think that the discrepancies between the various positions adopted are not as fundamental as would seem, and that they are merely a question of terminology and notation. In truth, theories have evolved considerably in the past decade, with a view to smoothing out mutual objections. Chomsky's standard theory probably led the trend by evolving into his extended standard theory. It should be expected that

this excessive, almost fickle-looking, mobility of linguistic theories
will persist for some time to come: indeed, most theories render an
account of data that are at best incomplete, and they contradict
eachother. They are then reviewed to atone the contradictions... Such a
state of affairs prompted the following comment by Lakoff: "It should be
clear to all that building a complete and non-fragmentary natural logic is
no immediate practical goal... Serious studies of grammar are at a mere
beginning. Moreover, the study of intentional logic has only just
begun..."

As far as the presentation of lexical questions is concerned,
it seems possible to maintain a fairly neutral position towards them; the
most important point being to circumscribe appropriately the tasks
incumbent to the lexicon. Given the present state of the art, it is only
possible to suggest a few directions, whenever well-defined objectives are
perceived.

As a mere matter of convenience, it can be considered that the
lexicon intervenes in grammatical matters at four different fundamental
levels: 1) semantico-logical (SL), 2) syntactical (SY), 3) morphological
(MO) and 4) phonological (PH). Various socio-cultural, stylistic, etc.
specifications are here neglected. In such circumstances, a lexical entry
will assume the form X = (SL, SY, MO, PH).

In order to select one of the elements between parenthesis, it
should be feasible to use   **sl**: X ---> **sl**(X)   (or: SL = **sl**(X)), and
similarly: **sy**(x) = SY, **mo**(X) = MO, **ph**(X) = PH.

As an example, let us take the French verb PLIER (English: to
fold). We have   X = "plier" (for the sake of clarity, both a lexical
entry and the spelling identifying it are made to coincide). The
corresponding lexical entry could look like this:

   ph(X) = /pli-/, "pli-" (respectively,phonological and graphic
                              roots).
   mo(X) = first regular group French conjugation.
   sy(X) = verb, transitive ... .
   sl(X) = V(x,y), agent (x), object (y), T(x), R(y), I.
            T: human **or** (folding)machine **or** ... .
            R: (oblong object **or** flat object) **and** (malleable **or**
               articulated).
            I: idiosyncratic specifications of V.

At the semantico-logical level, there appear items of information that are
related to definitions within an appropriate logic: Lakoff's natural
logic, Tesnière's actantial logic, Fillmore's case logic, etc.

For a more concrete grasp of the above, and while remaining
within the neutral formalism we previously adopted, let us consider the

following instance: let   z   be an object verifying the property
feuille(z) [sheet(z)], and Marie about whom we want to make an assertion
such as: "Marie plie la feuille"[Mary is folding the sheet]. In order to
arrive at this statement while respecting both meaning and context, we
must:

        a) Substitute Marie to x, z to y; something we can do since
Marie can be an "agent" and is "human", while z being a sheet has to be
oblong or flat, and no doubt malleable (and within the lexical entry for
feuille, we should therefore find the information: [plausible,
(malleable)], a piece of semantico-pragmatic information). At this level,
therefore, we have:

        V(Marie, z) , feuille(z) (plausible: malleable(z)).   (1)
        V(Marie, feuille) (elimination of the variable z)   (2)

        b) Activate the syntactical rules, choose the present
indicative tense as the default option --and it is at this level that the
syntactic field of the elements used intervenes. From (1) it is possible
to extract both:

        Marie V(pres. indic., 3rd pers. sing.)   (3)
        Art(def., fem. sing.) feuille(sing.).

(Noting that the agent is made to function as subject, in compliance to a
well-known case grammar property).

        c) Execute the morpho-phonological processes, using both
fields within the lexicon or syntactic-word table. We should then,
spellingwise, obtain the statement sought:

        Marie plie la feuille.   (4)

        This example is obviously quite simplistic. However, it is
fairly representative of the tasks cropping up in computer-automated
generation of sentences -- for the more general problem of text generation
see Mc Keon (1985).

4 LOGICAL PROPERTIES OF LEXICON AT SEMANTICO-LOGICAL LEVEL

        To one and the same subjacent logical form, there can
correspond several surface forms. This is the general problem of
paraphrase, although sometimes such choice-alternatives are settled
through a lexical choice.

        The simplest of cases involves two synonymous words within one
given context (for example: "Marie est l'épouse de Jean / __ la femme de
Jean" [Mary is John's spouse / __ John's wife]. More complex cases crop up

modulo certain systematic grammatical transformations.

We shall examine two transformation classes leading to equivalent statements.

4.1 Lexical equivalence

Let us consider:

"il n'entend pas"	[he can't hear],	(1)
"il est sourd"	[he's deaf].	(2)

Obviously, because of some "lexical synonymy theorem", generating these two statements will pose the problem of having to choose between two equivalent logical forms. Such a theorem could be stated as follows:

$$(\forall x)\ (\hat{e}tre(x,sourd)\quad <==>\quad non\ (entendre(x))\qquad (3)$$
$$[(\forall x)(to\ be(x,deaf)\quad <==>\quad not\ (\ to\ hear(x))],$$

where **non** [**not**] is a logical negation. Subsequently the universal quantifier $\forall$ will be implicit.

Relation (3) can then be stated in an equivalent way by writing:

$$(non\ \hat{e}tre\ (x,sourd)\quad <==>\quad entendre(x))\qquad (4)$$
$$[(not\ to\ be\ (x,deaf)\quad <==>\quad to\ hear(x))],$$

which underlies realizations obtained through (1) and (2):

"il entend" /	"il n'est pas sourd"	(1a) / (2a)
[he can hear]	[he is not deaf]	

More generally, it is possible to define a relation between certain adjectives and certain verbs by:

$$\textbf{RAV}\ (A,\ V)\ \text{if and only if:}\qquad \hat{e}tre\ (x,A) <==> V(x);\qquad (5)$$

where   is either the assertion (not a symbol) or the negation (stated by **not**), A is a predicative adjective and V a verb.

In order for the relation to be asserted, it is both necessary and sufficient that we may equivalently say:

"x est A / x V";	[x is A]	(6)

being appropriately transcribed (cf. (1) and (2)). The same goes for (7a, b and c) as follows:

{ (a) "il est ennuyeux / il ennuie"		
{ [he is boring] [he bores]		
{ (b) "il est vivant / il vit"		(7)
{ [he is alive] [he lives]		

```
{  (c) "il est mort / il ne vit pas"
{        [he is dead]  [he does not live],
```

which asserts **RAV**(ennuyeux,ennuyer), **RAV**(vivant,vivre), **RAV**(mort, **non** vivre),... and as well **RAV**(sourd, **non** entendre), **RAV**(aveugle, **non** voir). On the other hand, a pair such as (mort, mourir) is not suitable (il est mort <=/=> il meurt).

Considering (7b and c), three relations --two of which implying the third one-- can be extracted:

      (i)   **RAV**   (vivant, vivre)
                [alive] [to live]

      (ii) **RAV**   (mort, **non** vivre)
                [dead]   [**not** to live]

      (iii) être(x, vivant) = **non** être(x, mort)
           [to be] [alive]   [**not** to be] [dead].

Introducing some convenient notation, let: A <===> -A' (or **OPPOS**(A,A')) <u>if and only if</u>: (être(x,A) = **non** être(x,A')).
We then have, for example:

     <u>if</u> **RAV**(A, V) & **RAV**(A', non V) <u>then</u> A = -A'.   (8)

The set of relation (i), (ii) and (iii) is therefore <u>redundant</u>.
Let now **RNV**(N, V) for pairs such as (life, to live), in the case of which statements of the

         "il a la vie"   /   "il vit"   (9)
 [he has (the gift of) life]   [he lives]

kind are equivalent (in general: avoir(x, N) <==> **V**(x). Also let **RNA**(N, A) for pairs such as (serene, serenity); statements of the

        "il a la sérénité"   /   "il est serein"   (10)
   [serenity is in his person]   [he is serene]

kind being equivalent (in general: avoir(x,N) = être(x,A)). Here again we have lexical redundancy. For example, with (vue, voir, voyant) [sight, to see, seeing], if we know that **RNV**(vue, voir)[sight, to see], **RNA**(vue, voyant)[sight, seeing], then we subsequently have **RAV**(voyant, voir)[seeing, to see]. As well, we are allowed the statements: **RNN**(vue, cécité)[sight,blindness](because: "il n'a pas la vue"[he does not have sight] / "il est atteint de cécité"[he is stricken with blindness], **RAN**(aveugle$_1$, aveugle$_2$) [blind$_1$, blind$_2$]("il est aveugle$_1$" / "c'est un aveugle$_2$" [he is blind$_1$][he is a blind$_2$ man]) -- subscripts specify different.

The example just developed above is as simple as it is incomplete. Many others are possible, some of which we will take up later when dealing with morphological transformations (such as 7(a) and (b)). We merely meant, here, to illustrate the notion that lexical entries can entertain mutual logical relations, including redundancy with respect both to vocabulary and to a total set of relations --while some of them can be predicted from or built on others. In the Combinatorial Dictionary of Russian, compiled to assist automated text understanding, Mel'chuk resorts to relations of this type (for an analysis of this work, see Magnus (1985)).

4.2 Lexical Decomposition

What we have just seen is only a part, actually, of the general question known under the name of "Lexical Decomposition".

Up to now, only two entries in the lexicon were set in mutual correspondance by a relation. Other more complex transformations, allowing us to derive a word from several others, have been studied by generativistic semanticists such as Katz, Fodor, McCawley, Lakov, Ross, Babcock, Shibatani, and yet others.

Within this perspective,the lexical insertion problem --i.e., how to insert lexical entries into statements-- is made more difficult insofar as word-equivalent expressions have to be found. A few examples are in order.

Using the verbs "faire"[to make, to cause] and "devenir"[to become] and the adjective "mort"[dead], we want to express the verb "tuer"[to kill]. In the following formulae we omit to write the universal quantifier and we underline those terms which are supposed to be primitive ones (elements of $V_{.}$).

tuer (x,y)	<===>	faire (x, devenir(y, mort)).

Similarly:

amener (x, y)	<===>	faire (x, venir(y))
[to bring]		[to cause] [to come],

publier (x, y)	<===>	faire (x, paraître(y))
[to bring out]		[to cause][to come out],

etc. These examples are adapted from Lakoff who quotes them while writing about the systematic relations existing between "bring" and "come", as studied by Fillmore and Binnik.

Furthermore, a number of entries using "to cause, to make" raise a number of questions that have an impact upon semantic representation within the lexicon.

Indeed, the second argument used in connexion with "to make" has to be either an activity (some doing), an object, etc., while the suggested decompositions line up this argument under the form of a predicate. Obviously, the latter should not be interpreted as a truth value ("Peter makes true (false)" does not use "to make" in the same sense but in the one of "to appear").

In order to tackle this type of difficulty, it is possible, to any predicate $R(\ )$, to make correspond the element $A.R(\ )$, fact, event, etc., resulting from the truth of this predicate.

Now, with the verbs "refroidir" [to cool down], "réchauffer" [to heat up, to warm up], "liquéfier" [to liquefy] and "fondre" [to melt, to thaw], with the adjectives "froid" [cold], "chaud" [hot, warm] and "liquide" [liquid], the nouns "oxygène" [oxygen] and "beurre" [butter], and the preposition "pour" [for, in order to], let us assume we have:

$$\text{refroidir}(x, y) \iff \underline{\text{faire}}(x, A. \underline{\text{devenir}}(y, \underline{\text{froid}})), \qquad (14)$$
$$\text{réchauffer}(x, y) \iff \underline{\text{faire}}(x, A.\underline{\text{devenir}}(y, \underline{\text{chaud}})), \qquad (15)$$
$$\text{liquéfier}(x, y) \iff \underline{\text{faire}}(x, A.\underline{\text{devenir}}(y, \underline{\text{liquide}})) \qquad (16)$$
$$\& \underline{\text{être}}(y, \underline{\text{gaz}}),$$
$$\text{fondre }(y) \iff \underline{\text{devenir}}(y, \underline{\text{liquide}}) \qquad (17)$$
$$\& \underline{\text{être}} (y, \underline{\text{solide}}),$$

We consider the abstract statement:

$$\text{pour }(\underline{\text{faire}}(\text{Pierre}, A.\underline{\text{devenir}}(\text{l'oxygène}, \underline{\text{froid}})), \qquad (18)$$
$$A.\underline{\text{faire}}(\text{Pierre}, A.\underline{\text{devenir}}(\text{l'oxygène}, \underline{\text{liquide}}))),$$

where: pour $(R, A.S)$ means: condition R performed in order to result in the consequence A.S.

(14) and (16) can be used once (y/l'oxygène) is substituted in:

$$\text{pour }(\text{refroidir (Pierre, l'oxygène)},$$
$$A.\text{liquéfier (Pierre, l'oxygène)})$$

then:

"Pierre refroidit l'oxygène"
"pour   "
"Pierre liquéfier l'oxygène"

and finally:

"Pierre refroidit l'oxygène pour le liquéfier".

(The immediate introduction of an infinitive in connexion with A is noteworthy).

If we now consider a similar statement at the abstract level:

$$\underline{\text{pour}} \ (\underline{\text{faire}} \ (\text{Pierre}, A.\underline{\text{devenir}} \ (\text{le beurre}, \underline{\text{chaud}}) \qquad (19)$$
$$A.\underline{\text{faire}} \ (\text{Pierre}, A.\underline{\text{devenir}} \ (\text{le beurre}, \underline{\text{liquide}})),$$

we successively obtain:

$$\underline{\text{pour}} \ (\text{réchauffer (Pierre, le beurre)},$$
$$\underline{\text{faire}} \ (\text{Pierre}, \text{fondre (le beurre)})).$$

Then ((pre-)supposing that the butter in question is in the solid state to start with):

> "Pierre réchauffe le beurre"
> "pour   "
> "Pierre faire fondre le beurre"

and finally:

> "Pierre réchauffe le beurre pour le faire fondre"
> [Pierre warms up the butter to cause it to melt].

Lexical availability is not the same in both examples, and this prohibits exactly transposable surface formulations of the statements.

4.3 Semantico-Logical Features

Let us first briefly go over the more widely used characterizations achieved by means of features. Many of these features are by nature semantic, although they bring about clear syntactic implications. For example, the features [+animate][+feminine], which in French characterize the lexical entry "jument"[mare], will carry both of the following implications: (i) the mare is a female, (ii) this confers the feminine gender upon the nominal syntagma it regulates (e.g., la jument grise [la = the (f.), grise = gray (feminine counterpart of masculine gris)]. Whereas (i) definitely corresponds to a semantic characterization, (ii) is a syntactic property.

For a discussion of the various feature types, cf. Chomsky (1965). We will make a note, here, to the effect that these features refer to general properties (ones relative to human societies). These properties are structured, and therefore entail redundancies. For example: [+human] ===> [+animate], so much so that, whenever [+human] is considered, additional specification of the feature [+animate] becomes superfluous.

With respect to a predicative statement, these features allow us to set up types both of predicates ([-transitive] relates to the number of arguments a verb has), and of predicative arguments (For instance, [+animate subject] confers a type upon the first predicative argument).

On the whole, these features have a relatively formal character to them, since they control the formal acceptability of a statement; namely, as regards the adequacy of types of variables.

4.4 Lexical Presuppositions

Presuppositions can, as well, be considered logical specifications that are, in some cases, affixed to lexical entries. Generally speaking, these specification problems are extremely delicate ones. For a discussion of this, cf. Chomsky, Lakoff, Lyons.

An example borrowed from Lakoff:

"Sam realizes that Irv is a Martian".

Here, "Irv is a Martian" is being presupposed. In general, "to realize" presupposes its object to be true.

Previously encountered examples, such as (16) and (17) for instance, display conditions which actually are presuppositions; namely:

liquéfier (x, y)$\Longleftrightarrow$ faire (x, A.<u>devenir</u> (y, <u>liquide</u>))   (16c)
                     presupposition: <u>être</u> (y, <u>gaz</u>)
fondre (x, y) $\Longleftrightarrow$ devenir (y, <u>liquide</u>)   (17c)
                     présupposition: <u>être</u> (y, <u>solide</u>).

It is clear that understanding a natural language entails taking into account the complex notions involved in presupposing; particularly those which result from lexical items. Here again, any specific application of A.I. (even a complex one) allows us to tackle these questions appropriately.

4.5 <u>Semantic</u> <u>Structure</u> <u>of</u> <u>the</u> <u>lexicon</u>

One theoretical position, capable of taking advantage of the above (call it "Position$_1$" or "Primitive Natural Vocabulary Position"), could look like this:

(i) at a **deeper (logical)** level, statements make use exclusively of a **"primitive natural" vocabulary V.**,

(ii) if one word, in **V.** is such that any abstract statement using it can be paraphrased through another statement not using it, then this word is redundant. Whenever **V.** does not contain any such redundant word, it is considered minimal —although this is not absolutely necessary.

(iii) the set **V.** is a subset of the overall vocabulary set **V**.

The lexical theory developed by Wierzbicka (1972) illustrates this position —See also Fabb (1985) for an analysis of this theory.

A theoretical position opposed to that (call it "Position$_2$" or "primitive logic vocabulary position") could be the one in which (iii) is replaced by:

(iv) the linguistic vocabulary sets **V** and **V.** do not intersect, or less radically stated: $V \not\supset V.$.

In IA, however, many works proceed from Position$_2$ (For example, Schank on conceptual dependency (1975), Wilks on semantic primitives (1977)).

Whatever position is adopted, the lexical entry of an element

of **V** not belonging to **V.** will include a formula that is expressed
exclusively in terms of **V.** elements; e.g., (14) above for the entry
"refroidir".

To many linguists, the question still remains wide open, for
there does not yet exist a semantic theory making it possible to approach
natural language. From the examples just dealt with, a glimpse can be
caught of the immense complexity of the problem. Merely to illustrate
this, we can look at the example of the relations concerning very specific
uses of words.

Although, to be sure, within the frame of computer
applications, the number of units can be greatly reduced, and the number
of their respective uses as well. This points to a new approach to lexical
redundancy and to the logical relationships that can be established among
them.

Furthermore, it should be noted that previously observed
redundancies --concerning features of case structures and relations-- can
be taken advantage of in order to make lexical entries simpler. Besides
requiring the availability of a lexical store, this also assumes the
availability of a "lexical semantic grammar".

5 MORPHONOLOGICAL TRANSFORMATIONS AND LEXICAL RELATIONS

Many words are formed upon other words by using various
affixes. When thus derived, a word has a meaning and a syntax that are
somewhat predictable from the components involved in its synthesis.

For example, the French word "indéfini", constructed both on
the prefix "in-" and the adjective "défini" [defined], has a meaning that
can be predicted from the one of "défini"; namely, "non défini". At the
same time, within the domain of syntax, it is well-known that "in-" allows
the forming of predicative adjectives from other predicative adjectives.

Yet, the most current acceptation of "indéfini" is the
contrary of one of the meanings of "net" [clearcut]; a usage that is not
exactly foreseeable from prefixing "défini" with "in-". Although less
current, this perfectly predictable meaning of "indéfini" still does
coexist with the much more usual acceptation.[4]

The above is a fairly widespread occurrence (in French):
compound terms often have a linguistic content that is partially or even
totally idiosyncratic and, therefore, dictionaries should provide suitable
entries for them.

However, it should be possible to form words --not currently
in use-- that could be exclusively interpreted from their components. For

example, "reredéfaire" (re-re-dé-faire) [to re-re-un-do] could have but
only one meaning, and certainly no dictionary is about to include terms of
this type within its repertory. The same could be said of an English word
such as "neo-non-con-form-ist", the meaning of which can clearly be
deduced from that of "conform" (or, better even, from that of
"conformist").

Thus, it becomes clear that achieving systems, capable of
allowing a man-machine dialog in natural language, involves tackling the
problems of locating the relations and transformations, alluded to above,
within the understanding and generating process sought --both questions of
productivity and of various irregularities, to which we return later,
should meanwhile still be taken into account.

5.1 General Principles of Morphological Transformations

Essentially, linguists make a distinction between three types
of morphological processes: composition, derivation and flexion (Examples
of detailed studies of them can be found in Nyrop (1936), Dubois (1962),
Guibert (1972), in the introduction of Le Grand Larousse, 7 vol., in Dell
(1970), Catach (1981), etc. And in English, in Chomsky, in both Aronoff
(1976) and Strauss (1982) on nominalization and lexicalism).

a) **Composition** consists in linking lexical elements together
(most often in making a pair) to form nouns or adjectives (e.g.,
"garde-barrière"[(railroad level-crossing) gate-keeper], "portemanteau"
[coat-hanger], trait d'union" [hyphen], "musicophile" [music lover].
Graphic transliteration of the composition process is not consistent:
either the welding into one unit or the use of a hyphen is resorted to,
whenever composition is explicitly marked. However, a good many instances
of composition simply go unmarked --e.g., "trait d'union" [hyphen].

One of the combined terms can be of foreign origin --e.g.,
from Greek as in "musicophile", or from Latin as in "centrifuge".

Word formation mechanisms are several and various, often
escaping the reach of ordinary syntactic rules. Thus "by heart" is
ill-formed in that, usually, "heart" in the singular requires an article
(cf. Weinreich(1966)) --and similar observations could be made from French
compound words; e.g., "timbre poste" [post office stamp].

The important thing with these compounds is that they
sometimes can be analysed into their components by means of certain types
of paraphrases. An example: "musicophile" can be analyzed by means of "qui
est l'ami de la musique" [(one) who is a friend of music] or "qui aime la
musique" [(one) who loves music]. Such a paraphrase can be symbolically

written: P(x, y) with x = musique, y = aime [loves]. Thus:

    "musicophile" <==> P(musique, aime)

    "xenophobe"   <==> P(étranger, déteste) [stranger, detests]

    "garde-barrière" <==> P(barrière, garde) [gate, watches on]

Such analytic processes should, of course, be perfected by means of idiosyncratic specifications.

When considering the relations dealt with above, the morphophonological form of a compound word can be predicted from that of its components. Basically, it is a chain with morpho-phonological variants at both ends.

In general, for a compound word Z belonging to a syntactic class S, and obtained from both X belonging to U and Y belonging to V, the following notation is adopted:

$$[Z]_S = [[X]_U + [Y]_V]_S . \tag{1}$$

Thus, for "garde-barrière", we have:

$$[[gard\partial \ ]_V + [barj\varepsilon r \ ]N]_N \ ,$$

where V is a verb and N a noun (an oral phonological transcription being used).

Here, since gender as well as number marks are located on internal boundaries, further problems of flexional morphology crop up. Thus "monsieur" [sir] becomes "messieurs" [sirs]. These questions of inner agreements, within French compound words, remain delicates ones; often resting upon arbitrary considerations having sometimes no impact whatsoever on pronounciation. Thus "garde-barrière" [gate-keeper] and "gardes-barrières" [gate-keepers] have the same pronounciation: [gardbarjɛr] (A fairly complete examination of these problems in French can be found in Catch).

b) Derivation by prefixing is achieved by choosing a prefix and a lexical entry. The result is a new lexical entry belonging to the same syntactic category. On their own, prefixes are not lexical entries; they only morphophonologically materialize lexical transformations. Whenever a prefix u is combined with a lexical entry X that belongs to a category S, the result Y also belongs to S and is written:

$$[Y]_S = [U[X]_S]_S . \tag{2}$$

For example, with $[faire]_V = [X]_S$ and "dé-" = u, we get:

$$[défaire]_V = [dé[faire]_V]_V . \tag{3a}$$

In turn, with "re", we also get:

$$[red\acute{e}faire]_V = [re[d\acute{e}faire]_V]_V \qquad (3b)$$
$$= [re[d\acute{e}[faire]_V]_V]_V, \text{ etc.}$$

It should be noted that, in the case of derivation, the two elements u and X do not figure at equivalent notational levels, as opposed to what happens with composition.

In the phonological domain, this allows for a control of some phonological rules, tonic stressing in English, depending on the kind of morphological boundaries involved (on this problem, see Chomsky and Halle(1968)). We will merely illustrate, here, the question of this dependence at different types of boundaries by the example of nasals --more specifically by the way the prefix "in-" can be dealt with. In the morphophonological domain, the following rules can be evoked (for the sake of clarity, phonemes and not features are used):

in ---> in / ___ [V   (V: vowels),   (a)

   ---> $\tilde{\varepsilon}$ / ___ [C   (C: consonants other than   (b)
                                 nasals or liquids)

   ---> iK / ___ [K   (K: liquids or nasals).   (c)

A few examples:

for (4a):   "inobservé" (/inɔbsɛrve/, in phonological notation)
            [unobserved]
for (4b):   "incorrect" (/ɛ̃kɔrɛkt/),
for (4c):   "illégal" (/illegal/), "immatériel" (/immaterjɛl/),
            "inné" (/inne/),"irrésolu" (/irrezoly/).
            [innate]   [irresolute]

Rules (4) can be applied only within the context ___[;i.e., at the boundary of a prefix. This prohibits an erroneous application of rewriting procedures in (4) to instances such as, for example, "fin limier"[fine sleuthhound] ([fin]$_A$ # [limje]$_N$), since here "in-" is found within the context ___]$_A$ and not ___[.

However, not all dictionary entries comply with (4), as examples like "innocuité" [innocuousness], "inlassable" [indefatigable], "inracontable" [unrelatable (that cannot be told)], etc., demonstrate. And other derivations of the same type, that cannot either be found in a dictionary, are often observed. Therefore, inasmuch as a word --e.g., "im̲matériel" instead of "*in̲matériel"-- is present within the lexicon, it should be possible to specify it by means of [-rule (4)]. If, however, a word does not figure in the lexicon, how are we to deal with a derivation contradicting (4)? This is the most difficult part of the problem --See Tranel(1981).

In the semantico-logical domain, it is possible to associate specific relations to prefixes. For example, if the prefix "in-" is considered within one of its functions --namely, negation-- it corresponds to the relation **OPPOS** --defined in 3., (8), above. From this point of view, it can be seen that:

OPPOS(correct, incorrect)   or: correct <===> - incorrect.

Calling T(in-, X) the transformation obtained by applying the prefix "in-" to X, and letting Y = T(in-, X):

$$\{ \quad \mathbf{sl}(Y) \quad \Longleftrightarrow \quad -\mathbf{sl}(X) \tag{5}$$
$$\{ \quad [\mathbf{mopho}(Y)]_A \quad = \quad [in[k\mathfrak{d}r\varepsilon kt]_A]_A,$$

where mopho is the phonological form with its marks of morphological transformations (We would therefore have: $\mathbf{sy}(-Y) = A$, $\mathbf{mo}(Y) = \mathbf{mo}(X)$), $\mathbf{pho}(Y) = /\tilde{\varepsilon}k\mathfrak{d}r\varepsilon kt/$.

c) Derivation by suffixing is achieved by choosing a lexical entry and a suffix. The result is a new lexical entry, the syntactic category and the morphology of which are entirely determined by the suffix. In general, therefore, they will differ from those of the initial word.

The notation adopted is similar to the one used with prefixes. Therefore, taking a lexical entry X of the E-class and a suffix s that is a transformer into the F-class, a term Y of the F-class is obtained , and we can write:

$$[Y]_F \quad = \quad [[X]_E \, s]_F \, . \tag{6}$$

For a given transformation by prefixing, not only is F steadily determined, but also is E. To give a more concrete idea of this suffixing, a few typical instances are supplied below, presented graphically:

$$[[X]_A \, is]_V \qquad \text{example: "fertile"} \longrightarrow \text{"fertiliser"} \tag{7}$$
$$[\text{to fertilize}]$$

(The French infinitive ending -er is added to reconstitute the usual verb form, but the radix of the obtained verb would here be "fertilis").

$$[[X]_V \, tion]_N \qquad \text{example: "absorber"} \longrightarrow \text{"absorption"} \tag{8}$$

(same remark as previously, concerning the infinitive).

$$[[X]_V \, age]_N \qquad \text{example: "assembler"} \longrightarrow \text{"assemblage"}. \tag{9}$$

$$[[X]_V \, able]_A \qquad \text{example: "manger"} \longrightarrow \text{"mangeable"}. \tag{10}$$
$$[\text{to eat}] \qquad [\text{edible}]$$

To all these forms there correspond typical paraphrases that determine

relations between the initial and the resulting words. For example:
with

   FD (X,Y) if and only if: $Y(u,v) <===> faire(u, A.devenir(v,X))$,
letting

   X = "imperméable"

(7) yields

   "imperméabiliser"(u,v) <===> faire(u,A.devenir(v,imperméable)).

This kind of relation does not necessary involving suffixing in "is", as
examples (14), (15) and (16) in 4 do show.

   d) Flexional Morphology also involves suffixing. However, it
is particular in that, on the one hand, it is systematic and, on the other
hand, it ends word formation; i.e., no additional flexional suffix can be
placed beyond it on the same word, although it does not preclude further
prefixing of flexions.

   The semantic value of a flexion consists in actualizing
linguistic variables such as either gender and number of nouns and
adjectives (in French, gender is most often a priori regulated by nouns)
or tense and person of verbs.

   As can be observed on the following examples, verb-ending
irregularities result from phonological forms being affected, not only by
the values taken by linguistic variables, but also by the lexical entry
involved:

       le roi / les rois   }
       [the king]   } nouns
                                  } sing./ pl.
       le cheval / les chevaux }
       [the horse]   }

       je chante / ils chantent }
       [I'm singing]   }
                                  }
       je sais / ils savent   } verbs in pres. indic.
       [I know]   } 1st pers. sing./ 3rd pers. pl.
                                  }
       je vais / ils vont
       [I'm going]

   It follows that the lexicon must, for each entry incurring
flexion, supply an indication as to either its conjugation type (for
verbs) or its gender and number mark-type --unless, whenever it is the
case, an entry belongs to the most frequent type, selected as the
by-default type.

   Another type of irregularities with verbs, though an
infrequent one, shows up in the case verbs that are defective tensewise
and/or personwise.

Unless such defectivity can be semantically predicted, it is necessary to have it figure in the corresponding entry.

The case of "pleuvoir"[to rain], which can include the feature [-animate subject] prohibits "je pleux"[I am raining, I rain]. This is the case of a verb that should not be marked [+defect] in the lexicon. On the other hand, the defectivity, tensewise, of "clore"[to close] cannot be foreseen and should, therefore, be indicated in the lexicon.

The usual notation employed for flexional suffixes goes as follows:

let d be the suffix attached to the radix $[X]_E$, the result is written $[X + d]_E$. A few examples:

(in English) $[dog + s]_N$, $[govern + ed]_V$,
(in French) $[chien + s]_N$, $[gouvern + é]_V$.

The inflected unit may happen to be a complex one, as in:

$[nation]_N$ ---> $[[nation]_N al]_A$ ---> $[[[nation]_N al]_A is]_V$

---> $[dé [[[nation]_N al]_A is]_V]$

---> $[dé [[[nation]_N al]_A is + eront]_V]$
(dénationaliseront)
[will denationalize, 3rd pers.pl., indic. fut.]

It is possible here to permute the order between flexion and prefixation. The latter, however, cannot occur while generating the verb.

5.2 Morphological Irregularities

Morphological irregularities (already alluded to; see above: 2.2., bottom paragr.) can be neither phonological nor syntactic nor semantic ones. Furthermore, these transformations may, in an unforeseeable manner, happen to be unacceptable. A few examples:

(i) phonological irregularities, written:

$[in[X]_A]_A$ irréel / inracontable ,
                      [unreal] [unrelatable]

(ii) syntactic irregularities (cf. Dell), written:

$[[X]A]_V$ sèche   ---> sécher (1st group conjug.)
                   [dry,f.]   [to dry]

                   sale   ---> salir (2nd group conjug.)
                   [dirty]   [to soil]

$[[X]_V oir(+e)]_N$ arroser ---> arrosoir
                   [to water]   [watering-can]

                   passer ---> passoire

$$[a[X]_A]_V$$

	[to filter]	[strainer]
	proche --->	approcher
	[close]	[to come closer]
	grave --->	aggraver ;
		[to worsen]

noting that "approcher" can be [-reflexive,+intransitive], but "aggraver" cannot ("ça approche / ça s'aggrave / *ça aggrave").[2]

(iii) Semantic irregularities: almost all of the derived words, making it to standard usage, acquire one or more special derived meanings that are more or less remote from the meaning obtained directly by transforming. One example:

$$[re[X]_V]_V$$

	faire --->	refaire (faire de nouveau
	[to do]	ou bien duper)
		["to do again", but also "to fool"]

(iv) Irregularity within production:

(French examples)

$[[X]_V \, eur]_N$ *docter   --->   docteur

$[in[X]_A]_A$ rapide   --->   *inrapide (lent)
              [rapid]   [slow]

(English examples)

$[[X]_V \, or]_N$ to *doct   --->   doctor

$[[X]_A \, er]_A$ right   --->   *righter (more right)

(v) Suppletion:

$[[X]_A \, er]_A$ good ---> *gooder (better)

In English "better" being the suppletive form of *gooder". Examples of this type abound in the third-group conjugation of French verbs. Thus, v- and i- are suppletive radices of "aller"[to go].

Irregularities (ii), (iii) and (iv) are the ones raising the greatest difficulties, whenever we set out to make of morphology a part of syntax; for we are led to perform transformations which are actually prohibited within the scope of syntactic structure.

Thus, upon concluding his analysis of the nominalization process, Chomsky leaves derivational morphology outside of syntax. In turn, it is incumbent upon the latter to supply all the necessary alternative syntactic forms, so as to be able to cover such cases as:

"j'exige votre démission / ___que vous démissionniez".
[I demand your resignation]   [that you resign]

Others have gone as far as suggesting that this lexicalist position be further strengthened by expelling even flexional morphology from syntax; founding their contention upon the existence of idiosyncrasies such as: "woods" (forest) # "wood + s" (similarly in French, "les bois" is not necessarily the plural of "le bois") -- see Halle (1973)[]. However, this position might be somewhat extreme, if only because there are actually few instances of type (ii) and type (iv) flexional irregularities.

5.3 Transformational Recurrence Within Derivational Production

Some morphological transformations can be applied again and again, an unlimited number of times, upon one and the same word.

For example:
"il fait, il défait, il refait, il redéfait, il rerefait,..."
[he does, he undoes, he redoes, he reundoes, he re-redoes,...]

shows that $[re[X]_V]_V$ has no limit on the number of its reiterated applications $([re[re[...[X]_V...]_V]_V]_V)$.

Instead of figuring as individual terms in a string, other transformations can be regrouped into complex transformations having a global effect, and whose application can be reiterated an unlimited number of times. For instance:

$$[[[X]_V \text{ able}]_A \text{ is}]_V = [[X]_A \text{ abilis}]_A ,$$

where able$]_A$ is ---> abilis. This yields, for example:

"flot-abilis-abilis........abiliser"
[float(ing)................to (en)able = to make buoyant]

In practice, only a fractional use is made of this reiterative applicability of some transformations. It does show, however, that words —as much as phrases— have an infinite synthetic potential.

Consequently, attempting to store all possible words is out of the question; instead, a **grammar of words** is **necessary,** in order to derive complex words from already stored lexical entries.

It should be noted that the notion "creative ability of a language", raised by Chomsky, does extend to its lexicon; indeed, any individual who can speak, for example French, is fully able to understand words he/she has never heard before ("reflotabiliser" <==> "rendre de nouveau possible de flotter"[to make buoyant again], was probably never uttered in the presence of a great majority of French speakers, and yet all of them can spontaneously understand it).

This points to the relevance of a distinction to be made

between **actual words** (validated by their presence in dictionaries) and **potential words** (See example above). In this matter, it is urgent to realize that the line to be drawn between these two categories of words is a very fine one, indeed. An appropriate attitude, in this respect, might consist in storing only those derived words that have already acquired one or several current meanings. On this point, dictionaries display largely inconsistent attitudes, as is shown in this example from Dell: "indécollable"[that cannot be unglued] is an entry in Le Petit Robert dictionary of the French language, but "indéroulable"[that cannot be unreeled] is not. Yet, neither one of these two words has any special current meaning. The only justification this inconsistency can be granted is that it reflects upon how frequently a word is used, although this kind of information could be more economically released.

It is well known that the generative aspect of grammar has to contend with the ambiguities of certain surface forms ("La belle ferme le voile"[meaning either "The beautiful one draws the veil" or "The beautiful farm-house veils it (from sight)"] can be both understood and generated in two different ways, according to whether "ferme" (resp. voile) is N(resp.V) or is V(resp.N)). The same applies also to derived surface forms (cf. Dell: "piqueter" can mean either "to stake out" --i.e., when it results from $[[piquet[stake]]_N]_V$-- or "to dot" --from $[[piqu[to sting]]_V et]_N)$.

5.4 Nature of the Lexical Entry

Taking into account morphological transformations requires that the notion of lexical entry be accurately defined.

As is the case in Chomsky's work, **lexical item** can refer to the minimum element conveying one meaning, while displaying a unique morphosyntactic characterization.

In that case, to one and the same phonological form can correspond several lexical items, which can be regrouped into one vocabulary unit. Thus, for example, to the unit "sensible" will correspond two different items "$sensible_1$" and "$sensible_2$" ("qui peut être senti"[that can be felt] and "qui peut sentir"[that can feel = sensitive]), but only "sensible2" can yield the derivation "sensibilité"[sensibility (normal ability to feel) or sensitivity (above normal to excessive ability to feel)] ($<==>$ $[[sensible_2]_A ité]_N)^3$. The following examples, taken from Dell, illustrates this:

* "la sensibilité des variations de température",
  [sensible temperature variations]

"la sensibilité de cet appareil aux moindres
variations de température".
[the sensitivity of this equipment to the
smallest of temperature variations]

Thus it can be seen that the unit incurring derivational
morphological as well as synthetic constraints is none other than the
lexical item.

The regrouping of items into vocabulary units is a very
complex matter of affinity upon which both identity of phonological form
(cf., however, the question of flexional suppletion) and syntactic and
semantic kinship come to bear.

In a lexicon geared to assist automated understanding of
natural language, such questions are paramount. Indeed, it is impossible
to achieve a suitable analysis of speech, if the whole set of lexical
items, relevant to a specific application and pertaining to the same
vocabulary unit, is not at every moment available.

6 THE LEXICON AND PHONOLOGY

The function of the phonological component of a grammar is to
make explicit the relations that exist between, on the one hand, the
surface structures issued from the works of the syntactic component and,
on the other hand , the phonetic structures describing what is pronounced.

Within a generativistic perspective, a surface structure
displays a morphemic sequence that is endowed with a labeled parenthetic
structure translating an organic construction into words and syntagmas. A
concrete example of this can be:

$$[[["Jean"]_{Np}]_{NS}[[["jouer"]_V + t + sg \qquad (1)$$
$$+ 3^e \, p.]_V[["habile]_{Adj} \ "ment"]_{Adv}]_{VS}$$

$$[[[["John"]_{Np}]_{NS}[[["play"]_V + tense + sing.$$
$$+ 3rd \, pers.]_V[["clever"]_{Adj} \ "-ly"]_{Adv}]_{VS}]$$

where morphemes are referred to in a graphic form, Np (proper noun), V
(verb), Adj (adjective), Adv (adverb) are syntactic classes, NS (nominal
syntagma), VS (verbal syntagma) and S (phrase) are syntagmatic classes.

Within such structures, words show up as maximal
sub-structures that are delimited by pairs of parentheses tagged as
syntactic classes. Thus $["habile]_{Adj}["clever"]$, is not a word since it is
not maximal; it is included within $[["habile"]_{Adj} \ "ment"]_{Adv}$ which is a
word. Similarly, $[["jouer"]_V + t + sg + 3^e \, p]_V$ is, indeed, a word. But
$["jouer"]_V$ --not being maximal-- is not a word.

To structure (1) there corresponds a phonetic structure which --as a first approximation-- is to be selected within:

[zãzu(:)(ʔ){a,ɑ}bil({ø,ə,œ})mã(:)]

where () express the optional character and {} a selection --while, in the present example, t is the present of the indicative.

Given the above, the contribution made by the lexicon to the conversion of surface structures into phonetic structures is crucial, since in the end it is from the lexicon that both the phonological forms of words and various conditioning factors affecting the phonological-component rules are issued.

6.1 Various **Types** of **Phonological Rules**
Their **Impact On** the **Lexicon**

Various types of phonological rules can be brought out (see , for example Hooper(1976)):

a) Phonetically conditioned rules, spelt out solely in terms of phonological features --thoroughly excluding syntactic marks or even boundaries. For instance, a rule making use of both voicing and consonantic features, respectively [±voi] and [±cons]:

[+cons, +voc] --> [+cons, + voc, +αvoi] / [+cons, -voc, +αvoi]___   (2)
(where α∈{+,-}).

Such a rule makes it possible to foresee the variant of a liquid occurring behind a strong consonant (marked -voc). Thus, [ɹ̥] behind [t] in "trois"[three] drops its vocalic character to become unvoiced (-voi).

At the lexical level, such rules express a redundancy that can be put to use when cancelling out useless terms within the underlying phonological form. This way, it becomes possible to consider only one /ɾ / and one / ʎ / for the purpose of lexical forms.

b) Morpho-phonemic rules entail morphological, syntactic and lexical conditioning occurrences --e.g., 2.3.1.(4) above. Rules dealing with nasalization [±nas] in French belong to the same type, as can be seen from the way Schane(1968) spells them out. Example:

(3) NASALIZATION: V   --> [+nas] / ____ [+nas]{#, C} ,
(4) NASAL DELETION: [C, +nas] --> ø / [V, +nas]____ ,

where V = vowel, C = consonant, ø = empty segment, # = word-end mark and with the meta-rule: Apply (3) before applying (4).

It becomes obvious how [bɔnami] is derived from /bɔn#ami/ ("bon ami"[i.e., good friend, boyfriend]) and [bõtami] from /bɔn#tami/

("bon tamis"[good sieve]). Or again *[ɔkynami] can be obtained from /
ɔkyn#ami/ ("aucun ami"[no friend whatsoever]) instead of [ɔkɛ̃nami]. One
way or another the lexical entry for "aucun"[none] will have to include a
specific prohibition of (3) and (4). Let us write it [-(3), -(4)].
Implicitly (3) and (4) will be respectively subjected to the following
additional constraints: "if not -(3)" and "if not -(4)".

Thus, not only will the lexicon have to supply phonological
representations, it will also have to supplement each of these with
specific indications likely to call in or to block out certain rules.

c) Via-rules (cf. Hooper (1976)) are actually formal links
between two related lexical entries that cannot, however, be easily
derived one from the other by means of natural and productive procedures.
Thus, for example, it should be useful to maintain some kind of tie
between "empereur"[emperor] and "impératrice"[imperatrix], as would be
done   between   "instituteur"[primary-school   male   teacher]   and
"institutrice"[____ female teacher]. But, whereas in the latter case
there exists a productive morpho-phonemic transformation linking the two
words together, in the former case the initial parts of the two words
alternate with eachother in a way that is not regularly found elsewhere.
Therefore, in the former case, two different lexical entries must be set
up, while some link between them must be there to report their kinship.
The latter case, on the other hand, should adequately be covered by one
single entry, so long as the regular alternation (of gender: -eur/-ice) is
specified.

6.2 Underlying Representations

In a general way, the question of selecting the underlying
form lies in between to opposite exigencies: abstraction and 'realism' (or
'naturalness').

The abstraction principle (cf. Chomsky and Halle, for example)
stipulates that the phonetic variations of a word can be covered by one
single representation or form, whenever phonological rules making it
possible to derive such variations from the unique form are actually there
to allow it.

Thus for example, in French, it is permissible to gather the
various   pronounciations   of   "lundi"[monday]   under   one   single
representation. With /lœ̃ di/, while taking into account both the confusion
that might arise around (œ̃ /ɛ̃) and the either partial or total
pre-consonantic kinds of denasalization, it is possible to foresee the
various pronounciations: [lœ̃ di], [lɛ̃ di], [lœndi], ...

On the other hand, it seems hardly natural or very uneconomical to attempt a unification of the various realizations of the verb "aller" (je vais[I'm going], nous allons[we are going], qu'il aille[let him go], nous irons[we'll go]) --and similarly, of its English counterpart "to go" (I go, I went). The lack of economy, in such attempts, is owed to the necessity of introducing a large number of ad hoc rules. There exist a great number of cases that lie in between two extremes, and the solutions resorted to are, themselves, intermediate ones lying between two extremes as well.

One of these solutions, which could be called the extensional one (extensional form in set theory), consists in having a lexical entry for each form assumed by a lexical item, whether this form is derived or inflected. Such a radical solution may appear to solve all problems of morphological irregularities; however, it is not an economical one from the point of view of storage. And moreover, it requires that all relations --both derivational and flexional ties-- between words be made explicit. Arguments in favor of such solutions have been developed by Vennemann (1974), Thompson (1974).

The opposite tendency, Chomsky's and Halle's (1968), consists in having one single lexical entry for different words which are tied together by either a flexional or a derivational relation. This conforms to an economical direction; at leeast, so long as the description of either derivation or flexion processes does not become too complex, and neither do phonological rules.

The ideal compromise between these two types of solutions remains difficult to achieve, and whichever suggestion is put forward will be open to criticism. Meanwhile, for a well-specified application, certain theoretical positions can already be rejected.

CONCLUSION

Various questions brought up in the present exposé supply a number of pre-requisites to devising lexical components:

- Lexical items are defined with respect to at least four different types of domains: semantico-logical, syntactic, morphological (flexion and derivation) and phonological.

- Lexical items are non-ambiguous and regrouped into classes called vocables (words).

- Some lexical items are primitive. The other items must receive a semantico-logical definition making use of primitive elements.

- Some lexical items are simple, others --obtained by either derivation or composition-- are complex.

     - Some words are actually validated, others are only potentially achievable through composition and/or derivation --others still being impossible to achieve through composition and/or derivation.

     - Constructions can be either regular or idiosyncratic, or even can deviate (cf. Dell: idiosyncratic applies to derived words whose characteristics are unforeseeable. For example, in French, the gender of derived words with the "-oir(e)" ending cannot be foreseen. Deviant words are those whose meaning deviates from the one a transformation would normally confer upon it).

     - Morpho-phonemic transformations can be either regular or irregular (whence the recourse to specific features).

     - Phonological forms can be either simple or polymorphic.

     The above various influences underpin the inner organization of a lexical component. But there are yet other imperatives that must also be taken into account; namely, those dealing with access to lexical information.

     A number of works in psycho-linguistics or natural phonology offer models in which phonological units of lexical access basically are concrete phonemes (as opposed to the abstract units in Chomsky's and Halle's theory). Also, results obtained by Klatt (1981) --who uses statistical analysis of pronounciation errors-- point in the same direction.

     Meanwhile, Morton (1983)'s observations lead to neuro-linguistic models within which the lexical function appears to have been exploded into a large number of separate, specialized functions: input and output, written, oral, etc.

     Juxtaposing the above remarks to various observations already made, throughout the present article, we may wonder whether the structure of a lexicon should not be made modular, with varying degrees of modular autonomy. This way, whenever a morphological transformation is irregular at the semantic and phonological levels but regular at the syntactic one, it might be possible to take advantage of this partial regularity, on the condition that the lexicon possesses a purely morpho-syntactic module.

     A lexical unit would then be an abstract relation between components drawn from each of the modules: phonological, morpho-phonological, morpho-syntactic, logico-semantic, etc.

     Thus the lexicon would entail abstraction levels corresponding, on the one hand, to those abstract relations that link the concrete components of lexical entries together and, on the other hand, to what can be called lexical grammar regulating word transformations.

ACKNOWLEDGEMENT

Due thanks are owed to Prof. J.F. Malet, California State University, Sacramento, for his prompt translation of the original French text.

FOOTNOTES

[1] These terms figure only within a specific positive- or negative-mode context. Thus "croyable" is represented in the negative mode: "cette proposition n'est pas croyable /* cette proposition est croyable,"[This proposition is not believeable /* this proposition is believeable]. To take an example in English: "I would rather go /*I would not rather go" --See Baker (1970) and Lakoff (1971).

[2] Unlike its English counterpart (for the sake of translation) "aggraver" must display the appropriate mark of the reflexive (se, s') whenever "to worsen" is used intransitively --i.e., verb without a stipulated object. Transl.'s Note.

[3] The English "sensible$_3$"[having good sense] is not covered by the French "sensible" but by "sensé". Transl.'s Note.

[4] Transl.'s Note : French "indéfini" can, in English, correspond either to "undefined" or to "indefinite". For a discussion of "un-" vs. "in-", see Oxford Dictionary. In general, as it would seem, the English language solves the type of semantic ambiguity, here dealt with, by resorting to two different derivations.

BIBLIOGRAPHY

Aronoff, M.H. (1976). Word Formation in Generative Grammar. MIT.

Baker, M. & Speas, P. (1985). Dictionary Entries for Motion Verbs. In Lexical Semantics in Review, ed. B.Levin.

Catach, N. (1981). Orthographe et lexicographie. Nathan.

Chomsky, N. (1957). Syntactic Structures. Mouton.

Chomsky, N. (1965). Aspects of the Theory of Syntax. MIT.

Chomsky, N. (1972). Studies on Semantics in Generative Grammar. Mouton.

Chomsky, N. (1984). Lectures on Goverment and Binding. Dordrech: Foris publications.

Cohen, P.S. & Mercer, R.L. (1974). The Phonological Component of an Automatic Speech Recognition System. Proc. IEEE Symposium Speech Recognition, 177-88.

Dell, F. (1979). La morphologie dérivationnelle du français et l'organisation de la composante lexicale en grammaire générative. Revue Romane, XIV, 2, 185-216.

De Mori, R. (1983). Computer Models of Speech Using Fuzz Algorithms. Plenum Press, New York and London.

Dubois, J. (1962). Etude sur la dérivation suffixale en français moderne et contemporain. Larousse, Paris.

Fabb, N. (1985). Review of Wierzbicka's Work. In Lexical Semantics in Review, ed. B. Levin.

Fauconnier, G. (1977). Polarité syntaxique et sémantique. Linguistica Investigationes, T1, fasc. 1, 1-37.

Fillmore, C. (1968). The Case for Case. In Universals in Linguistic Theory, eds. E. Bach & R.T. Harny, New York, Holt, Rinehart & Wiston, 1-88.

Gross, M. (1975). Méthodes en syntaxe. Hermann, Paris.

Guibert, L. (1971). De la formation des unités lexicales. In Introduction of Grand Larousse de la Langue Française, T1, IX-LXXXI, Larousse, Paris.

Halle, M. (1973). Prolegomena to a Theory of Word Formation. Linguistic Inquiry, 4, 3-16.

Haton, J.P. (1979). The Representation and Use of a Lexicon in Automatic Speech Recognition and Understanding. In Spoken Langage Generation and Understanding, ed. J.C. Simon, Reidel Publication Compagny, 311-36.

Hooper, J. (1976). An Introduction to Natural Generative Phonology. Academic Press, New York.

Jelinek, F. (1976). Continuous Speech Recognition by Statiscal Methods.

Proc. of IEEE, vol. 64, 4.

Kay, M. (1983). When Meta-Rules Are Not Meta-Rules. In Automatic Natural Language Parsing, eds. K. Sparck Jones & Y. Wilks, 94-116.

Kiparsky, P. (1968). How Abstract Is Phonology?, distribued by Indiana University Linguistics Club.

Klatt, D. H. (1981). Lexical Representation For Speech Production and Perception. In The Cognitive Representation of Speech, eds. T. Myers, J. Haver & J. Anderson, North-Holland.

Kramer, S.N. (1975). L'histoire commence à sommer. Arthaud, Paris.

Lakoff, G. (1970). Linguistics and Natural Logic. Synthese, vol.22, 1 & 2.

Levin, B. (ed.) (1985). Lexical Semantics in Review. MIT.

Lieber, R. (1981). On the Organisation of the Lexicon. Reproduced by Indiana University Linguistics Club.

Lyons (1980). Sémantique linguistique. Larousse.

Magnus, M. (1985). Review of Gruber's 'Look and See' and Jackendoff's 'Grammatical Relations and Functional Structure'. In Lexical Semantics in Review, ed. B. Levin, MIT.

Martinet, A. & Walter, H. (1973). Dictionnaire de la prononciation française dans son usage réel. France-Expansion, Paris.

McKeon, R.K. (1985). Text Generation. Cambridge University Press.

Morton, J. (1983). Le lexique interne. La Recherche, 143.

Patterson, K.E. (1978). Phonemic Dyslexia: Errors of Meaning and the Meaning of Errors. Quaterly J. of Exp. Psychology, 30.

Perennou, G. (1980). Lexique et traitement automatique de la parole. Revue d'Acoustique, vol. 13, 53, 2/4.

Perennou, G., de Calmès, M. & M'ghafri, Y. (1984). Rapport GRECO de Communication Parlée, CNRS.

Pierrel, J.M. (1981). Etude et mise en oeuvre de contraintes linguistiques en compréhension automatique du discours continu. Thèse d'Etat, Université de Nancy 1.

Schanck, R.C. (1975). Conceptuel Information Processing. North-Holland, Amsterdam.

Shane, S.A. (1968). French Phonology and Morphology. MIT.

Simon, H.A. (1958). Heuristic Problem Solving. The Next Advance in Operation Research, vol. 6.

Strauss, S.L. (1982). Lexicalist Phonology of English and German, Dordrecht: Foris (Publications in Language Science 9).

Tesnière, L. (1959). Eléments de syntaxe structurale. Klincksieck, Paris.

Thomson, S.A. (1974). On the Issue of Productivity in the Lexicon. In Approaches to the Lexicon, eds. S.A. Thompson & C. Hord, 1-25,

Papers in Syntax, $\underline{6}$, University of California, Los Angeles.

Tranel, B. (1981). Concretness in Generative Phonology: Evidence from French. University of California Tren.

Venneman, T. (1974). Phonological Concretness in Natural Generative Grammar. In Toward Tomorrow's Linguistics, eds. R. Shroy & C.J. Bailey, Washington, DC: Georgetown University Press, 202-19.

Vergnaud, J.R. (1973). Formal Properties of Lexical Derivations. Quaterly Progress Report of the Research Laboratory of Electronics, $\underline{108}$, MIT.

Weinreich, U. (1966). Explorations in Semantic Theory. In Current Trends in Linguistics, vol. 3, ed. T.A. Sebeok, Mouton, La Haye, 395-477.

Weizenbaum, J. (1976). Computer Power and Human Person. San Francisco and London: W.H. Freeman and co.

Wierzbicka, A. (1972). Semantic Primitives. Athenaum, Verlag, Frankfurt.

Wilks, Y. (1977). Structures and Language Boundarier. IJCAI $\underline{5}$, 151-57.

ASPECTS OF MAN-MACHINE VOICE DIALOG

J.M. Pierrel
CRIN, University of Nancy, BP 239, F-54506 Vandoeuvre Cedex

1. INTRODUCTION

Over the past decade, research on man-machine dialog has become an increasingly important branch of computer science. Until the early 1970's users accepted, without much resistance the handling of their applications by major computing centers. The coming of mini- and micro-computer (with computing and storage capacities comparable to those of the previously dominant large size computers) and of new means of communication, now allows for the establishment of direct contact with the machine. These new possibilities, accessible to non-experts, have led to the definition of new man-machine interfaces.

Thus, during the past decade, apart from specific auxiliaries necessary for the development of computer-applications (studies into programming-methodology and software engineering or information systems) new forms of automatic perception (pattern recognition, image/speech processing), interpretation of more and more natural messages (natural speech processing) and reasoning (artificial intelligence) have come to light. All this has thghroughly transformed the dialog between man and machine.

After a brief typology of developments in man-machine dialog, we will concentrate on voice dialog. We will endeavor to outline the principles of continuous speech recognition, essentially limited to sentence recognition, before proceeding to the characteristics of voice dialog from two aspects, namely the dialog situation to be processed and the expedients to be used.

We will conclude by presenting the studies of CRIN, studies which are, aimed at defining and shaping a new man-machine voice dialog system.

2. ELEMENTS OF A TYPOLOGY OF MAN-MACHINE DIALOGS

It is not our intention to offer an exhaustive typology of the various existing man-machine dialog systems, but rather to present some of the major features of these dialogs, viewed from the aspects of the expedients used, and the type of dialog-storage.

2.1. Expedients

Programming languages, or specialized control languages, continue to be the principal means of communication between man and machine. These languages offer computer specialists numerous advantages :
- their standardization makes them international languages. The UNIX system for example is compatible with various hardware,
- their adaptability to the machine makes it possible to optimalize, if desired, the use of material resources,
- their diversity allows for a maximal adaptation to the diverse possible applications with a minimal loss of efficiency,
- the available development tools enable the machine to make an increasing number of static, c.q. dynamic checks (type control e.g.)

These languages, however, have their drawbacks, and require :
- an often fairly long training period and
- adaptation of the human reasoning process (algorithm).

Moreover, they lead to an operator-machine dialog which is often restricted to keyboard and screen. It is for this reason that various systems have been studied and applied so as to open the door to other means of communication, that is, natural language, vision and speech. The figure 1 indicates some advantages and inconveniences of these three means.

2.2. Machine Controled Dialog vs Operator Controled Dialog

Within the framework of man-machine dialog's using speech or written messages, the following dialog-categories may be distinguished :

a- Question-Answer Systems. The principal advantage here is one of operator-simplicity. On the other hand they are often cumbersome and do not provide a global vision of alternatives, or of the structure of the dialog which is imposed entirely by the machine.

b - Menu-driven Systems. Easily applicable, these systems permit, in the context of question-answer systems, the clearest possible vision of local choices. On the other hand, they are limited to a machine-

Communication channel	Advantages	Limitations or inconvéniences
Natural language	– no training – natural medium for communication	– Ambiguity inherent in natural language – Use of Keyboard-screen necessary
Vision	– natural sense of perception of out outside world – pluridimensional representations possible	– cumbersome input (receptor) and output (screen) procedures
Speech	– cf. natural language – multi-directional medium for communi-cation – limited input-output hardware (microphone and loudspeaker)	– ambiguity of speech

Figure # 1. Some advantages and inconveniences of natural
language, vision and speech

directed dialog and, always require a screen to present the menus.
Also, they can become somewhat overrefined for an operator not accus-
tomed to a given system. To limit this, the most frequently used system
(to date) is the definition of hidden menu-driven systems that respond
directly to the operator's request and do not offer the underlying
menus except when the "HELP" key is pressed.

c - "Natural" Dialogs. Much more difficult to apply, this type of dialog
is characterized by a communication control which is more or less divided
between operator and machine. These dialogs require techniques which
are more complex, and ones which often draw upon artificial intelligence.
They are, without doubt, more satisfactory than menu-driven or question-
answer systems.

In all, from the point of view of computer science and
information storage, two types of dialogs can be distinguished. There
are dialogs which deal with static tasks, where dialog evolution is
not required, and those concerned with dynamic tasks, such as robot

control or industrial processes, which require a much closer link
between modules of dialog interpretation and task-engineering.

In this article, we will essentially concentrate on finalized
voice dialogs of type (c). It is necessary, however, to call to mind
the most widely applied principles of automatic speech understanding.

3. MAN-MACHINE COMMUNICATION AND SENTENCE-UNDERSTANDING

3.1. Research on Various Types of Man-Machine Voice Communication

Research on various recognition, and/or understanding
systems, shows four different types of man-machine voice dialogs, each
with specific applications :

i) Word for Word Communication. To date, this is the only system which
is industrially operational, and can be expected to hold up under certain
specific applications, such as oral input of numerical data, multiple
response questions, or the control of simple industrial processes.
In these cases, no genuine dialog system would be used. A recognition
system would suffice and, depending on the extent of the vocabulary
to be used, a global (sizable vocabulary) or analytical (exhaustive
vocabulary) method would be applied. The algorithm of word comparison
is in most cases based on the principle of dynamic programming (Sakoe
78 ; Haton 82).

ii) Communication Using Artificial Languages. This is particularly
well suited for industrial use (process-handling). Oral communication
of this type uses a language wholly defined by an extracontextual grammar
(comparable to programming languages). This language serves a syntax-
guided recognition system. In this area two main systems exist :

= Extension of the principle of dynamic programming : what
is important here is that the field of research on dynamic programming
be limited, in terms of syntactic constraints provided by an automat
(Levinson 80 ; Sauter 84 ; Charpillet 84).

= Syntactic analysis using an bottom up (KEAL - Mercier
80) or top-down (HEARSAY I - Reddy 73 ; MYRTILLE I - Pierrel 75, Haton
76 ; LITHAN - Sakaï 76 ; ESOPE - Mariani 82) strategy.

Here, the dialog procedures followed correspond in general
to the activation of relatively simple automats. They do, however,
allow for the storage of those dialogs useful for validating recognition
(see figure 2).

Figure 2. Example of Dialog in the MYRTILLE I System.

Dialog Opened

"AUTOMATIC OPERATOR OF[+++], WHAT CAN I DO FOR YOU ?"

x : "I WOULD LIKE TO TALK TO MONSIEUR DURAND, PLEASE".

"DID YOU ASK FOR MONSIEUR DUPONT ?" (ambiguity pertaining to the name of requested person).

x : "NO, MONSIEUR DURAND". The system expects an answer thus formulated and the pragmatic information will simplify the analysis of the answer).

"MONSIEUR DURAND IS BUSY. SHALL I PUT YOU ON HOLD ?".

x : NO, THANK YOU, I'LL CALL BACK LATER". (other example of a sentence subject to simplified analysis).

Dialog closed.

iii) Communication in a Natural Language, Limited to an Area of Expertise (pseudo-natural languages). Here, use is made of natural language with minimal restrictions, which opens the door to public use (e.g. information systems). This requires the application of more highly complex understanding processes and dialog procedures than with type (ii). The majority of the systems defined in the ARPA project belong to this category, in particular C.M.U.'s HEARSAY II (Lesser 75) and B.B.N.'s HWIM (Woods 76). The system developed at CRIN, MYRTILLE II (Pierrel 82) is also in this group.

All the aforementioned systems focus on the sentence understanding stage, without really integrating it in a more general dialog process. Furtheron we shall concentrate on man-machine voice dialog systems in pseudonatural languages.

iv) Dictating Machines. No restriction can be imposed on natural language other than that of elocution. Recognition procedures activated do not make use of pragmatic (context-related) information, and dialog procedures are bent on validating recognition results using, if need be, external means of communication other than voice.

Research on this issue, and in particular on a designation system enabling swift correction of errors of recognition, is presently being conducted at CRIN (Charpillet 85). We have, however, elected not to present it here with regard to the dialog used.

The problem of which type of communication to choose depends to a great extent on the intended application and the extent to which certain language constraints are acceptable. This article essentially focuses on systems to be adopted by information centers for the general public, or for a semi-professional public. In both categories thorough training in the language and dialog used would not be practical. This corresponds to another type of communication (iii), i.e. dialog in semi-natural language restricted to a certain area of expertise.

Such a system requires an in-depth study of the characteristics of aim-dialogs, which, alone, make it possible to draw up an inventory of necessary expedients. One must note, however, that an oral dialog is of interest only if it represents a natural way of interaction leading to a certain satisfaction on the side of the operator, with zero losses at the level of message-content. This implies that one cannot confine oneself to systems which totally steer the dialog and reduce exchanges (with the operator) to a series of simple questions and answers. Extensive research has been conducted on interhuman communication. Are the obtained results applicable to man-machine voice dialog ? In the case of finalized dialogs, one is tempted to answer this question in the affirmative. Can man-to-man communication models, however, such as the one defined in (Grice 75) serve as a basis for research on a man-machine communication system ? Would it not be preferable to define a model specifically for man-machine voice dialog ?

3.2. Sentence Understanding

Before venturing into the specific problems connected to the definition and use of dialog systems, a quick survey of the existing sentence recognition and understanding systems seems appropriate, since these represent useful tools for the definition of a new generation of systems. For a more detailed presentation of these systems see (Lea 80). As such, we will only briefly refer to the general principles and organizations in use.

a) General Principle

Sentence recognition is the main target of the various systems, whether they be conceived for artificial languages (cf. 3.1 (ii)) or subcategories of natural languages, restricted to an area of expertise. The limits of acoustic-phonetic decoding, which to date allows for a maximal recognition of sentence-phonemes of 75%, have proved an incentive for the definition of new systems. These use a maximum of linguistic data (lexical, syntactic, semantic and pragmatic) to compensate for the hiatuses in phonetic recognition.

This multitude of data-sources required to process a statement is schematized in figure 3. Here the core of the systems corresponds to an internal representation of the statement in the course of being processed and to a control of sorts, that would activate the various sources of knowledge (SC_i) using mechanisms (M_i) apposite to each type of data.

<u>Figure 3</u>. Theoretical Flow-chart Of An Understanding-system

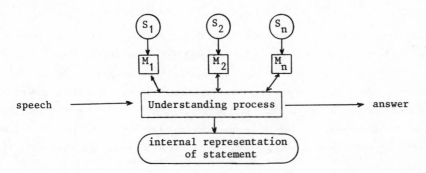

The practical difficulties encountered in using such an understanding-process, as well as the influence from hierarchic models for human perception (cf. Libermann 70) have resulted in the following three-step "staging" :

- <u>Acoustic-phonetic recognition</u>.

  Passage from signal to a lattice of pseudo-phonemes.

- <u>Sentence-understanding</u>.

  The minimal segment lattice is used to set up a syntactic-semantic representation, incomplete c.q. multiple, of the original sentence.

- <u>Dialog storage and interpretation</u>.

  Recognition results are validated and the operator's request complied with.

Strong interaction exists between these three steps and they should be considered as one single stage, even if in the majority of systems they follow each other in a certain order. Agreement exists on the need to further integrate the three steps.

We will now focus on the second and third steps before venturing to define genuine dialog systems.

b) <u>Possible Approaches For Sentence Recognition</u>

To alleviate the shortcomings of acoustic-phonetic recognition, and deal with non-determinism stemming from possible errors at this stage, most systems rely on the principle of hypothesis-test-validation, using all available data within the framework of a given application. Two theories, each with its own approach to the problem, exist.

- <u>Bottom-up approach</u> : starting from the signal or lattice of pseudo-phonemes, the sentence is rediscovered while ascending the various levels of abstraction : lexical, syntactic, semantic, etc. This procedure, while providing relative immunity against noise or lowlevel errors, requires a lattice of all possible words, based on the lattice of pseudo-phonemes. If a large vocabulary is required, this lattice rapidly becomes very extensive. Such an analysis, when not operational, becomes too costly.

- <u>Top down approach</u> : starting from the highest possible abstraction level (syntactic-semantic data) those words which may appear at a given position in a sentence are identified and tested via a phonetic recognition procedure. This predictive method eliminates a certain number of hypothetisized words and becomes a necessity when vocabularies are vast.

On the other hand, this approach is much more sensible to noise than an bottom up approach. In case of error, a much more cumbersome procedure is required to resynchronize operator and input channel. Diagram ≠ 4 (source Mari 79) compares the hypothetisized words in both approaches in the MYRTILLE I system. (Haton 76).

V ∂ v U u b Ɛ e p a r e a m a b a m a ℓ b e

Z a ʒ Y ∂ d i Ɛ t e ℓ ∂ ∂ b o d o ã o r d Ɛ

ʒ e Z o o g e i k ∂ e a e d ∂ g ∂ õ e   g i

"j' voudrais   parler à   madame   Albert"

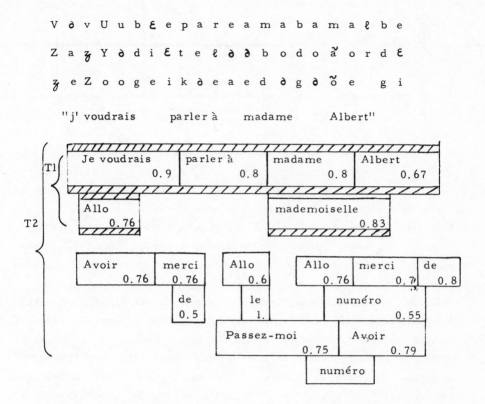

T1 : recognized words following top-down strategy
T2 : total lattice of words which could be recognized

Comparison of word lattice following top-down strategy-
possible lattice

Figure 4

To remedy the inconvenience and limitations of strictly bottom-up/top-down methods, mixed procedures have been conceived, for several understanding systems such as HEARSAY II (Erman 77), HWIN (Wolf 77) and MYRTILLE II (Pierrel 82). The strategy used in the MYRTILLE II system for example, would then give the following :

Definition of language (linguistic data)

Test to reduce

non-determinism   Hypotheses   Definition of
                                   (set of words)
                                                         resumption
                                   ⇕ RECOGNITION
                                                         points
                                   Phonetic lattice

Vocal signal (after analysis and parametrization)

These vertical organization methods are always used in conjunction with one of two horizontal strategies.

≠ 1. With the "left-right" method, it is possible to take the predictive character of speech production into account (used in HARPY, LITHAN, KEAL, ESOPE, MYRTILLE et al.). Application is often problematic because of noisy passages in the statement disrupting the analysis.

≠ 2. The "center-sides" or "anchoring points" method (HEARSAY II, HWIN, S.R.I. (Walker 78) and a version of MYRTILLE) construes partial representations of the sentence starting from different, well-recognized words, to alleviate the difficulties encountered with the "left-right" strategy. The main difficulties with this "center-sides" method are the necessity to fuse the aforementioned partial interpretations of the sentence into one final sentence and, the choice of key words or anchoring points.

c) Knowledge Used

The principal sources of information in the sentence understanding stage are vocabulary, syntax and semantics. The material can be represented in two different ways :

≠ 1. Maximal integration of sources, ultimately resulting in a unique precompiled network containing the phonetic transcriptions of all authorized sentences (adopted for HARPY - Lowerre 76).

≠ 2. Modular structuring of material respecting the traditional classification : vocabulary, phonetics, phonology, syntax and semantics.

Although maximal integration techniques have proved particularly efficient (HARPY is undoubtedly the ARPA-affshoot closest to real time) they do exhibit important drawbacks :

- language modification is difficult, necessitating complete recompilation of the network.
- the extent of the language is limited due to the size of the network, which rapidly becomes over-extended.
- the language is rigid, or highly incompatible with free expression.

It is necessary, in the case of pseudo-natural languages, to maintain a more classical structure of these data-sources, in particular between

- a phonetic glossary, encompassing the various possible phonological alterations, in precompiled form or not,

- a syntax which requires high-performance models when applied to natural languages. In artificial languages these models may be replaced by contextfree grammar, contiguity matrices or limited stage automats. To date, the most widely used models are based on the network idea. Its most well-known exponent, ATN (Augmented Transition Network), was defined by Woods in 1970 for the analysis of written messages (Woods 70) and employed in the HWIN system (Woods 75) where it has exhibited capacity and flexibility.

For the MYRTILLE II system a slightly different model has been conceived : Procedural-Node Network (P.N.N.) (Pierrel 82). In this system, the arcs stand for words or non-terminals, references to subnetworks, and the nodes symbolize procedures. The role of the latter is to determine which trajectory will be followed to cover the arcs that have sprung off the node in analytic context and phonetic, prosodic or semantic testing. Unlike A.T.N., which regroups grammar definition and syntactic analysis in one structure, P.N.N. is monitored by an external procedure of syntactic analysis.

- semantic description, often revealing two components, i.e. local semantic constraints and semantic-pragmatic knowledge pertaining to the statement as a whole.

The local semantic constraints in the various systems manifest in terms of two forms :

* an arborescent representation of the hierarchized vocabulary using semantic data, as is the case of MYRTILLE II and the S.R.I. system, or

* a semantic grammar, simultaneously defining syntax and local semantic constraints, as in HEARSAY II and HWIN.

This second solution, though highly efficient, requires an entire redefining of syntax and semantics for each applicational modification.

These local semantic constraints do not, however, suffice for an in-depth syntactic-semantic analysis. Deduction should be made of semantic and programming data. This becomes possible when a grammar-associated semantic network (S.R.I. system) or a case-grammar model, following Fillmore (MYRTILLE II - Haton 82b) is used.

d) Organizations

A distinction exists between hierarchical and non-hierarchical organizations.

- Non-hierarchical organizations allow for an expedient, that is, an elective access to data sources. In this system, used by HEARSAY II, the diverse sources of knowledge are independant processes communicating by means of the 'blackboard', a structure of external data.

- Other systems have produced an explicit and predefined hierarchy concerning sources of knowledge. The functioning of these systems is supervised by an external device (HWIN, KEAL, MYRTILLE).

J.P. Haton notes that "it is remarkable that such apprarently different systems such as HEARSAY II and HWIN widely differ on the point of organization. Both systems use a semantic grammar, a strategy of 'islands of confidence' and similar lexical search processes. The communication mechanisms between knowledge sources and their instantiations are, however, extremely different. Here lies an initial dilemma. Should the structure of complex data (blackboard-type) be defined as representing knowledge, or should the organization of the system and of associated control structures be emphasized ?" (Haton 84).

4. SPECIFIC ASPECTS OF MAN-MACHINE VOICE DIALOG

4.1. Dialog situation

Various elementary dialog situations exist (Neel 83) as messages which may not be recognized or may be unintelligible, partially understood, incomplete, or ambiguous. Even in the case when they are wholly recognized, it is necessary to detect incorrectly interpreted or incoherent messages as well as those which cannot be complied. Each

type of message corresponds to a particular dialog situation and it
would be erroneous to think that a voice dialog system only distinguishes
"well" or "badly" recognized messages.

i) Non-recognized or Unintelligible Messages

The causes of unintelligible messages can be : excessive
noise, input or transmission error, overlap of system-output and
operator-input, or simply, bad pronounciation. A message is
classified as unintelligible if the system cannot even recognize it
partially. In that case, a total repetition is requested. If the system
can detect the cause of failure, the request is worded as an advice.
Example : "Please repeat your message louder."

The total number of statement-repetitions should be limited
and if necessary one should switch to manual control.

ii) Partially Understood or Incomplete Messages

The sentence-understanding stage often results in a syntactic-semantic structure representing the original statement. Sometimes,
and especially when a center-sides strategy is applied, only part of
the original statement is rendered. This can be due to bad recognition
or to the use of a word not included in the glossary. Even with correct
recognition, the operator may have forgotten to specify a necessary
attribute. Rather than systematically foreseeing requests for repetition
or additional information, the system could contain a set of argument
values, confined in the dialog case-history or in a reservoir of implicit
values. In that case, it would be necessary, of course, to build in
a confirmation which could be explicit, as follow :

O : What's the price of a ticket to ? Paris

S : From Nancy to PARIS ?

O : Yes

S : The price of the ticket NANCY-PARIS is ...

or implicit :

O : What's the price of a ticket to PARIS ?

S : The price of the ticket NANCY-PARIS is ...

In the case of implicit confirmation a possible contention on the side
of the operator could be :

O : No, from TOULOUSE to PARIS.

iii) Ambiguous Messages

Speech understanding may encounter two kinds of ambiguity. One is the ambiguity inherent in natural languages (homonyms and polysemic words), the other one is due to the recognition process (minimal pairs and homophones).

Ambiguity could be eliminated in two different ways :

1. The systems asks a question.

2. The system determines the most probable interpretation, which it later validates, as in the preceeding case, by means of an implicit/ explicit request for confirmation. In this case the use of a dialog-context or case-history may often be useful, since an isolated statement may appear ambiguous, but may become unequivocal when set in the dialog.

If the ambiguity pertains to a word, it is preferable to have the machine make an interpretation, followed by a request for confirmation, rather than having the operator make the choice. If the choice were the operator's, the ambiguity might reappear in the ensuing dialog-stage and generate a never-ending cycle, as follow :

O : Pass me Monsieur Dutronc
                          Dupont

S : Did you say Monsieur Dupont or Dutronc ?

O : Monsieur Dutronc
             Dupont

iv) Wholly Recognized Messages

Messages for which the level of sentence recognition is able to provide an unequivocal syntactic-semantic structure are defined as wholly recognized.

Categories.

1. Badly interpreted messages.

The sentence-understanding level is unable to distinguish correct from incorrect. To solve this problem, an explicit confirmation could be set up at each step. This, however, may needlesly encumber the dialog. An implicit confirmation if used would, make it impossible for the operator to disagree. In process-control applications, explicit confirmation by the user before the activation of physical systems becomes, necessary.

2. Incoherent Messages.

After recognition, two types of incoherence may be detected. Semantic incoherence is linked to the appearance of a contradiction between the formulated request and the task-universe. Pragmatic incoherence is related to a contradiction between statement and case-history. Although incoherence often points to incorrect interpretation by the system, it may also be due to the operator, especially when hesitation or repetition occurs. Incoherence should always be registered and should trigger a request for clarification as soon as the lexeme to which the incoherence pertains is used by the dialog system to answer or make a further deduction.

3. Messages That Cannot Be Processed

When requests fall ouside the expertise of the system, they may trigger a message reminding of the system's limited possibilities.

The use of diversified sources of knowledge is necessary if one is to define not only the language to be recognized but also the task and the dialog.

4.2. Sources Of Knowledge

Knowledge used in a dialog system falls apart in predefined, or static, and evolution knowledge.

4.2.1. Predefined Knowledge

a) Language model

This model, needed for recognition and answering, would include a syntactic and a lexical element, similar to those used in sentence understanding (cf. § 3.2.c).

b) Task model

The following are necessary if a system is to function properly.

- a semantic-pragmatic definition of the objects that are part of the task and of the relations between these objects. This knowledge, often linked to lexical entities, can be regrouped into various distinctive glossaries, according to desired application.

- a definition of targets and secondary targets, specifying how access to the necessary data is obtained. Various models can represent this. Particularly apt are script- or framelike declarative representations, or semantic networks. Expressions of generality also should be defined at this level. These application-stipulated expressions often take the form of implicit values for the various attributes.

c) Dialog Model

The dialog model specifies the control and storage strategies of the finalized dialog and the possible interference between different dialog stages. It can consist of declarative rules, which lead to the defining of the dialog storage module as an expert system of sorts. It may also take the form of a procedure comparable to the use of a supervisor module.

d) Operator Model

The model should not only describe phonological or prosodic features valid for the majority of potential operators; but also those limited to certain individuals. In the case of operational applications it is expecially necessary to define the system's behavioral rules. Thus, in an information-system, a distinction should be made between those operators authorized to modify the underlying data-bank and those who are not. This information permits different types of knowledge to be processed. These may include consultations, updating, et al.

4.2.2. Evolutive Knowledge

a) Task Universe

Where an evolutive process is used, the task universe, being an indispensable complement of the task model, corresponds to the data bank, in the case of an information-center, or, in the case of robot-control or industrial application, a precise description of the process.

This information is necessary to determine the most suitable action or answer, and to detect statements that the system cannot handle.

b) Dialog Case-History

The dialog case-history should conserve, in a structured form, pertinent facts and possible interpretations of previous exchanges within a single dialog. It covers the detection of incoherences and above all, allows for a natural dialog which contains repetitions and certain elliptic or anaphorical features of speech.

c) Partial or Temporary Solutions

Functioning as a short term dialog-process memory, this source of information allows for the provisional storage of, a.o.

- entire hypotheses put forward by the sentence understanding processor in the course of a single dialog-stage (syntactic-semantic structure of the statement and possible lexical representation of the last statement).

- diverse temporary solutions pending confirmation.

4.3. Functions

The diversified functions that are to be used in a man-machine voice dialog system do not necessarily correspond to different modules.

a) Control of Communication Channels

This guides the opening and closing of the dialog, triggers repetition of question when overly long silences occur and transmits "please wait" signals when the system requires a processing time which exceeds real time.

b) Sentence Understanding

Syntactic, semantic and lexical constraints are transmitted to this module in the form of parameters (cf. § 3.2.).

c) Contextual Interpretation

The syntactic-semantic representation of the statement is integrated in the dialog-context (case-history). This module discerns those statements that have a bearing on

* task :

- request for information or instructions
- supply information or instructions in an implicit/explicit manner, in response to a question.

* dialog :

- contention concerning a previous statement by the same operator (repetition, correction) or to a statement by the machine.
- request for implicit/explicit restatements using elements from an oral context : "I beg your pardon", "Hello ?".

d) Dialog-Processing

Intervention by this module becomes necessary when disagreement occurs, when there is a request for restatement and confirmation. This action is maintained in close interaction with the dialog case-history. Each type of statement calls for a different treatment. This often leads to a restatement, or bouncing of the dialog to the operator or, after a negative statement, to a request for reconfirmation or restatement.

e) Generation

Generation (a reverse function of recognition and interpretation) allows for the production of the surface structure of the questions and answers of the system, and for the activation of a speech synthesis/restoration module.

f) Reasoning

Drawing on the dialog case-history, the reasoning module
- detects incoherence,
- resolves ambiguity, and
- detects and/or traces a given theme.

It also determines, according to theme and goal, if the operator's request is explicit enough to single out the requested information or to trigger the action corresponding to the operator's instructions. In the case of incomplete information, it determines the secondary target and directs the dialog in that direction by means of question.

In the case of dialogs limited to simple tasks reasoning may be left to an automat. An opposing situation would conversely require an expert system.

5. CRIN's DIALOG SYSTEM

After having defined the systems MYRTILLE I (Pierrel 75) for the processing of limited dialogs in artificial languages, and MYRTILLE II (Pierrel 82) showing the feasability of sentence recognition in pseudo-natural languages, CRIN is working on studies for a voice dialog system (Carbonell 84) which would integrate a maximum of functions (cf. § 4). This research was begun two years ago and is being conducted in close connection with the "Dialogue Oral" (Oral Dialog) team of the C.N.R.S. G.R.E.C.O. "Communication Parlée" (Speech Communication).

Our objective is the definition of a system capable of understanding and satisfying requests coming from operators who express themselves naturally (no -language- training required), within a finalized oral dialog. The system is expected, in part, to process and structure dialog and acquire limited, predefined expertise. The ultimate goal is to have system consult the data bank (the Application Test used pertains to administrative information, as given on the pink pages of the French telephone directory).

In this article we will not describe the procedures to be followed for the application of this system. We will, therefore, limit ourselves to a brief survey of the data sources used (excluding acoustic and phonetic information), processors and their interactions.

5.1. Selected Representation of Information

5.1.1. Predefined Information

Three categories can be distinguished :

a) Language elements, comprising

- information on the structure of the language. We have opted for a Procedural Node Network representation (Pierrel 82), entailing a center-sides analysis,

- a lexical component, that is, a subcategory of the general vocabulary (grammatical- or toolwords) specifying for each of the words its syntactic attributes (grammatical class) and phonetic representation, and

- a description of the different prosodic structures of a statement, i.e. elementary patterns and complex structures.

b) Knowledge of finalized dialog control and storage strategies, presented through dialog flow-charts. The most frequently appearing dialog situations are formally described in scripts or scenarios.

c) Information proper to the application,

Notably

- a definition of the vocabulary proper to the application. Each word would be associated with a syntactic (possible grammatical classes), semantic (general features, e.g. "animated", "inanimate") and phonetic (phonetic representation and rules for phonological alteration) component.

- an application-and task description, sufficiently precise to satisfy operator request (the system being the expert), and comprising

* <u>a definition of the concepts used</u>, specifying for each of them its identifier with reference to the associated lexical entity, its profile, which determines the manner in which the concept is used and, its class.

Example : Sex (person) |male, female|.

The concepts may be combined. With "formula" an elementary combination of concepts and operators (or, and, no) is meant. The formula corresponds to a fact or lexem and is represented, in our system, by an arborescence AND/OR.

* <u>the relationships between concepts</u> (other than class-adherence) are written in the form of rewriting rules. Several deductions are thus allowed for. These could be :

Nationality (person, $\neg$ France) $\Rightarrow$ nationality (person, foreigner)

Father (x,y) $\Rightarrow$ (son(y,x) / daughter (x,y)) & male (y).

* <u>the formulation of the data-bank</u> which pertains to the application, in the form of a list of instantiated formulas.

For example :

Term (procure (person, ID card), 10 days)

Color (driving-license, pink)

* <u>pragmatic information</u>, request-linked within the task-universe.

Example :   aim : procure (x, ID card)

             cond : minor (x)

             sol : accompany (x,y) & parent (x,y)

* <u>a set of implicit values</u>. This information, like that concerning the data-bank, is given in a declarative manner :

      Nationality (operator, French),

      Town (Nancy).

5.1.2. Dynamic Information

Processors have access to this information in order to consult or update it. The information consists of hypotheses and interpretations concerning the statement or the dialog it has been taken from. In other words, it represents the syntactic-semantic interpretation of the statement and the dialog case-history.

5.2. Processors

Five different processors have been selected to cover the successive steps of the understanding process.

a) Acoustic-Phonetic Processing

Objective : the construction of a lattice of units which represents the statement, which is received in the form of a digitalized acoustic signal. This lattice is used at other levels to work out interpretations.

It is imperative to provide, for each segment an -exhaustive-list of hypotheses including the pronounced phoneme rather than the most plausible interpretations at the risk of excluding the correct one.

In short, the signal segmented into phonemes and the detected segments are identified (phonetically labeled), which requires an expert decoding system (Carbonell 84b, 84c).

b) Prosodic Processing

Objective : a regrouping of the segments in a string of hierarchically structured prosodic units. Only the unequivocal prosodic information is retained, that is, those markers (pauses or melodic switches) whose presence has been detected with a maximum degree of certainty. This information may be used by the lexical and syntatic-semantic components to elaborate hypotheses. For the evaluation of hypotheses the information is an indispensable tool since a syntactic-semantic interpretation will not be stored unless it is compatible with the prosodic markers in the statement.

c) Lexical processing

The phonetic units are regrouped in lexical units (words), following either of two strategies :
- The possibility for a given word to occur at a certain position in the statement is assessed.
- The appearance of certain hypothetisized words, belonging to a given glossary, in the original statement, is detected.

d) Syntactic-Semantic Processing

The lexical units are restructured in a hierarchy of syn-tactic-semantique units (syntagms) and the structural links between syntagms are assessed. An upward strategy, processing the sentence from left to right can be followed, or a mixed, centersides one (upward and downward), using keywords (cf. § 2.2.).

e) Dialog Processing and Interpretation

An interpretation of the statement is conducted. This interpretation is linked to the ones that have been elaborated in the course of earlier statements and stored in the dialog case-history. Also, it is linked to the dialog-objective and application-universe.

The reaction of the system at the occurrence of operator-intervention is determined, e.g.

- request for production of information,
- request for confirmation or restatement,
- dialog retriggering.

The contents and structure of an operator statement are predicted, based on the dialog situation of a given moment. The other processing levels (acoustic, syntactic-semantic and lexical) use these predictions to limit their scanning-range.

5.3. Interaction Between Processors

The nature of the above processors seemingly imposes a sequential order of processor-activation, with the exception of the prosodic element. A strictly sequential process, starting with phonetics and finishing with dialog-interpretation (or v.v.) yields a meager result. It is, however, the option chosen in the majority of continuous speech understanding systems. From one level to the other, the hiatuses amplify and incertainties increase, entailing the multiplication of local hypotheses and subsequently the emergence of competing representations. To reduce the risk of hiatuses and multiple interpretations, interaction between the different processors, in the form of information-exchanges, has been allowed for. (cf. figure 5).

5.4. Developments

Initially, emphasis was put on defining the information in view of its uses and internal (system-useable) and external (accessible to operator considering the system's parametrization) representations. The above has been integrated in an Application-Test bearing on administrative information. Simultaneously the details of the system's various processors and its general organization have been presented. Presently the employment of diverse processors is under study. The first partial validation tests are expected within the next 6 to 12 months.

Processors → Information sources →

Destinataire ↓

	PHONETICS	PROSODICS	LEXICAL	SYNTACTIC-SEMANTIC	DIALOG.
PHONETICS	hypotheses : – phonetical – of segmentation facts : – energy variations (bands) – spectral information		hypotheses : – phonetic pattern – lexical reference forms		
PROSODICS	hypotheses : – segmented signal – average vowel length	hypotheses : – prosodic facts : – global energy variations – FO variations			
LEXICAL	hypotheses : – phonetic	hypotheses : – word limits	hypotheses : – lexical	hypotheses : – sub-lexicon determined by grammatical or semantic criteria	hypotheses : – sub-lexicon (keywords linked to application or dialog-stage)
SYN/SEM		hypotheses : – syntagm limits – assertion/interrogation (at statement level)	hypotheses : – lexical	hypotheses : – syntactic-semantic	hypotheses : – statement structure
DIALOG	facts : – lenght of statement		hypotheses : – application-linked keywords	hypotheses : – semantic	hypotheses : – on dialog being processed (case-history)

Figure 5. Interaction between processing levels of man-machine voice dialog.

6. <u>CONCLUSION</u>

The introduction of the oral element in a man-machine communication system requires dialogs which are as natural as possible. This article has sought to describe the diverse elements of such a dialog system. First the general principles of automatic continuous speech understanding systems were summed up. This was followed by a presentation of the principal features that characterize man-machine voice dialog systems, from the aspect of processed dialog situations, functions and sources of knowledge to be integrated. Finally the outline of the dialog system project now being defined at CRIN was described. If, until recently, most research was limited to sentence understanding, it seems that now the time has come to concentrate on voice dialog understanding and processing as an important step toward the realization of intelligent oral interfaces between man and machine.

Acknowledgements

During the preparation of this article I have greatly benefitted from the numerous talks I have had with my colleagues of the "Dialogue Oral" team at CNRS G.R.E.C.O. "Communication Parlée", and from the research on man-machine dialog being conducted at CRIN.

In particular I would like to thank N. Carbonell, B. Mangeol, P. Mousel and A. Roussanaly, who work with me on the definition of the CRIN system. Finally I would like to thank C. Peek for his help in presenting my ideas in a language which I do not command to perfection.

REFERENCES

Carbonell, N., Cordier, M.O., Fohr, D., Haton, J.P., Lonchamp, F., & Pierrel, J.M. (1984.a). Acquisition et formalisation du raisonnement dans un système expert de lecture de spectrogrammes vocaux. Colloque ARC, Paris-Orsay.

Carbonell, N., Fohr, D., Haton, J.P., Lonchamp, F. & Pierrel, J.M. (1984.b). An Expert System for the Automatic Reading of French Spectrograms. Proc. IEEE-ICASSP 84, San Diego.

Carbonell, N., Haton, J.P., Pierrel, J.M. & Co. (1984.c). Dialogue oral homme-machine : bilan du projet MYRTILLE et perspectives. In Pierrel, J.M., Haton, J.P. & Néel, F., editors (1984). Dialogue homme-machine à composante orale.

Charpillet, F., Haton, J.P. & Pierrel, J.M. (1984). Apport de la pro-
    grammation dynamique en reconnaissance automatique de la
    parole continue. 4ème congrès Int. Reconnaissance des Formes
    et Intelligence Artificielle, AFCET, Paris.
Charpillet, F., Haton, J.P., Pierrel, J.M. (1985). Un système de recon-
    naissance de la parole continue pour la saisie de textes
    lus. 5ème Congrès AFCET-INRIA, R.F.-I.A., 1985.
Erman, L.D. (1977). A Functionnal Description of the HEARSAY II Speech
    Understanding System. Proc. IEEE-ICASSP 77, Hartford.
Grice, H.P. (1975). Logic and Conversation. In Cole and Morgan, Syntax
    and Semantics, Speech Acts, Academic Press, New-York.
Haton, J.P. & Pierrel, J.M. (1976). Organization and Operation of a
    Connected Speech Understanding System at Lexical Syntactic
    and Sementic Level. Proc. IEEE-ICASSP 76, Philadelphia.
Haton, J.P. (1982.a). Speech Recognition and Understanding. Invited
    paper, 6th Int. Conf. Pattern Recognition, München, pp.
    570-581.
Haton, J.P., Pierrel, J.M. & Sabbagh, S. (1982.b). Semantic and Prag-
    matic Processing in Continuous Speech Understanding. In
    Automatic Speech Analysis and Recognition, Haton, J.P.,
    editor, D. Reidel.
Haton, J.P. (1984). compréhension de la parole et intelligence arti-
    ficielle : état des recherches. In Pierrel, J.M., Haton,
    J.P. & Néel, F., éditeurs. Dialogue homme-machine à compo-
    sante orale.
Klatt, D.H. (1977). Review of the ARPA Speech Understanding project.
    J. Acoustic. Soc. Am., 62, pp. 1345-1366.
Lea, W.A. (1980). Trends in Speech Recognition, Printice Hall, Signal
    Processing Series.
Lesser, V.R. and Al. (1975). Organization of the HEARSAY II Speech
    Understanding System. IEEE Trans. ASSP, 23, pp. 11-23.
Levinson, S.E. & Shipley, K.L. (1980). A Conversational Mode Airline
    Information and Reservation System Using Speech Input and
    Output. Bell Syst. Tech. J., 59, n° 1, pp. 119-137.
Liberman, A.M. (1970). The Grammars of Speech and Language. Cognitive
    Psychology, 1, pp. 301-323.
Lowerre, B.T. (1976). The HARPY Speech Recognition System. Technical
    Report, Carnegie-Mellon University, Dep. of Computer Science.
Mari, J.F. (1979). Contribution à l'analyse syntaxique et à la recherche
    lexicale en reconnaissance du discours continu. Thèse de
    3ème cycle, Université de Nancy I.
Mariani, J. (1982). The AESOP Continuous Speech Understanding System.
    Proc. IEEE-ICASSP 82, Paris.
Mercier, G. and Al. (1980). The KEAL Speech Understanding System. In
    Spoken Language Generation and Understanding, Simon, J.C.,
    editor, D. Reidel.
Néel, F. & Béroule, D. (1984). Une approche des problèmes de la commu-
    nication parlée homme-machine. Congrès AFCET, Paris.
Pierrel, J.M. (1975). Contribution à la compréhension automatique du
    discours continu. Thèse de 3ème cycle, Université de Nancy I.
Pierrel, J.M. (1981). Etude et mise en oeuvre de contraintes linguis-
    tiques en compréhension automatique du discours continu.
    Thèse de doctorat, Université de Nancy I.
Pierrel, J.M. (1982). Use of Linguistic Constraints for Automatic Conti-
    nuous Speech Understanding : the MYRTILLE II System, T.S.I.,
    Vol. 1, n° 5, pp. 329-346, North Oxford Academic.

Pierrel, J.M. Haton, J.P., Néel, F., Editeurs (1984). Dialogue homme-machine à composante orale. Actes du séminaire GRECO-GALF, Nancy.

Reddy, D.R., Erman, L.D., Neely, R.D. (1973). A Model for a System for Machine Recognition of Speech. IEEE Trans. A.U., 21, pp. 229-238.

Sakai, T. & Nagakawa, S. (1976). Speech Understanding System LITHAN and some Applications. Proc. 3th Int. Conf. Pattern Recognition, Coronado.

Sakoe, H. & Chiba, S. (1978). Dynamic Programming Optimization for Spoken Word Recognition. IEEE Trans. ASSP, 26, pp. 43-46.

Sauter, L. (1984). RAPACE : un système de reconnaissance analytique de parole continue. 4ème congrès int. Reconnaissance des formes et intelligence artificielle, Paris.

Wolf, J.J. and Woods, W.A. (1977). The HWIM Speech Understanding System. IEEE-ICASSP 77, Hartford.

Woods, W.A. (1975). Syntax, Semantic and Speech. In Speech Recognition, Reddy, D.R., editor, Academic Press.

Woods, W.A. and Al. (1976). Speech Understanding System. Final Progress Report, Report n° 3438, Vol. I-V, BBN.

INDEX